D0890134

Date: 3/11/14

944.035 BAS
Bashor, Will.
Marie Antoinette's head : the
royal hairdresser, the queen,

PALM BEACH COUNTY
LIBRARY SYSTEM
3650 SUMMIT BLVD.
WEST PALM BEACH, FL 33406

MARIE ANTOINETTE'S HEAD

Marie Antoinette's Head

The Royal Hairdresser, the Queen, and the Revolution

Will Bashor

LYONS PRESS
Guilford, Connecticut
An imprint of Globe Pequot Press

As always, for Norma Blanche, Bertina Faye, and Randall Scott

To buy books in quantity for corporate use
or incentives, call **(800) 962–0973**
or e-mail **premiums@GlobePequot.com.**

Copyright © 2013 by Will Bashor

ALL RIGHTS RESERVED. No part of this book may be reproduced or transmitted in any form by any means, electronic or mechanical, including photocopying and recording, or by any information storage and retrieval system, except as may be expressly permitted in writing from the publisher. Requests for permission should be addressed to Globe Pequot Press, Attn: Rights and Permissions Department, PO Box 480, Guilford, CT 06437.

Lyons Press is an imprint of Globe Pequot Press.

All images public domain unless otherwise noted.

Family tree on p. vii by the author.
Map on pp. viii–ix by William R. Shepherd, *Historical Atlas* (NY: Henry Holt, 1911), 149.

Project editor: Meredith Dias
Layout: Casey Shain

Library of Congress Cataloging-in-Publication Data

Bashor, Will.
  Marie Antoinette's head : the royal hairdresser, the queen, and the revolution / Will Bashor.
    pages cm
  Summary: "For the better part of the Queen Marie Antoinette's reign over France, one man was entrusted with the sole responsibility of ensuring that her coiffure was at its most ostentatious best. Marie Antoinette's Head tells the story of Leonard Autie, Marie Antoinette's hairdresser and confidante, the man responsible for the style that made her the envy of France and for the uproar that dragged her to the guillotine"— Provided by publisher.
  ISBN 978-0-7627-9153-8 (hardback)
  1. Autié, Léonard, 1751?-1820. 2. Marie Antoinette, Queen, consort of Louis XVI, King of France, 1755-1793. 3. Marie Antoinette, Queen, consort of Louis XVI, King of France, 1755-1793—Friends and associates. 4. France—History—Louis XVI, 1774-1793. 5. France—History—Revolution—1789-1799. 6. France—Court and courtiers—Biography. I. Title.
  DC137.19.B37 2013
  944'.035092—dc23
  [B]

                                                                    2013019803

Printed in the United States of America

10 9 8 7 6 5 4 3 2 1

CONTENTS

CONTENTS

AUTIÉ FAMILY TREE

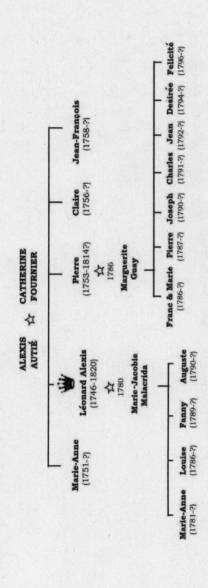

ALEXIS AUTIÉ ☆ CATHERINE FOURNIER

Marie-Anne (1751-?)

Léonard Alexis (1746-1820) ☆ 1780 Marie-Jacobie Malacrida

Pierre (1753-1814?) ☆ 1786 Marguerite Guay

Claire (1756-?)

Jean-François (1758-?)

Marie-Anne (1781-?) Louise (1786-?) Fanny (1789-?) Auguste (1790-?)

Franc & Marie (1786-?) Pierre (1787-?) Joseph (1790-?) Charles (1791-?) Jean (1792-?) Desirée (1794-?) Felicité (1796-?)

☆ Marriage & date

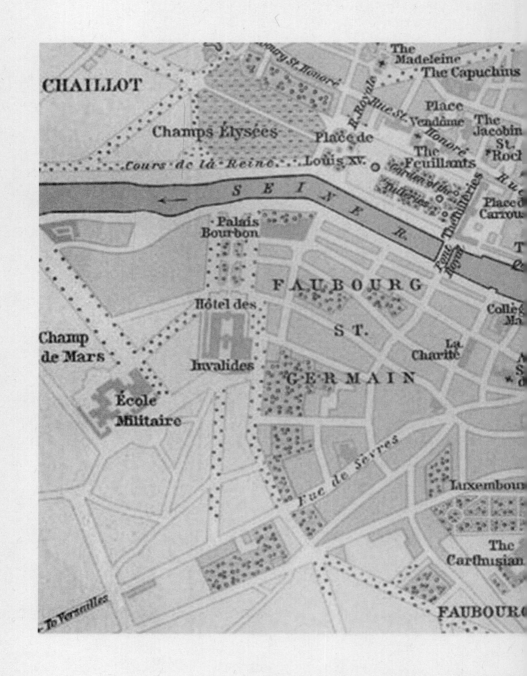

CHRONOLOGY

Cast of Historical Characters

D'Aiguillon, Duke (1720–1788). *French general exiled for his notorious relationship with Madame du Barry.*

Alexander I (1777–1825). *Czar of Russia (1801–1825).*

D'Angoulême, Duke (1775–1844). *Louis Antoine d'Artois, son of the Count of Artois. Last Dauphin of France (1824–1830).*

Arnould, Sophie (1740–1802). *Famous actress and singer of the French stage.*

Artois, Count of (1757–1836). *Youngest brother of Louis XVI. King Charles X (1824–1830). Last Bourbon ruler of France.*

Autié, Jean-François (1758–?). *Léonard's brother and second hairdresser to Marie Antoinette.*

Autié, Léonard Alexis (1746–1820). *Royal hairdresser, valet, and confidant to Queen Marie Antoinette.*

Autié, Pierre (1753-1814?). *Léonard's brother and hairdresser to Madame Élisabeth, Louis XVI's sister.*

D'Avaray, Duke (1759–1811). *Antoine Louis François de Bésiade, favorite of Louis XVIII.*

Bailly, Jean Sylvain (1736–1793). *First mayor of Paris in 1792. Guillotined in 1793 for defending Marie Antoinette.*

Balbi, Countess (1785–1852). *Anne Jacobé de Caumont la Force. Presumed mistress of Louis XVIII.*

Barras, Paul François (1755–1829). *Deputy of the Convention; he voted for the death of Louis XVI.*

Bault, Monsieur. *Served as concierge of Marie Antoinette's prison with his wife.*

Beaumarchais, Pierre (1732–1799). *Playwright whose best-known work was* Le Barbier de Séville.

Bertin, Marie-Jean Rose (1747–1813). *Milliner and dress designer to Queen Marie Antoinette.*

Bezenval, Baron Pierre (1722–1794). *Last commander of the Swiss Guards.*

Blache, alias Dumas. *Spy sent to London to keep watch over Madame du Barry.*

Boehmer and Bassenge. *Parisian jewelers who created the notorious diamond necklace.*

Bouillé, Marquis de (1739–1800). *French general who helped plan the royal family's flight to Varennes.*

Breteuil, Baron de Preuilly (1730–1807). *Last prime minister of Louis XVI.*

Busne, François de. *Knight of the Legion of Honor who was Marie Antoinette's last bodyguard.*

Calonne, Charles-Alexandre de (1734–1802). *Statesman responsible for the economic crisis of 1789.*

Campan, Jeanne-Louise-Henriette (1752–1822). *Marie Antoinette's lady-in-waiting from 1774 to 1792.*

Choiseul-Stainville, Duke of (1760–1838). *French colonel who assisted in the king's flight to Varennes.*

Coigny, François-Henri (1737–1821). *Soldier who served against the Republic in the Revolutionary Wars.*

Condé, Prince of (1736–1818). *Royal who left France to lead the counter-revolutionary army.*

Dillon, Édouard. *Marie Antoinette's favorite, known for his handsomeness.*

Drouet, Jean-Baptiste. *Postmaster of Ste. Menehould who helped capture the king in Varennes.*

Du Barry, Madame (1743–1793). *The last favorite of Louis XV; she was guillotined on December 8, 1793.*

Duthé, Mademoiselle. *Opera dancer and courtesan at the end of the eighteenth century.*

Élisabeth of France, Madame (1764–1794). *Princess and younger sister of Louis XVI.*

Feodorovna, Maria (1759–1828). *Empress of Russia and wife of Paul I.*

Fersen, Hans Axel de (1755–1810). *Swedish count and presumed lover of Marie Antoinette.*

Frémont. *Léonard's friend and partner of the Académie de Coiffure.*

Gluck, Christoph Willibald von (1714–1787). *German composer who taught Marie Antoinette the harpsichord.*

Guéménée, Princesse de (1743–1807). *French aristocrat and governess of Marie Antoinette's children.*

Guimard, Marie Madeleine (1743–1816). *Star ballerina of the French opera and wealthy socialite.*

Joseph II of Austria (1741–1790). *Holy Roman Emperor from 1765 to 1790. Marie Antoinette's brother.*

Julien. *Léonard's assistant, also known as the "handsome Julien."*

Lafayette, Marquis de (1757–1834). *French aristocrat and general in the American Revolutionary War.*

La Motte-Valois, Jeanne de (1756–1791). *Thief who stole the diamonds in the Necklace Affair.*

Lamballe, Princesse de (1749–1792). *Superintendent of Marie Antoinette's household, the court's highest rank.*

Langeac, Madame de. *Eccentric widow, also known as Madame d'Urfé.*

Larsenneur, Sieur. *French hairdresser to Marie Antoinette before Léonard's arrival in Paris.*

Lauzun, Armand Louis (1747–1793). *Later Duke of Biron, he commanded the anti-revolutionary army.*

Legros (de Rumigny). *Hairdresser in Louis XV's court, and writer of work devoted to the art.*

Limpérani, Marianna. *Renowned singer of the French stage in the late eighteenth century.*

Louis Joseph (1781–1789). *Dauphin of France. Second child and eldest son of Louis XVI.*

Louis XV (1710–1774). *King of France from 1715 to 1774. Grandfather of Louis XVI.*

Louis XVI (1754–1793). *Dauphin of France from 1765 to 1774. King from 1774 to 1791.*

Louis XVII (1785–1795). *Dauphin of France from 1789 to 1791. Uncrowned king 1791 to 1793.*

Louis XVIII (1755–1824). *Count of Provence during reign of Louis XVI. King from 1814 to 1824.*

Lucette. *Léonard's mistress. An actress and political activist.*

Malacrida, Marie-Louise Jacobie (1752–1837). Wife and mother of Léonard's children. Divorced ca. 1794.

Maria Theresa (1717–1780). *Empress of Austria from 1740 to 1780. Marie Antoinette's mother.*

Marie Antoinette of Austria (1755–1793). *Dauphine of France (1770–1774). Queen of France (1774–1792).*

Marie-Thérèse of France (1778–1851). *Louis XVI and Marie Antoinette's eldest daughter.*

Mercy-Argenteau, Count of (1727–1794). *Arranged marriage of Marie Antoinette and the Dauphin Louis.*

Montansier, Mademoiselle (1730–1820). *Versailles's theater director and investor in Léonard's theater.*

Necker, Jacques (1732–1804). *Louis XVI's finance minister who was banished from court in 1787.*

Nicolet, Jean-Baptiste (1728–1796). *Opened Nicolet's Theater, where Julie Niébert and Laura performed.*

Niébert, Julie. *Actress of Nicolet's Theater and member of the Grands Danseurs troupe.*

Noailles, Anna (1729–1794). *Known as Madame Etiquette in Marie Antoinette's court.*

D'Oliva, Nicole Leguay. *Prostitute who impersonated Marie Antoinette in the Necklace Affair.*

Paul I, Czar (1754–1801). *Emperor of Russia from 1796 to 1801.*

Polignac, Duchess of (1749–1793). *Beautiful favorite of Marie Antoinette from 1775 until her exile in 1789.*

Pompadour, Madame de (1721–1764). *Courtesan and mistress of Louis XV from 1745 to her death in 1764.*

Provence, Count of. *Title of Louis XVIII during the reign of his brother Louis XVI (1770–1791).*

Rochefoucauld-Liancourt, François (1747–1827). *Estates-General deputy who warned Louis XVI of revolt.*

Rohan, Prince de (1734–1803). *Cardinal who was duped in the Affair of the Diamond Necklace in 1785.*

Sophie Hélène Béatrice of France (1786–1787). *The youngest of Louis XVI's four children.*

Vandenyver, Baptiste. *Dutch banker who transacted the sale of Marie Antoinette's diamonds.*

Vaudreuil, Count of. *One of Marie Antoinette's favorites and the Duchess of Polignac's lover.*

Vigée-LeBrun, Louise Élisabeth (1755–1842). *The most important female painter of the eighteenth century.*

Viotti, Giovanni Battista (1755–1824). *Italian violinist and Léonard's partner in the Théâtre de Monsieur.*

A Note on Sources

Exaggeration and hyperbole always pose problems when constructing a biography, especially one that relies on centuries-old memoirs, letters, and secondhand accounts of events. Even government documents can be misleading when they are written in the midst of the type of regime and social change that took place during and after the French Revolution.

The literature on the Revolution is vast, but that which focuses on Marie Antoinette's hairdresser, Léonard Autié, is somewhat limited. The amazing hairstyles were a big story in their day, with extensive coverage in the press, but little was written about the man behind these creations. Fortunately, Baron Lamothe-Langon published Léonard's memoirs, *Souvenirs de Léonard, coiffeur de la reine Marie-Antoinette*, eighteen years after his death in 1838. The ghostwriter purported that he used Léonard's journals and notes to achieve the two-volume work, but his critics claimed that it was apocryphal, embellishing the hairdresser's role in history.

Nevertheless, I relied heavily on *Souvenirs de Léonard*, using its timeline and cast of characters. But, keeping its critics in mind, I also extensively consulted the court memoirs and letters of Léonard's contemporaries to investigate any doubtful claims and resolve any conflicts. Any discrepancies are duly noted in this biography. Unless otherwise noted in the endnotes, the dialogue retrieved from the *Souvenirs de Léonard* is unverifiable because the work itself has been deemed unreliable in its original form. However, all dialogue has been transcribed verbatim from original sources, and dialogue from any French sources has been diligently translated into English. All references have been cited with endnotes and a comprehensive bibliography.

Since 1838, only Louis Péricaud and Gustave Bord have revisited Léonard's story in any detail, focusing on his theater venture and his role in the royal family's affairs, respectively in 1908 and 1909. Although this book addresses the famous hairdresser's life and is not intended to be a reference in French history, it does shed light on the trials and tribulations of the last Queen of France from another angle—that of her confidant and coveted hairdresser.

A Note on Titles of Nobility

In the eighteenth century, it was the custom in France to address any gentleman, Monsieur; any married woman, Madame; and any young lady, as well as any unmarried woman, Mademoiselle. The plural was Messieurs, Mesdames, and Mesdemoiselles. Nobility, however, had certain privileges attached to it, and social etiquette required that its members be addressed properly.

The rules followed at the court of Versailles until 1789 have been respected in this work. The king is addressed as *Sire* or *Votre Majesté*, Your Majesty, with the queen addressed as *Madame* or *Votre Majesté*. The king's children and grandchildren are called *Enfants de France* (Children of France). The king's eldest prince, however, is addressed as *Monsieur le Dauphin*, the title used for the heir apparent to the throne. In speaking of him, one would say *Monseigneur* only; he is never called His Royal Highness as other princes. His younger brothers have various titles, according to their appendages, such as the Duke of Burgundy or the Duke of Anjou. They are addressed as *Monseigneur* or *Votre Altesse Royale*, Your Royal Highness. If one is speaking about the king's oldest brother, he can only be referred to as *Monsieur*.

The princes of the royal blood, *princes de sang*, but who are not sons of the king or his brothers, are addressed as *Monsieur le Prince*, with the second son being called *Monsieur le Duc*. As to the princes who are not of the royal blood, they are called *Mon Prince* or *Votre Altesse*. The princesses of France, the king's daughters, are called *Mesdames de France* as soon as they are born. The dauphin's wife is called Madame la Dauphine; for example, Marie Antoinette is addressed as Dauphine of France, until she becomes queen.

The marshals of France, lieutenants-general, and ambassadors are all addressed as *Monseigneur* or *Votre Excellence*. Any other person of rank, such as marquis, baron, or chevalier, is simply addressed as *Monsieur*.[1]

PROLOGUE

"To tell the truth, I think your head-dress is too fragile to bear a crown."
—EMPEROR JOSEPH TO HIS SISTER MARIE ANTOINETTE
VERSAILLES, 1777

Paris, France
October 1793

Captain de Busne, Marie Antoinette's last bodyguard, took her back to the cell where she awaited the hour of her execution. He had just accompanied her to the revolutionary tribunal where she was tried and convicted, but on this occasion, Captain de Busne was also guilty of unpardonable crimes. He had held his hat in his hand while escorting the fallen queen, he had taken the trouble of fetching a glass of water for her, and finally, he had offered his arm to help her down the dark staircase leading to her fetid prison cell. Later that day, Captain de Busne was denounced by the tribunal and arrested for his criminal behavior.[1]

Even the dark, dungeon-like Conciergerie prison was thought too good for Marie Antoinette. After hearing the revolutionary court pronounce the sentence of death a few minutes past four o'clock in the morning, the widowed queen, now a haggard old woman at thirty-eight, was escorted back to her cell. It was a small, narrow cell with no chimney, where the guards burned juniper to cover up the smell of the primitive sanitation—a far cry from her extravagant chambers at the court of Versailles just four chaotic years earlier.

How things had changed! When the young princess first arrived at the magnificent palace in 1770 to wed the future King Louis XVI, she was led to a bedchamber that would have been the envy of all of Europe. The ceiling had been freshly gilded and adorned with cherubs and doves. Behind a majestic banister, a brocade canopy was spangled with gold, screening the princess's lavishly decorated bed. Every detail in her private life, the choice of her marvelous clothes, even the style of the ribbon for her hair, was determined by the château's unbending traditions of decorum, dating back to the reign of the Sun King, Louis XIV, who not only constructed the enchanting palace of Versailles and its gardens, but also imposed rigid rules of etiquette. These rules prescribed the behavior of the courtiers and the king himself; even his grandsons, Louis XV and Louis XVI, who preferred family to court life, could not escape the strict codes of comportment, manners, and dress at Versailles.

When the prison maid, Rosalie, arrived at eight o'clock in the morning, only two candles were burning in her dark quarters. Marie Antoinette sighed and put on a white morning gown, draping a muslin handkerchief around her neck.[2] Long forgotten were the magnificent gowns and accessories of her designer Madame Bertin at Versailles, where the queen's *toilette* took place every morning in the presence of the court nobles. The ritual was a masterpiece of etiquette; the ladies-in-waiting had prescribed duties for dressing Marie Antoinette, while the maids of honor followed strict procedures for bathing. The honor of presenting her dress was granted to the noble lady present with the highest rank.[3] Afterward, the princess would retire to her sumptuous private apartments. On each side of the bed were two doors, which gave access to a royal suite of private rooms including her library, her bathroom, and a salon where she enjoyed reading her novels.

Now sitting on her prison cell bed, a rotting straw-filled mattress covered with a tattered woolen blanket, Marie Antoinette turned to Rosalie, who had promised to fulfill her last requests, and asked for paper and a pen to write a letter to her sister-in-law Madame Élisabeth, which was never to be delivered:

> *It is to you, my sister, that I write for the last time. I have just been condemned, not to a shameful death, for such is only for criminals, but to go and rejoin your brother . . .*[4]

Marie Antoinette signed and handed Rosalie the letter, which was covered with the fallen queen's tears. Suddenly, the cell door opened with a deafening clank. Marie Antoinette almost fainted at the sight of the red-hooded executioner. She recoiled with horror when he asked her to turn around so he could cut her hair, necessary to ensure that the guillotine's blade would work properly.[5]

Her hair. It would be the last thing to go. Marie Antoinette's hair, the talk of all Europe when she held her elaborate court at Versailles, had almost always been the sole responsibility of the eccentric Léonard Autié, the hairdresser with the "magical comb." Léonard, often taken for nobility, would enter the queen's private salon soon after her entourage of ladies-in-waiting dressed her. It was he who fashioned the ever-fantastic edifices of hair, sometimes adding feathers and accessories to create elegant hairstyles up to four feet high. But it could also be said that Léonard was indirectly responsible for the very first attacks upon the queen, found in inflammatory pamphlets circulating as early as 1775.[6] The attacks were prompted by Léonard's incredibly fanatical hairstyles, concoctions that reached such a height that it was necessary for ladies to kneel on the carriage floor—or hold the towering hairpieces outside the coach windows en route to balls and the opera.

Noble ladies of the court of Versailles felt obliged to imitate the queen's new and daring hairstyles, despite the danger of becoming burning infernos when they brushed against the candles of the palace chandeliers. The young ladies of Paris were also enthralled with the newfangled trends, drastically increasing their coiffure expenses and incurring large debts. Mothers and husbands grumbled, family fights ensued, and many relationships were irreparably damaged. In all, the general consensus of the French people was well publicized—the queen was bankrupting all the women of France, financially and morally.

The queens of France were always of foreign birth for political reasons, but Marie Antoinette was a princess from Austria, France's longtime enemy. Although it was vital for her to appear as French as possible, her fashions and hairstyles increasingly alienated her subjects. Attacks on the queen's hair were soon followed by damaging accusations ranging from sexual promiscuity to high treason. When incest was added to the list, the revolutionary court was able to finally make its case to condemn the queen to death.[7]

Léonard Autié, her celebrated and loyal hairdresser, was in exile in Germany when the executioner arrived at Marie Antoinette's prison cell, scissors in hand, on that chilly October morning in 1793. He tied her hands behind her back and, roughly grasping her hair, cut off the iconic locks that Léonard had made so legendary.

At eleven o'clock Marie Antoinette left the Conciergerie—where she had been confined for more than two months—and mounted the cart which was to carry her to the guillotine, passing along the streets of Paris and amidst lines of soldiers. According to witnesses, her face was pale and her eyes were bloodshot. She was nearly unrecognizable. Her once beautiful and envied coif, whitened by fear and grief, had been cut short around her cap.

Minutes later, the executioner would exhibit the severed queen's head to the crazed crowds at the foot of the scaffold. Nothing but the continuous roar of "Vive la nation!" could be heard as he held it up, victoriously, by her hair.

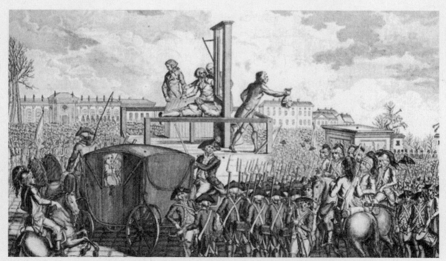

Scene at the Place de la République, October 16, 1793

PART ONE

The Mania

CHAPTER 1

Léonard the Magician

"Within three years Léonard shall be the foremost hairdresser in the universe!"
—Léonard to his friend Frémont
Café Procope, 1770

June 1769
Paris, France

Having made the long journey from Bordeaux, Léonard finally arrived in Paris on a summer's evening in 1769 after an arduous day of traveling. He was tired, he wrote in his journal, but he would not allow himself to appear so. His only luggage was but a "big bundle of vanity," which would hide the fact that he had just covered some 120 miles in two weeks *on foot* in the last leg of his journey.[1]

On the day that he arrived, all of Paris was out on the streets to observe the long-awaited transit of Venus across the face of the sun.[2] Crowds filled the squares, observing the spectacle through pieces of smoked glass. King Louis XV's château must have been packed, because when a sudden shower interrupted the transit, a large throng of sightseers pushed into the observing pavilion "with much noise and confusion."[3]

Louis XV was fascinated by astronomy, and the press reported that His Majesty had observed, in the company of his mistress, Madame du Barry, the passage of Venus across the sun, giving rise to some verses by a courtier: "What shall we be told by this telescope, this Venus, and this sun?"

The courtier was referring to Madame du Barry as Venus, the goddess of beauty, and the king as the great-grandson and heir to the throne of Louis XIV—known as the Sun King because of the splendor of his court at Versailles.

"It's a good omen!" Léonard noted in his journal. Destined to seek his fortune in beauty, he was certain that he would thus succeed through the "graces of the fairer sex."

In the meantime, he found lodging at No. 15 rue des Noyers, near the Place Maubert, for the modest rent of just six francs per month. Léonard must have been

Place Maubert, circa 1750

either short on funds or too exhausted to find better lodging, because the area had always been known as a gathering place of rowdy youths and beggars, once described as "poor devils who tramp the streets, go to bed with an empty stomach, wake without knowing where they will eat, pass the whole day in hunting for a half crown, and are always shabby, ragged, and down-at-heel."[4]

Pewter shops, taverns, and thieves' kitchens surrounded the square. If No. 15 was in keeping with the rest of the street—dirty, ragged, and ancient—it would have been one of many tall, leaning houses with "mildewed, irregular façades."[5]

At ten o'clock the next morning, Léonard was still stretched out on his hard straw pallet, a contraption that his hostess generously called a bed. As he fixed his eyes on the ceiling, he noticed that the meagerly furnished room was decorated with two spiderwebs. Léonard was unfazed; present circumstances aside, he had finally made it. Nothing was going to disturb his planning for his future.

Admitting to himself that he would never find his fortune in the sciences or assume a position in government, he appeared confident that he could take advantage of his two talents—his charisma and his artistic genius. "Greedy for gold and fame," he wrote in his memoirs, "I may very well decide the destiny of my whole life with just a single stroke of my comb!"

Upon arrival in Paris, Léonard would have noticed that Parisian men dressed in accordance with their rank, wearing small wigs to which they applied powder sparingly. Men of higher society wore waistcoats with breeches that reached down to their calves. Stockings were then held up with garters buckled just below the knee. Men of lower ranks normally dressed in the clothes discarded by the wealthier classes, which considerably lessened the contrasts between upper and lower society; only the cleanliness of the clothes spoke the difference. The less fortunate, for example, would wear a nightshirt day and night, hardly ever changing or washing it. Underwear was a luxury item that was usually beyond their means.[6] A young man's poverty follows him wherever he goes, the French proverb claims; yet, much of Léonard's rise in the European capital of fashion would hinge on his ability to confirm to a certain aesthetic—or at least, preserve the illusion of it. Unable to afford any powder, Léonard styled his hair and whitened it with a billowing gust of flour. With his fine gray waistcoat brushed until it shined and the folds of his tie artistically arranged for any amateur eye, he pulled his tightly drawn stockings up to show the calves of his legs. Now he could surely be taken for a gentleman. If he wasn't quite there yet, he was destined to become one soon enough. After all, Paris awaited him.

Not wanting to wake the porter, Léonard left his newfound lodging on tiptoe, carrying underneath his arm a hat that had been bleached by the scorching sun of the highways. Although he was in his mid-twenties, he wore a sword on his side for the first time in his life, like any other noble gentleman of France. He strutted down the rue des Noyers and the rue Saint-Jacques with the pretentiousness and haughtiness common to a young man his age.

In his pocket he held a receipt for two weeks' rent for his room, along with five large six-franc coins, a beautiful shell comb, and an "ample supply of confidence" in himself. He was planning on dining at an inn on the rue de la Huchette for twenty-five centimes, less wine, of course. Hopefully, by dining in the company of several illustrious knights of Saint-Louis he could "make up in vanity for what the stomach lacked" in such economical eateries.

Léonard reports in his memoir that he had hardly been walking for ten minutes when he began to hear comments from passersby:

"What a handsome youth!"

"What beautiful blue eyes!"

"Really a marvelous head of hair!"

"And I should think so!" Léonard smugly added.

From these comments it is natural to assume that the young Léonard was what was then called a *miroir à fillettes*, a sparkle in any young lady's eyes. With Léonard and his story, the truth is always somewhat mysterious. It is the classic tale of a young man coming from the provinces to make his way up in the grand society of Paris, but Léonard was from Gascony, and anyone outside this province would describe a Gascon as being cocky and vainglorious. In fact, the French word *gasconnade* means telling unlikely stories. Léonard was indeed given to exaggeration and bragging, as he himself admits, and he was quite dramatic in almost everything he shared. Although history indeed has confirmed that all of the events did take place, the role he played in them may not have been exactly as he would have everyone believe.

Léonard was not only known to occasionally stretch the truth, but at times he also conveniently failed to reveal the entire story. He did dress hair in Bordeaux, but he neglected to mention his rather long stops in Marseilles and Toulouse, serving as an apprentice there before taking the latest fashions in hair to Bordeaux. Although respected for his talent, his seductive flattery and flamboyant flair were insufficient to gain the patronage of the grand dames of Bordeaux. Unwilling to dress the hair of ladies of lower rank and status, Léonard then traveled from Bordeaux to Paris.

Although the exact year of his birth has been debated, Léonard Alexis Autié was probably born sometime between 1746 and 1751. He was born in the medieval town of Pamiers, in the mountainous region of southwestern France, and it is likely he spent his childhood near there; his parents, Alexis and Catherine, were domestic servants. Leaving home, he learned and practiced his craft while traveling in southern France before coming to Paris. It would not have been unusual for a young man with Léonard's ambition and talent to flee the rural, perhaps dreary, life of Pamiers.

Léonard Alexis Autié

Not coming from a good family, failing to make a name for himself in Bordeaux before coming to Paris, and ever conscious of his provincial status, Léonard would perfect his trademark arrogance—to the delight, fortunately, of his future clientele.

A short time before his arrival in Paris, Léonard had corresponded with a barber student by the name of Frémont, an acquaintance from Bordeaux, who had been employed as a hairdresser for the past six or seven months in Paris. Léonard revealed that his friend had secured a position with the well-known Monsieur Legros, a "manipulator" of hair who had gained a rather esteemed reputation in the splendid capital. When Léonard finally paid Frémont a visit, he had the opportunity to meet the hairdresser, whom he immediately found to be pompous and bloated with a sense of his own genius.

Legros, wrapped in a magnificent dressing gown, and almost lying prone on a large armchair, was supervising Frémont at the moment Léonard arrived. Frémont was styling the hair of a Parliament official who, unable to obtain a sitting from Legros at his own residence, had come to his salon for suggestions of a hairstyle most suitable to his features.

Frémont, now Legros's first assistant, held the government official's head in his hands and made it turn slowly from side to side for his master. Legros, wrapped in profound meditation, seemed unaware of all that was going on around him; he hadn't even noticed when Léonard entered the room.

At last, after a good quarter of an hour of deep thought, the master hairdresser finally blurted out in a resounding voice: "Curl this man's hair!"

While the man's hair was being curled, Frémont introduced Léonard to Legros without leaving his parliamentary customer's side. Legros then called the newcomer to his armchair, in as condescending a manner as he could muster.

"Is it true, my boy," he said to Léonard while toying with the frill of his gown, "that you intend to take up hairdressing?"

"Yes, sir, I have come to Paris to perfect myself in this art," replied Léonard.

"To perfect yourself! Upon my honor!" he said. "The word 'perfect' is exceedingly funny coming from such a young country boy."

Léonard was offended by the slight. "Sir," he said, "I'll have you know that I have styled hair in the grand cities of Bordeaux, Toulouse, and Marseilles."

"You have only frizzled and powdered hair in those cities, that is what you mean. I want you to know that the art of hairdressing exists only in Paris—and only since I appeared here on the scene!"

"I thought that the legendary Monsieur Dage . . ."

"Dage!" interrupted Legros. "Nothing but a chance hairdresser, a reputation he created between two of Madame de Pompadour's curling papers, when he happened to mention that he had dressed the hair of one of the king's other mistresses. Such reputations are despicable. Come, come, my friend, it would be much better if Dage had never existed. He was a man without genius, a man who could not train a single pupil and who allowed hairdressing to fall into the hands of females."

Legros stood up and continued, "Have you not read my book?"

"*The Art of Hairdressing*? Yes, sir, I have read it," said Léonard.

"Very good, young man; then we might make something of you after all!" Legros walked past Frémont to observe his apprentice's hair curling technique.

Legros, formerly a cook, told Léonard he only found women hairdressers in Paris when he first arrived, so he decided to open an *académie de coiffure* for ladies near the Bastille. He then published *The Art of Hairdressing for Ladies* in 1768.[7]

Léonard had indeed leafed through this whimsical treatise on hairdressing, which he described as being "written like a cookbook." Legros had ornamented it with his own quirky drawings, representing a number of the hairstyles that he had created. In fact, it was precisely because of this somewhat unprofessional manual of hairdressing that Léonard was convinced that hairdressers were "nothing more than clumsy barbers." This realization is what made Léonard enter the profession, hoping to surpass this "master of sham" as well as all of his ostentatious followers.

As soon as Legros had given Frémont permission to leave the salon for the evening, Léonard left with him. He thanked Legros, both for his promise of employment and for his contributions to the art of styling. He did not add that it was the old master's ineptitude that gave Léonard the confidence to come to Paris as a hairdresser.

The two friends then made their way to the Café Procope, located on a street near the theater district. Coffee was served while Léonard glanced through the *Gazette de France*, a biweekly paper in Paris at the time. He was absorbed in it for about ten minutes when, jerking with a sudden start, he struck the table with his knee and upset his nearly full cup of coffee. Wiping the coffee off his own trousers, Frémont shouted at Léonard, wanting to know what was wrong with him.

Léonard had found an article on the art of hairdressing, and he discovered that it was not Legros who had first understood the importance of an "awe-inspiring" hairstyle. It was actually a lawyer, and he began to read the article to Frémont:

> *The art of dressing a lady's hair is a free art like poetry, painting, or sculpture. By means of the talents that we possess, we bestow new charms on the beauty of which the poets sing.*[8]

Frémont told him that the article actually concerned a legal case that was being brought before the higher court. The wigmakers were defending their authority of a so-called exclusive privilege, which turned over to them the styling of all clients, both male and female.[9] Léonard quickly continued reading:

Drawing from *L'Art de la Coiffure des Dames Françaises* by Legros

A forehead more or less broad, a face more or less round, requires very different treatment. Everywhere it is necessary to improve nature or repair its blemishes. Moreover, it is proper to reconcile hairstyles with the flesh-tone's color under which the hairstyle is to be presented. It is necessary to know the shades, the use of lighteners, and the distribution of shadows so as to give more life to the complexion, more expression to the eyes, and more attractiveness to the charms.

Léonard had felt the very same way about hairdressing, he later wrote, but he could never have expressed it in such an eloquent manner. "Within three years, Léonard shall be the foremost hairdresser in the universe!" he told Frémont. He was determined that his hairstyles would one day "express, modify, or disguise one's innermost passions." With the fountain of youth springing from his comb, women would never be old before reaching the age of sixty, and the lives of young beauties could be lived, or even wasted, without ever showing it.

Frémont began to mock Léonard. *The world's foremost hairdresser? Him?* Didn't he live in that dreadful neighborhood on the rue des Noyers? Frémont would have been stunned had he known that Léonard arrived in Paris with only thirty francs in his pocket. When Léonard asked his friend to help him find a position in a salon, Frémont was taken aback. *How could the foremost hairdresser in the world find his beginnings in a common salon?*

Frémont proposed that Léonard should freelance; there were many "pretty little nymphs" in the grand capital who earned more than three hundred francs' salary. In fact, the performers from Nicolet's Theater could give a country boy like him a great opportunity. If Léonard would accept such a life while waiting for a better one, he would also be able to try out his daring experiments on Nicolet's actresses.

The actresses of Nicolet's Theater, established in 1760 by Jean-Baptiste Nicolet, first entertained its audiences with rope dancing, acrobatics, and balancing acts. When Nicolet had the honor of performing for King Louis XV, his troupe took the title of *Grands Danseurs du Roi*, or the King's Great Dancers.[10]

The plan certainly made a lot of sense—it would be much more auspicious an entry into Paris than slaving away in a common salon. Léonard may not have been wise about the ways of the theater when he first arrived in Paris, but at Nicolet's, he was soon to be thrown in the deep end.

Frémont planned to introduce Léonard to Julie Niébert, a beautiful actress from Nicolet's. After a long dinner that included the choicest cuts of meats washed down with a bottle of Clos-Vougeot, they were slightly tipsy; they clandestinely slipped past the theater's watchful manager into the dressing room. The women were getting ready to appear in a new pantomime that evening.

Madame de Pompadour styled *à la tête de mouton*

Frémont introduced Léonard to Julie and Laura (last name unknown), his lady love, as a "seductive youth and a clever artist all in one, who knows how to style or, at least, knows how to turn a woman's head." Julie immediately begged Léonard to style her hair—she was to play a fairy in the pantomime. Léonard lost no time in flattering the young maiden by letting her know that she was already a fairy in his eyes.

He rolled up the sleeves of his coat and motioned Julie to the seat in front of her dressing table, where she surrendered to the hairdresser's inspiration. He dexterously divided Julie's beautiful ash blonde hair into long flowing locks. When he asked Julie if she had any pearls, flowers, or tinsel at hand, she handed him a small case of imitation jewels.

When finally freed from its curling papers and Léonard's comb, Julie's hair took on a bewitching charm. He had divided it into zones with each one presenting different visions: here emeralds, there pearls with a little flower, and a few blossoms that seemed to pierce through the curls. But the most ingenious, the most original attribute of the hairstyle, was an array of stars which "in no way seemed to be part of the head which it crowned." Léonard succeeded in giving his creation the magic that could only be created by the fairy's wand.

Léonard's hairstyle would certainly have been over the top and far ahead of its time. Hairstyles of this period were generally petite and arranged close to the head. The *tête de mouton*, or sheep's head, style was particularly popular at the time and was characterized by soft curls with little or no height.

The sheep's head style received its name one day when Louis XIV was hunting with one of his ladies of the court. Her hair became disheveled during the chase, so she pulled it back and secured it with her garter—securing the bed of the king that night as well. This traditional style, featuring defined twists of curls that were arranged in rows across the front and top of the head, was popular throughout Europe and commonly included a *pompom*, an ornament such as small ribbons, pearls, jewels, flowers or decorative pins styled together. The pompom was named for Madame de Pompadour, the former mistress of Louis XV.

Léonard's creation would have been an outlandish diversion, but the means he used that day, and he would later ride to fame and fortune, were rather simple. He fastened his stars to a circle of extremely fine wire, and to this he attached two pieces of the same wire that he fixed in the hair; the golden stars seemed to arch themselves as a crown on his fairy's head without any visible attachment. "From two steps away," he wrote, "my illusion was complete!"

When Julie's hairstyle was entirely finished, Frémont looked at it pensively. Léonard noted that there was more than one detail to which he obviously objected, but considering the whole, his friend didn't dare express any criticism. Julie was visibly delighted when she saw the "contraption" that he had just erected on her head.[11]

Up to this time the petite dancer had received very little praise for her work on the stage. According to the reviews, she was somewhat awkward in her gestures and she showed little grace in her motions on the stage. Although theatergoers did find her charming, Julie's success on the stage had been, to say the least, somewhat limited.

That very night, things changed for the fairy.

When the fairy, fresh out of Léonard's hands, appeared on the stage, the audience immediately took notice. *What a strangely original hairstyle!* They tried in vain to discover how the aureole of stars was held above her head. It was perhaps admired because it was not understood, and Julie, who had never before been applauded on the stage, was enthusiastically greeted every time she appeared on stage thereafter. This unaccustomed reception encouraged her immensely. Moreover, something which had never occurred in her performance in *The King's Great Dancers*, she was recalled twice after the performance to accept her accolades.

When Julie and Laura later joined Léonard and Frémont in their dressing room after the play, Julie ran to Léonard and embraced him heartily. The couples then decided it was now time for "supper," which then implied something much more promising—especially when the party was composed of two lively actresses and two eager young men. Léonard recounted that it was a supper where knees touched, where the seats became closer and closer, and the candles soon began to flicker.

Léonard may just have been in the right place at the right time; the hairdressers à la mode in Paris at the time were usually young and good looking. But Léonard, often referred to as the "beau Léonard" or the "handsome Léonard," was more than just pleasing to the ladies' eyes. He was charmingly seductive in the art of flattery, sometimes spending hours caressing and flittering about his lady's tresses. It should not be surprising that the time for hairdressing might end at *l'heure du berger*, an expression for twilight when lovers meet.

The next morning, Julie and Léonard joined the other couple in Laura's room, where they were having breakfast, sipping liqueurs, and discussing Léonard's living arrangements. It soon became unanimous that the budding new artist should leave the "wretched" rue des Noyers, and take up residence on the boulevard where Julie and Laura resided. They were certain that Léonard would soon achieve a distinguished role in society, and they argued that it was paramount that he should live in a more fashionable and respectable area of Paris.

Léonard confided that it was not financially possible for him to move, but Julie begged him to ignore his scruples and accept her help. If she would share with him, he would in turn someday be able to share with her.

Laura and Frémont, agreeing with Julie, asked Léonard to take a cab to fetch his baggage. They wanted to move him into a nice furnished room on the boulevard that very evening, but Léonard objected. Ever conscious of concealing his provincial roots, he did not want Julie to discover that the only worthwhile item still left in his room on the rue des Noyers was his prized tortoiseshell comb.

When Julie then reminded Léonard that he would have to create a new fairy that very same evening, he hastened to the rue des Noyers to begin moving. While Léonard was fetching his magical comb, Frémont began searching for a new room for him.

French theater had changed drastically since the reign of Louis XIV fifty-five years earlier. The *Théâtre Français* and the *Opéra*, long devoted to the aristocracy, no longer had a monopoly on performances; new theater troupes were being created in the fairgrounds of Paris. This deregulated type of theater began to evolve from acrobatics and tightrope walking to sketches and plays. When Jean-Baptiste Nicolet took the fairground theater to the streets, opening his Nicolet's Theater on the boulevard du Temple, the new venue became an instant success.[12] The working class Parisians, who cared more for the theater than any other form of amusement, flocked there night after night.[13]

Royal patronage of the earlier venues had resulted in a monopoly over the theater, shielding the king from criticism and ridicule. With the rise in independent theaters and the increase in attendance of the working classes, the audience evolved from that of passive spectators to active participants, especially in the often disruptive parterre section on the theater floor. Politically, this was an early sign of the coming rebellion.

The reign of Louis XV also saw a change in the way the public regarded the profession of acting. Actresses were ordinarily looked down upon up to this point, often linked to prostitution. However, the new boulevard theaters required talented actresses who could sing, dance, and read—all attributes of a good upbringing in a formerly male-dominated profession. These actresses were thus often recruited from "good" families.

Léonard's fairy, Julie, would have performed in the afternoons for the public and in the evenings for higher society, requiring extensive rehearsals and the ability to learn many different parts each season. The perception of actresses gradually changed, and the increases in their wages paralleled the increased demand.

For the second performance of the new pantomime at Nicolet's, Léonard made Julie a hairstyle even more extraordinary than the first. The prodigious concoction of hair, tinsel, imitation stones, and everything else he had at hand, was so large that it couldn't have fit in a bushel basket. Accordingly, the audience again received the actress with a crescendo of enthusiasm.

The *Gazette de France* had only mentioned his first masterpiece in the morning edition. In the evening edition it revealed that a considerable number of nobility and higher bourgeoisie had flocked to the boulevard to enjoy the new spectacle. At the door of the theater stood a long, double line of carriages. In fact, Monsieur Nicolet had never seen such an illustrious audience in his smoky theater.

The next day, Frémont informed Léonard that the haughty Legros, having rushed to Nicolet's when he heard of Léonard's newfound fame, "had turned completely pale upon seeing the amazing hairdo of the fairy."

Legros told Frémont that the Gascon lad had dared to make use of "the strange, the exaggerated, and the outright ridiculous" in his fashions. It was a dangerous experiment, because an artist who gave in to such eccentricities either provoked hooting or cheers. Legros could not help but notice, though, that Léonard clearly had won acclaim for his efforts and was taking Paris by storm.

When Legros warned Frémont that his own days might well be numbered, Frémont tried to console him, telling him that his own unique style would always have its followers. But Legros could smell the future—he was fearful that this daring innovator would soon leave all other hairdressers with only the old dowagers of Paris.

Returning that same day from rehearsal, Julie revealed to Léonard and her friends that Nicolet's company was to play its new pantomime that evening at Madame the Countess of Amblimont's. It was just one more honor that the fairy's famous hairstyle had brought them. The king's minister, the Duke of Choiseul, had sent Monsieur Nicolet an order for them to appear, calling two companies together—that of the *Variétés amusantes* and theirs—at the countess's manor.

The fairy, her stars, and her hairstyle produced the same effect for the countess's guests as they had at Nicolet's. Not only did the countess ask to see Léonard in person, but after the play she took him through the salons, where he was introduced to her most illustrious guests. Haughtily ignored in one room, ogled through fans in another, and praised in a third, Léonard was at last conducted by the mistress of the house to a small room where a debonair nobleman and a pretty woman sat.

The couple on the sofa was none other than Monsieur the Duke of Choiseul, Foreign Minister of France, and his sister Madame de Grammont. Choiseul had gained the favor of the king's first mistress Madame de Pompadour by acquiring for her some letters that Louis XV had written to his cousin and paramour, the Duchess of Choiseul.[14] In 1757 the appreciative Madame de Pompadour was able to have him transferred to Vienna, where he formed a new alliance between France and Austria. His success in Vienna opened the way to a much larger career when, in 1758, he was named minister of foreign affairs, thus eventually controlling the policy of France. However, upon the death of Madame de Pompadour in 1764, Choiseul's enemies, led by the king's new mistress Madame du Barry, were maneuvering to remove him from the king's favor. His days were now numbered.

It appears that Léonard may very well have been aware of Choiseul's precarious situation when the Countess of Amblimont introduced him as the author of the hairstyle that was the talk of all the salons of Paris. The jolly minister was pleased to meet the celebrity, and he immediately asked him if he had ever dressed the hair of any abbesses. Léonard replied that he had indeed "accommodated several Episcopal heads" in the provinces. Then the illustrious minister rose and requested that Léonard follow him. Having gone through several apartments, they reached the rear of the stage on which a pantomime had just been performed. Choiseul knocked lightly at a little door, more announcement than request, and opened it right away; they found themselves in the midst of four young actresses busy making themselves up as abbesses.

The actresses objected to the intrusion but the minister informed the "pretty rogues" that he rather enjoyed slipping behind the curtain occasionally. When the young maidens saw that he had brought Léonard along, they were ecstatic. Léonard took each of them in hand, and soon made them "four of the prettiest abbesses that ever came out of a seminary," after which he slipped back into the salon for the show.

Léonard left the Amblimont residence with ten gold coins that Choiseul paid him for styling the abbesses' hair. The minister had also asked Léonard to visit him so he could recommend the new hairdresser to the ladies of the court; he added that his sister, Madame de Grammont, would surely grant him her support. Léonard knew that forming alliances with the right people in the right circles would be the only way to gain—and safeguard—any royal favor and patronage. However, a man's fame and fortune could also just as readily disappear by allying with a courtier who had lost the king's good graces.

While Léonard was riding home along the boulevard with Julie, she tried to speak between loud bouts of laughter. She was certain that she was something of a fairy because, since Léonard met her, he had become a man of society and even protected by noble lords. But Léonard chastised her, telling her that the only important result of the evening was "her caresses and Minister de Choiseul's ten coins in his pocket." Léonard was wise enough in the ways of the world to know that the minister was not a protector on whom one should depend.

Julie noted that Léonard seemed quite cynical, especially considering that only two days earlier he had roosted in a small room on the rue des Noyers. Léonard explained that the king's new mistress, Madame the Countess du Barry, would more than likely have the minister overthrown within a few months. By writing himself down as one of the minister's protégés, he ran the risk of displeasing the countess at the time when the good minister might very well be ruined.

Madame du Barry had become a prime minister in the court of Louis XV, a weak monarch who surrendered too easily to his mistresses. She had power, luxury, riches and the adulation of royalty. Lacking moral prestige only, she had her courtiers, her poets, and her pomp, all the while reigning over the king and the kingdom alike. If Léonard should ever desire to enter the splendid society of Versailles, knowing Madame du Barry's favorites—and her enemies—would be imperative. Having the magic comb, he now only needed the clientele, the noble ladies to supply him with all the royal tittle-tattle.

Within the week following Madame d'Amblimont's soirée, Léonard received some thirty scented notes demanding his talents. He didn't even know how these women had his address; clearly, word about him was spreading through the city. First it was a dancer, then a singer, then an actress of the *Théâtre français*, more often a nymph from the *Variétés amusantes*. The Sophie Arnoulds, the Duthes, and the Adelines and other sublime ladies were also soon on his numbered list; yet requests from women of real quality were still few and far between, which surprised him.

In the salons of Madame d'Amblimont he had heard the whispered praise of his physique, the brightness of his eyes and the whiteness of his hands. Considering this, he was astonished that an auspicious hairdresser such as himself should still languish in the dim light of the dressing rooms of Nicolet's Theater—especially at a time when other lackeys in high society were making their fortune. He began to wonder if it were not bad fortune at all, but rather some dubious plot by a rival.

Léonard finally discovered that someone indeed had done him a disservice. Legros, stunned by Léonard's quick success, had gone about venting his spite. Although Legros could not deny Léonard's superiority, the fairy's hairstyle had crushed him, and every day that another head of an actress or dancer was "Léonarded" (as it was called in the theater world), Legros became increasingly antagonistic. Having no way to attack Léonard's creations and aware of Léonard's illicit liaisons with the actresses of the boulevard, Legros turned to attacking his morality.

In order to understand more clearly the success of Legros's attack against Léonard, it is necessary to know that during this period in history the hairdresser was considered a "man of intimacy" and a confessor; there were no secrets in either the boudoir or the dressing room. One of the merits of a hairdresser was also to be a handsome man blessed with a fine physique. What the ladies thought of Léonard in that respect is well documented. Yet Legros, by means of slander, succeeded for a time in denying Léonard the honorable and noble dressing rooms of the Faubourg Saint-Germain, the Palais-Royal, and the Faubourg Saint-Honoré. In his memoirs, Léonard did not reveal any names nor the vile words sputtered by Legros, but from the context of his notes, it was clear Léonard had gone above and beyond in his role as hairdresser.

One morning Léonard received a small triangular note covered with a most delicate perfume, which read:

Madame the Marquise de Langeac requests Monsieur Léonard to call on her tomorrow at noon; she is to give a reception in the evening, and as a kindly fairy may be there, she will be delighted to come to an understanding with Monsieur Léonard on the hairstyle which may best suit that fairy, so that she may have nothing in common with that of Nicolet's.

Léonard decided to visit the Marquise de Langeac with the utmost secrecy; his instinct convinced him not to show the note to Julie. Perhaps he knew his affair with the actress was an obstacle to gaining access to the intimate boudoirs of the noblest of Parisian ladies. In pursuit of fame and influence, he could not be tied down; he would never allow a fleeting relationship with an actress to interfere with his machinations to move in the highest circles.

In Paris, in those days, it was possible to be fashionable with very little money. The noble lords only wore their clothes on two or three occasions, and it was great booty for the lackeys and valets when the lords discarded pieces of their wardrobes at bargain prices. Through these means Léonard had formed a rather fine, and especially varied, collection. He lacked nothing, not even the sword with its steel hilt, nor the cocked hat covered with black satin, for full dress. In short, Léonard could have been taken anywhere for the son of a good family. His character as a fashionable cavalier was questionable only when he opened his mouth.

He assuredly looked more like a marquis than a hairdresser, and when he had himself announced at the residence of the marquise, the chambermaid announced him as "Marquis de Léonard!"

Madame de Langeac received Léonard while lounging on her bed, as was the custom of women of society toward those whom they treated without any ceremony. Her subsequent flirtations are more likely indicative of the reason she greeted him this way. She immediately informed him that the court hairdresser, Larsenneur, had formerly arranged her hair, but due to Léonard's acclaim, she would choose him as his replacement.

Léonard was honored, but the marquise asked him to put honor aside. She mentioned that he was known for creating divinities out of "Nicolet's wretched dancers," and she reminded him that it was only his achievements that summoned him to her. The marquise had put great stress on the words "Nicolet's wretched dancers"; Léonard felt that they had the air of not just condescension, but jealousy.

Madame de Langeac's questions showed she was acquainted with the slanderous stories circulated against him by Legros. But she was willing to put aside the hearsay,

Hôtel de Langeac

and for good reason. She had just received news from the king that she was to be included among the ladies of the court who were acceptable to the young Dauphine Marie Antoinette, expected to arrive soon at the court of Versailles. In fact, the marquise was chosen to belong to the enviable group of the princess's select circle, an extraordinary honor.

The marquise boldly revealed that she intended to help him find his place in society. Léonard was taken aback, but grateful. He knew that a hairdresser soon deserved the confidence of the ladies who employed him. Better still, the marquise planned to place him with the celebrated dauphine.

She described Larsenneur as "dull and without imagination." He was a sort of wigmaker whose speeches, she said, "crushed our minds at the same time that his heavy hands crushed our heads." Such a servant would surely not suit the princess Marie Antoinette of Austria who had been described as quick, lively, and even a bit giddy.

Although the marquise had high hopes for Léonard to become hairdresser to the dauphine, she wanted him to be first most devoted to herself, warning him that she was a bit exacting. In other words, no more foolishness at Nicolet's Theater. She was anxious to have his fame increase, but told him to be forewarned: No one knew better than an actress how to ruin a reputation.

It was difficult for Léonard to conceal his grin when the marquise asked if there was anything about his relationship with the actresses that she should know. He assured her that there was absolutely nothing she should know. Léonard's memoirs tells us what he meant by this—he was speaking a bit too literally.

After the conversation, the marquise at first dismissed him, but then impulsively asked him to stay and arrange everything on her dressing table to dress her hair. She also asked him to wipe the mirror—but not to look into it.

Léonard did as he was told. He looked in the mirror, which stood opposite her bed, and the marquise got up with the most complete lack of precaution. He later noted in his journal, "Léonard, my friend, you are now launched into brilliant adventures, you lucky rogue!"

The Marquise de Langeac was a woman in her mid-twenties and petite with very attractive features. Without the assistance of her maid, she had put on an almost transparent muslin skirt, and rather carelessly wrapped herself in a cape with ornate lace. She sat down at her dressing table and Léonard prepared to style her hair.

He began by dividing her hair into silky locks and asked what type of gown the marquise intended to wear that morning. She told him that she was neither going out nor receiving anyone; she would remain in her morning lingerie. She informed Sophie, her lady-in-waiting, that she could have the morning off. Sophie obeyed and suppressed a smile as she was leaving the room.

The marquise said she was hopeful that Léonard was going to make her very pretty, but the Gascon flattered her by saying that there was nothing for him to do in that respect. At that moment, the marquise's cape opened, permitting Léonard to see what he thought was "the most beautiful bosom in the world." Bewildered, Léonard tried to distract his thoughts by focusing on the marquise's hair as though there was nothing else of import in the room.

When the marquise complained that he was pulling her hair, he apologized. He was extremely agitated, and she understood completely, after having glanced at herself in the mirror. Without covering up, she asked him to continue his work. But Léonard was unable to resist the temptation, and he planted a burning kiss on the marquise's bosom.

Very late in the evening, Madame de Langeac told her hairdresser that if she had the privilege of making nobles he would be a prince that very evening.

"Marquise, I considered myself lucky enough to be a bit of a marquis this evening, but, for mercy's sake, please do not *de-marquis* me too soon," he replied.

CHAPTER 2

The King's New Mistress

"This young man must come to see me at Versailles, and I shall guarantee his fortune."

—Madame the Countess du Barry
to the Marquise de Langeac, Paris

March 1770
Paris, France

After Léonard's first meeting with the Marquise de Langeac, she began to send for him at all hours of the night and day. One would have thought that she spent all of her time in the hands of her hairdresser, but according to one onlooker, her hair never seemed so badly arranged.

The toilette of noble ladies customarily took place in the morning and the evening. When the gentleman of the house sent word that breakfast was being served, the lady's reply was generally "do not wait for me." Her toilette was an intimate reception held in her boudoir where she received only a small circle of dearest friends. Her hairdresser would take an hour or more to complete his creation, during which time the conversation went on without interruption.[1]

The evening toilette, the hour when Paris and the court of Versailles normally had their hair curled up rolled in rollers, lasted almost as long as that in the morning, but no company was admitted. Whenever Madame de Langeac sent for Léonard for her evening toilette, there was always some concert to attend, or a ball at the Salle de Vauxhall, a new theater that resembled an antique circus. Otherwise, there was a reading of a comedy or a tragedy, which was to be given at the residence of an older countess who no longer had anything better to do. Madame de Langeac's porter, who was accustomed to seeing Léonard enter by the courtyard gate, never saw him come out again after her evening toilette.

Due to Léonard's frequent evening absences, Julie soon began to suspect something, and one night she had one of the theater boys follow him. The young lad saw Léonard enter the Marquise de Langeac's residence but he too never saw Léonard come out, having waited for more than five hours.

Early the next morning Léonard heard someone knocking at his door. He had just come in, and his bed was incriminatingly untouched. He opened the door, shocked to find Julie. The visit was such a jolt that he meticulously recorded the entire encounter in his journal.

"What a pleasant surprise!" Léonard exclaimed, perhaps unconvincingly.

"Pleasant surprise?" she asked as she entered the room. "Léonard, do you love me?"

"What kind of question is that?" asked Léonard. "After six months of sweet intimacy, it is a startling one, to say the least."

"Not at all," she said, "but I shall make it more clear by repeating it with an additional word—do you *still* love me?"

Léonard squirmed.

"I doubt it," Julie continued, "especially when I find you all dressed up so early in the morning, and your bed has not been touched!"

"Is that a reason to doubt my love!" asked Léonard.

"It's the best of reasons! However, I am not scolding you," she said, all the while looking at herself in the mirror. "As you know, there is no faithfulness clause in our treaty. When I fancy a man, I take him. Take the Petit-Diable, our head tightrope dancer, who is certainly the most seductive Adonis I know. Just as I expect you to overlook my tightrope walker, I myself will overlook your Marquise de Langeac."

"The Marquise de Langeac! Who told you?" he asked.

"That you go and arrange, or rather, disarrange her hair every evening, and that it lasts until morning, why, everybody knows it—it isn't the little woman's first affair! And she did not even think it worth her while to make a mystery of this one. However, we have to take arms and protest, we women of the theater, against such beauties of high society.

"To tell the truth, if this continues, it will be impossible for us to have any fairly decent admirers if these ladies continue robbing us of our hairdressers and lackeys. I can't stand it any longer, and I'm certainly going to start a revolt! Adieu, Léonard!"

Julie stormed out of the room.

In April 1770, a long procession of fifty-seven new French carriages, each drawn by six horses, left Schönbrunn on the outskirts of Vienna. The Archduchess Marie Antoinette of Austria was never again to see the palace's long yellow façade with its green shutters. The future queen of France, only fourteen years old at the time, was traveling to an island on the Rhine River to be officially handed over to her new French family. The trip would require a stable of more than *twenty thousand* horses and at least 132 servants. All along the route from village to village, bells pealed and artillery fired salutes.[2]

When the dauphine entered the "Austrian" entrance of the small house on the island, the little dauphine was not stripped naked (as historians have noted) so that she could not retain anything from her homeland; that old custom had long been abandoned. After putting on a ceremonial dress and attending a short recital, Marie Antoinette left through the "French" entrance. That was it—the princess was now French.

Months earlier, when the coaches to fetch the dauphine from her homeland had been constructed in Paris, they were the talk of the city and the court of Versailles. Everyone hoped to see them, and crowds were already gathering at the coach builder Francien's to admire the exquisite carriages. They were built at great expense by order of the Duke of Choiseul, who had also designed them.

Madame de Langeac was astonished that she had not yet seen the dauphine's coaches. When Léonard arrived, she asked her hairdresser to surpass himself—she wanted a very roguish, coquettish hairstyle. It was rumored that Madame the Countess du Barry, the king's new mistress, was planning to visit Francien's that morning, and the marquise hoped she might possibly see the countess there. She told Léonard

The royal coach
(BIBLIOTHÈQUE NATIONALE DE FRANCE)

that she did not want to lose a single glance from the gentlemen, whether the favorite made an appearance or not.

The marquise also invited Léonard to join her. She wanted to present him to Madame du Barry, hinting that it would be quite a "natural opportunity" from which he might profit. Léonard, neither wanting to upset Madame de Langeac nor refuse an opportunity to be introduced to anyone important at court, happily obeyed.

When the marquise added that it was possible that the countess might dismiss Monsieur Legros in order to take him on as her new hairdresser, she noted slyly, "But you must be no more than Legros's substitute!" She clearly feared that Léonard was to give the countess the same kind of services that she received.

When Léonard arrived, a small crowd was besieging the door of the renowned coach builder; it was almost impossible to enter the shed where the famed carriages were on display. One was covered with crimson velvet, on which the four seasons were embroidered in gold. The other was covered with blue velvet, and on its doors were displayed the four elements. All

Madame the Countess du Barry

the embroidery was in exquisite taste, and the roof of each carriage had bouquets of golden flowers that were so "supple that they nodded gracefully in the slightest breeze."

The flexibility of the coach springs was such that these carriages would rock at the slightest touch. Madame du Barry, the king's favorite, was there with the Duke of Aumont, first gentleman of the King's Chamber. She gave one of the carriages a light touch and, having started it into a gentle swing, remarked: "See, monsieur, this looks more suitable for tender love."

Madame du Barry noticed Madame de Langeac, and eagerly approached her: "Good day, dear marquise," she said. "What are you doing these days? You are no longer seen at court; you are ill, perhaps. You do look pale."

Madame de Langeac politely assured her that she was quite well and having spotted Léonard made a sign for him to approach. She presented him to the favorite of Louis XV, saying, "Here, Madame du Barry, is young Léonard, a hairdresser of great merit, who would already be famous at court if he were not so modest."

The countess had already heard of Léonard and replied, "Now, dear heart! There is nothing I should not do to oblige you. This young man must come to see me at Versailles, and I shall take care of his fortune."

When the countess asked the Duke of Aumont for his approval, he kissed her hand and agreed that they would be able to help the hairdresser further his career. Léonard noted, however, that the duke gazed at him with contempt when he said, "Only too glad, madame, only too glad to be able to please you, as well as our charming and mischievous marquise, in this matter."

The Duke of Aumont looked at Léonard with that patronizing contempt which noble lords were known to exhibit when meeting a noble lady's new protégé. These new protégés were often handsome young merchants, lawyers, or designers with enormous wealth; but to the nobles, who were not always wealthy, success in the late eighteenth century meant only status and privilege, not money. As these newcomers moved up in society, they often felt frustrated by the nobles—a class determined to keep everyone in their right place. Léonard was going to be no exception.

In the memoirs of her contemporaries and in her own letters, Madame du Barry is revealed to be not as elegant or refined as her predecessor, Madame de Pompadour. Neither was she as vindictive or as interested in politics. In fact, the opportunities for squandering public money were sufficient for Madame du Barry, so long as her drafts on the royal treasury were honored and she could retreat to her lovely château Luciennes. Her illustrious predecessor had been much more ambitious in the king's affairs.

While mourning the death of one of his earlier mistresses in 1745, Louis XV was introduced to Madame Jeanne Antoinette d'Étiolles by a group of courtiers. The king invited her to a masquerade ball at Versailles; one month later she was separated from her husband and was installed in an apartment at Versailles directly above that of the king's. Having no title to be presented at court, the king purchased the Pompadour marquisate, a tract of land with a title of nobility attached to it, and Marquise de Pompadour slipped into her role as the king's new favorite.[3]

Although she used her influence to promote the fine arts, which she herself cultivated with considerable success, her extravagance was unrestrained. Not only did Madame de Pompadour obtain a hefty pension, but she also interfered frequently in government affairs. Among other political intrigues, she was blamed for promoting a disastrous war with Prussia.

After the death of Madame de Pompadour, the next mistress, first known by the name of Mademoiselle Lange, belonged to the "establishment" of the notorious

Madame Gourdan. When she became the mistress of the Count du Barry, he had her appear before the king, who was instantly struck with her charms.

Once introduced at court, the newly named Countess du Barry immediately took full advantage of her new position, attempting to ruin the king's minister, the Duke of Choiseul, so she could promote her own minister, the Duke of Aiguillon. The duties of the king's mistresses were never confined to pleasing only the king. The *maîtresse en titre* received the homage of men of letters and, in return, bestowed upon them her patronage. As the coffers of the kingdom became her cash box, gold coins flowed to her milliners, goldsmiths, jewelers, furniture dealers, and artists who painted her portraits.

The Countess du Barry exhausted the royal treasury but, according to the French philosopher Voltaire, she also possessed beauty, a kind heart, and many amiable qualities. She was known to intercede on behalf of condemned criminals and to give generously to charities and the less fortunate, even in later years when her means were fairly limited.[4]

When Léonard made the trip to Versailles to visit Madame du Barry, he said he felt like a "poet who goes to a lord for permission to dedicate his work to him." The king was with her when Léonard arrived. While Léonard waited in the antechamber, he overheard Louis XV and his favorite's discussion in the next room.

"As to that which relates to magnificence," said the countess, "it seems to me that Louis, fifteenth of that name reigning, should see that the woman whom he honors with his favors should hold the premier rank everywhere."

"Well, then, are you telling me, countess, that Francien has made you a carriage more magnificent than those intended for the dauphine?" asked the king.

"Here is the design," she said. Léonard could hear the unrolling of a large sheet of paper.

"Look, sire," she continued, "is it possible to imagine anything more enchanting than a graceful coat of arms on a gold background? The sides represent, one, a basket with a bed of roses, on which two doves lovingly bill; the other, a heart pierced by an arrow, with quivers, torches, all the attributes of love; finally, a garland of flowers like a string of pearls, which runs around the panels to encircle them with its bright colors. Has Your Majesty ever seen anything finer?"

"It is perhaps too fine, countess," said the king. "The malicious may perhaps notice that one of the doves is well past sixty, and I do not know if people will not laugh at the roses, the quivers, and the torches."

"Nonsense, sire, do kings ever get old?" she asked. The king just laughed boisterously.

The king exited through another door, and Léonard was nudged by a gentleman in black into the boudoir. Madame du Barry was lying on a sofa with her head resting on her hand, a scene which Léonard noted, reminded him of Cleopatra. When she saw Léonard, she commented that he was dressed as well as any nobleman at court. She then remarked that the Marquise de Langeac showed very good taste in the choice of her protégés, but it was vital that she should become acquainted with what he could do. Léonard suggested that if the countess would send for him some morning, she would be able to see his talent firsthand.

She agreed. "Very well, you will find me at Luciennes tomorrow at noon. Wear that suit; it is very becoming to you. Goodbye, Léonard. You will mention your name to my maid, and she will have my orders."

While the humble carriage that was taking Léonard back to Paris shook him roughly on its worn cushions, he was already constructing a story to keep the news of his appointment from reaching Madame de Langeac. Perhaps Léonard was ridden with guilt: Was he using the marquise to make his way into the royal household? Or, knowing the marquise's attachment to his services, was he afraid to disappoint the very generous patroness?

Fortunately, when Léonard returned home, he found a note from the actress Mademoiselle Guimard, inviting him that very evening to her house at Pantin, where plays were often given. The celebrated dancer informed him that he would have a dozen or so ladies to style, and that he should therefore come with plenty of inspiration.

Léonard arrived at Mademoiselle Guimard's manor, and after he had dressed the hair of the performers, he decided to take a little rest in a salon near the stage while waiting for the performance. Maids, milliners, seamstresses, and flower girls occupied the salon, and he was somewhat surprised by their loose morals. Léonard had just entered the world of the Parisian *grisettes*.[5]

Grisettes were young girls who were separated from their poor families at the age of eighteen and lived in rooming houses, working hand to mouth to survive. However, the grisettes were living out their fantasy, unlike the young ladies of good families who were kept at home, or chaperoned by their strict mothers, devoted aunts, and brow-beating grandmothers. The grisettes were, in some sense, entirely free, and they never passed up an opportunity to meet a new friend.

When Léonard later decided to rest in the garden under the thick, darkening trees, he could hardly take a step without stumbling against something—in one spot it was a small foot in a white shoe of one of the grisettes, in the other it was a boot. He called the garden "Elysium," paradise in Greek mythology.

Léonard did not return to Paris until after midnight. While passing on the boulevard du Temple, he saw a light in Julie's apartment. He knew now she was certainly in love with the Petit-Diable, and probably no longer thought of him. Jealous and under the influence of Mademoiselle Guimard's champagne, he wanted to prove to

Mademoiselle Guimard

Julie that actors were not the only ones who could be ornery; he too could be as much of a devil as her dancer.

He knew that Julie lived in the little house with only two female servants, and if he broke her windows with stones, then the Petit-Diable would come running out if he were there. While the Petit-Diable was looking for him, he would then have time to slip through the open door.

At the first sound of breaking glass, the window opened and the fat, red face of Julie's friend, the abbot, appeared. Not seeing anyone below, the abbot closed the window; disappointed, Léonard decided it was time to make his way home.

Just then a nearby patrol arrived and formed a circle around him. When the police officer asked Léonard what he was doing there, he answered that he was a bit of an astronomer, and he liked to gaze at the planets on such a beautiful evening. The officer said he didn't believe that the love of astronomy ever authorized a person to break the windows of the good people of Paris.

When he asked Léonard to follow him to the guard house, Léonard cried out, "For mercy's sake, Monsieur le Sergeant, take me to the commissary of the district; I shall make myself known to him."

The officer refused his request, and made it clear that he intended to take Léonard to jail—until Léonard shouted out, "But, Monsieur le Sergeant, I am in the service of Madame the Countess du Barry!"

Upon hearing the favorite's name, the officer quickly removed his hat, saying, "If you belong to Madame du Barry, this is then a different matter. Still, you were breaking windows."

Léonard told the officer that he was only following the orders of Madame the Countess, and that Julie, the dancer before whose house they had met, had slandered Madame the Countess, and such was the manner in which she always took revenge, adding that the king also agreed to it.

"It is not such a bad idea after all," said the officer, "and it does give work to the glaziers of Paris."

"Good night, sir!" said Léonard, and he turned to continue his way home.

Léonard had good reason to feel on top of the world that evening. Welcomed in the boudoirs of the noblest ladies and in high demand by actresses and operagoers, Léonard could receive favorable treatment with just the mere mention of the royal favorite's name. Within a very short time, the brilliant new coiffeur had not only become the toast of Paris, but he was expected to be treated with the respect due any noble gentlemen.

"Finally Léonard arrived," said the Countess of Genlis, "He arrived and he was king."

CHAPTER 3

The Court of Versailles

"Happiness is seldom sober; it becomes elated, and it almost always runs away beyond the limits of moderation."

—LÉONARD TO FRÉMONT, 1772

May 1770
Versailles, France

King Louis XV often found himself more concerned with his mistresses than his kingdom. Living in the extravagance of Versailles, an opulent haven in comparison to the squalor and stench of Paris, the unpopular monarch rarely made the fifteen-mile excursion to the city. Rather, Parisians were forced to make the trip to Versailles to see him. Vendors, artisans, and purveyors eventually obtained the right to build stalls on the side of the grandiose château to supply the needs of its three thousand inhabitants. The general public had practically free access to the entire palace, roaming the corridors and even watching the royals dine. (Ironically, access for visitors then was much freer than it is today.[1])

A messenger could make the trip on horseback from Paris to Versailles in a little more than half an hour, but the excursion was much longer by coach. The coach departed from Léonard's door at nine o'clock, arriving at Madame du Barry's elegant pavilion at noon. He gave his name at the entrance, surprised to find everyone already expecting him. He was free to pass everywhere; after going through six rooms filled with paintings, decorated scrolls, and gilding, each more magnificent than the other, he entered a sort of temple whose altar was an extravagant and unmade bed. A young chambermaid informed him that the countess was in her bath.

Léonard confusedly told the maid that the countess was expecting him. She smiled and, having opened a small door of which she had the key, led Léonard into the next room without announcing him. The king's favorite had left her bathtub and had just slipped between two warm sheets. Only the end of her nose could be seen when she complimented Léonard for his punctuality.

Madame the Countess du Barry in her boudoir

She opened by asking Léonard if he had ever traveled in the Orient. It appears that a friend of hers, the captain of the king's navy, had told her about a unique custom that existed in Asia, and she was certain that it could improve one's health. Wealthy Asians were having themselves massaged upon leaving the bath, and it was supposedly a very pleasant experience. If it were introduced in France, it could become a very valuable tool for hairdressers.

Léonard, however, was not familiar with the word "massaged"; the countess explained that it consisted of applying a certain pressure on different parts of the body with the hands, as a kind of tonic. It was performed by a person of the opposite sex and, although the massage was normally performed by women in the Orient, she assured him that there should be no objection to just the opposite in France. Léonard began to blush. Noticing his reaction, the countess remarked that he should remember that it was a "question of therapeutic care" only.

Léonard, not one to disobey such requests, did exactly as the countess asked.

Once it began, she exclaimed various compliments, including, "Oh, yes, the Orientals are very wise!"

Léonard later returned to Paris quite proud of himself for his increased standing at court—however he came about it. He soon arrived at the residence of Madame de Langeac, and began to arrange her hair.

"Léonard," said Madame de Langeac, "tell me about your visits to Madame du Barry."

"The first was rather insignificant," said Léonard.

"And the second?" she asked.

"The second," he replied, "has proved to me that Madame du Barry is not less a friend of progress in the arts than the late Marquise de Pompadour."

"How is that, Léonard?" she asked.

"Madame the Countess received me in her bath," he said.

"A well-known habit of the favorite, it is there that she usually gives sittings to her painter," she said.

"Oh, but there was no question of painting this morning!" said Léonard, and he told the story about the intimate Oriental custom that the countess had asked him to try on her.

"And you obeyed her!" exclaimed Madame de Langeac, giving him a sharp fillip with her pretty fingers.

Fearing that her paramour might soon be snatched away, she continued, "Léonard, I forbid you to return to Luciennes. Come, promise not to return there."

Léonard, the Gascon who arrived in Paris with little but his dreams and his comb, was now in the enviable position of being claimed by two countesses. And this was only the beginning.

For hundreds of years the reigning house of France had to defend its borders from the house of Habsburg, which, consisting of Austria, Spain, and Holland, surrounded Louis XV's royal domain. When the Habsburgs were driven from Spain and the new house of Hohenzollern in Germany became a powerful threat, France and Austria were ready to forget their hereditary feud and forge a new alliance. King Louis XV and the Austrian empress Maria Theresa thus began plans for the young Dauphin

Louis Auguste of France, the young prince next in line for the throne, to marry the Austrian archduchess Marie Antoinette. Maria Theresa had selected her youngest daughter, hoping that "Marie Antoinette's beauty would gain more power in France than her soldiers had hitherto been able to achieve." The marriage had been arranged long before it was ever announced to the public.

When Marie Antoinette finally arrived in France from Austria to wed the Dauphin Louis, she made her entry in the magnificent coach that had been sent to Vienna by the Duke of Choiseul. Madame du Barry had demanded that doves and her trademark of Cupid's arrows be added to the already quite elaborate adornment on the carriage.

Marie Antoinette's reception in France surpassed all expectations. As she had been adored in Austria, all French hearts now turned toward her as she made her way to Versailles.[2] Peasants came from every direction, and the roads were strewn with flowers. Young girls surrounded her coach, offering her flowers and crying, "How lovely our princess is!"

The dauphine finally reached the château of Versailles in the evening on the 15th of May 1770; she was married to Louis Auguste the following day in the palace chapel. Kneeling at the foot of the altar, the new couple swore devotion to each other. The solemn ceremony was hardly over when a terrifying storm erupted. The villagers and the Parisians who had made the long trip scrambled in the gardens for shelter from the torrential rains. The plans to illuminate Versailles that evening with fireworks were cancelled.

After the disappointing wedding celebration in Versailles, the royal family was looking forward to the magnificent fête and fireworks in Paris. But on the day the dauphine entered the French capital, there was such a clamorous crowd of all ages and classes assembled to meet her that people literally trampled each other to get a glimpse of her. The crowds became uncontrollable after the fireworks at the Place Louis XV were cancelled due to mechanical problems. A fire that broke out on the scaffolding of the statue of Louis XV only added to the commotion. Many spectators were crushed to death or pushed into the river, hundreds were wounded; some thirty dead bodies were discovered once the chaos had ended. Heaping insult on top of the injuries, the lack of a sufficient police force created a haven for pickpockets; jewels, watches, and gold coins were removed from many of the dead bodies. Léonard's rival, the haughty Legros, was one of the victims crushed to death by the frenzied mob.

It was reported that the dauphin and dauphine were so saddened by the incident in Paris that they later donated money to his and other grieving families. It is hard for the superstitious not to view the tragic events surrounding the royal couple's union as an ominous sign of things to come, both for newlyweds and their country.

Wedding celebration in the King's Chapel at Versailles, May 16th, 1770

Returning to Versailles, the Dauphine Marie Antoinette was helped from the royal carriage in the grand marble courtyard. It was here that Léonard saw her for the first time. The portrait that he drew in his journals of this young archduchess hardly resembled those flattering ones that others have sketched. The hairdresser seemed mostly unimpressed with the young beauty; he found Marie Antoinette neither pretty nor attractive, yet there was a "promise of beauty." She was extremely slender and still lacked grace, but at least there was no sign of that "Austrian stiffness," which she had fortunately left on the banks of the Danube.

Most disappointingly, in Léonard's professional view, was her hair. Marie Antoinette's hair, which was then a pale strawberry blonde, seemed very "badly arranged" according to Léonard. His opinion was most likely biased by his rivalry with Larsenneur, the hairdresser who had been sent to Austria to coif the dauphine *à la française* before her departure.

It was no secret that the Empress of Austria was anxious, for political reasons, to secure the hand of the Dauphin Louis for her daughter—the over-arching goal was to secure an alliance with France; yet, the question of beauty and youth could not be overlooked as a plus in all of this. It was customary for monarchs to send "flattering" miniatures of their princesses and princes before marriages were arranged, as the future spouse would not have had the opportunity to see them in person before any engagements were negotiated. Although the marriages were for alliance purposes, the charm and intelligence of these political pawns were factors that could not be ignored—a princess would one day be queen of the realm after all, and would also have to provide heirs to the throne.

As early as 1768, the Empress had sent the Duke of Choiseul her wishes to have her youngest daughter's miniature painted. Although she would have preferred a life-size portrait, she wrote him that there was "no one here capable of undertaking such a work." Her own minister, the Count Mercy, proposed that a painter be sent to Vienna from Paris, but little did she know that he had other plans as well. He wanted to send for a *friseur* capable of showing off the fair locks of Marie Antoinette, while covering up a minor defect at the same time. He explained: "She has a rather high forehead with the hair growing badly. Her Majesty can assure herself that a man who is perfect at his trade will succeed in correcting, or at least in concealing, this small defect."[3]

This trifling imperfection might have been a considerable setback at a time when high foreheads were no longer in fashion. Very shortly after this, the Empress acquiesced to have a hairdresser brought to Vienna, but only if one could be found by the trusted Choiseul. A coiffeur was finally unearthed who had once dressed the hair of an Austrian princess who had resided at her country's embassy in Paris. When the recommended Monsieur Larsenneur arrived at court, he immediately began to "tug and pull" on the princess's locks to overcome the effects of the high forehead.[4]

Although Larsenneur would remain the coiffeur-in-chief at Versailles for some years, he would be remembered as the coiffeur belonging to the days when Marie Antoinette cared little for her personal appearance. Léonard severely criticized his new rival: "The princess was so little occupied with her toilette that she allowed one Larsenneur, who had joined her at Vienna, to coif her for some years quite inconceivably badly, and kept him on in order not to pain him." The eyes of the dauphine were azure blue with a quick, but somewhat bold, expression. She had a prominent nose, a small mouth, thick lips, and a complexion of dazzling whiteness, as well as the troubling forehead. Although Marie Antoinette carried her head high, there was a bit of arrogance in her countenance. Contemporaries often wrote of the high forehead and the Habsburg protruding chin that gave the princess a haughty, sometimes snooty, appearance. Others countered that this air of arrogance was tempered by her bright blue eyes and the captivating sweetness of her smile.[5]

Madame de Langeac was one of the first ladies presented to the dauphine. She found the princess to be gentle but somewhat peevish due to her young age. "As to the qualities of her sex," she wrote, "one may say that she was virtuous as a matter of principle, but sometimes frivolous and impulsive." It was quite difficult for Marie

Château de Versailles, eighteenth century
(BIBLIOTHÈQUE NATIONALE DE FRANCE)

Antoinette to resist any of her desires, as history has repeatedly noted about the young dauphine. Homesick for her family in Austria, often ignored by her new husband, and imprisoned by the rigid court etiquette of Versailles, the princess adopted a lifestyle full of enjoyable distractions such as gambling, visiting the theater, and taking scandalous nocturnal strolls—all unbecoming activities for a future queen of France.

Marie Antoinette was also known to make fun of courtiers and members of the royal family. Even the king's mistress, Madame du Barry, was not spared the princess's mockery. Because du Barry had a lower rank, etiquette forbade her from speaking to the dauphine first; Marie Antoinette despised her and refused to do so—until the king reprimanded her for her behavior.

The Countess de Noailles, a solemn woman well versed in the science of etiquette, was chosen as the dauphine's lady of honor. Her mission was to guide the dauphine in all that concerned the ceremonies of court. This task was difficult indeed; the dauphine was known to be excessively familiar with royal courtiers and often behaved in an undignified manner. She often shocked her aunts and governesses by yawning or giggling at royal functions, as well as disappointing respectable courtiers who were pressing forward to pay her homage.

On one occasion, the countess discovered that the future queen of France had called the two little children of her maid-in-waiting into her room, romping with them on the floor and soiling her exquisite clothing. "Madame Etiquette," as the princess called her, was always dismayed by the princess's dirty and noisy apartments, which were cluttered with clothes, broken furniture, and toys. Because the countess often reprimanded the princess, Marie Antoinette shunned her presence whenever possible.

To stir the pot even more, the princess once asked her chambermaid to dismiss the countess, which insulted and angered the countess to no end; she replied that she did not take orders from a servant well below her rank.[6] Madame de Langeac, on the contrary, was somewhat lax in morality, and she was able to quickly win over the young dauphine. In fact, Marie Antoinette let the court know that she could absolutely not get along without her, making it imperative that she take up residence in the palace.

Countess de Noailles

Madame de Langeac was herself a very frivolous woman, and her admission into the dauphine's circle brought loud protest from Madame de Noailles. She became even more agitated when the dauphine requested Madame de Langeac to form a social circle for her. It was composed of women fond of pleasure who laughed at everything, including the gossip regarding their reputations. The ladies of the small society recognized but one law: the necessity of spending their lives merrily behind a thin and deceptive veil of decorum, often on the edge of scandal.

Although she was aware that Marie Antoinette was still young, Madame de Noailles prophetically foresaw the downfall of the monarchy with the antics of the frolicsome princess. She once surprised the dauphine walking in the park, accompanied by a single lady and without an entourage. Madame de Noailles was speechless when she saw the royal princess running after a butterfly and, most distressing of all, when she lost one of her shoes while running in plain sight of common passersby.

Madame Noailles went to Louis XV and requested a private audience to discuss matters that closely affected the glory of his crown and the honor of the court of Versailles. After hearing the story, the king was visibly irritated that the governess was imposing so many courtly obligations on the young princess. To him, what she called obligations were "merely a succession of wearisome cares, and gatherings of toothless old maids dull enough to kill the poor child with boredom."

Considerably chastened, Countess de Noailles bowed deeply to Louis XV. She refused to drop the matter and hastened to tell all to the dauphine's chambermaid, the aptly named Madame de Misery. After the lady of honor, she was the most fervent supporter of court etiquette. To the great regret of the straitlaced spinsters, the dauphine was allowed to continue what they saw as unseemly pleasures not befitting a future queen.

Madame du Barry not only thought aloud, but also spoke more freely than other courtiers to the king about all matters. She boldly suggested that the Duke of Choiseul be removed as the king's minister and replaced with the Duke of Aiguillon. The reason was not political, though the king couldn't have known this; Choiseul had "scorned her charms," while Aiguillon had accepted them. It was Madame du Barry who had persuaded the king to keep the Dauphin Louis away from government affairs while she strove to turn the dauphine from the frolics of her youth to the wiles of flirting and intrigue. The dauphine, however, detested the king's mistress, which concerned the king. The position of Madame du Barry at court was a particularly sensitive issue, and she complained bitterly to the king for any slight—Marie Antoinette and her ladies absolutely refused to yield the favorite the precedence that she claimed.

Jealousy played a role in the court intrigues. When the dauphine heard that Madame du Barry was the person who most amused King Louis XV, she said, "Then I declare myself her rival; for I will try who can best amuse my grandpapa for the future. I will exert all my powers to please and divert him, and then we shall see who can best succeed." Madame du Barry was nearby when she heard Marie Antoinette's threat and she never forgave it.

Meanwhile, Madame de Langeac's rise as Marie Antoinette's favorite was rapid. Her ascent was merely but one example how one could rise in status quite quickly at the court of Versailles. The dauphine affectionately received Madame de Langeac and shared openly with her. In fact, Léonard learned from Madame de Langeac that Marie Antoinette spoke very casually with her in the "most uncommonly informal language" about certain conjugal matters.

The dauphine had no doubts about being queen one day, but she was less certain about giving birth to an heir, a future king. Most of the court had heard the embarrassing rumors regarding the dauphin's physical condition and the dauphine's apprehension about ever having a child. Mocking poems were being recited throughout Paris, the most scornful touting Marie Antoinette's lesbian relationship with her favorites. Madame Campan, a favorite chambermaid and noble lady by birth, would later emphatically deny these rumors in her memoirs, claiming that the dauphine's behavior was always honorable and proper with respect to her closest friends at court.[7]

The princess had obviously read about sexual attraction in her beloved novels, and was well aware that it was absent from her marriage. For a long period of time after the royal couple's wedding, Louis XVI appeared to be jealous of his new wife's popularity. The cries of the crowds would multiply whenever she joined her husband on the balcony. In turn, Louis would ignore his bride, and when he went to her bed at night, he would fall fast asleep without speaking a word. She knew that he preferred hunting and fiddling with locks in his workshop to fulfilling his marital duties, but she was unaware of the reason: The prince experienced tremendous pain when trying to fulfill such duties.

Louis suffered from phimosis, a penile deformity in which the foreskin is so narrow that it interferes with sexual intercourse.[8] In addition to preventing an heir to the throne, the malady was also quite embarrassing; the couple's bed sheets had to be humiliatingly checked every morning for blood or emissions. The intimate life of the couple was now public information, spurring layers of rumors, counter-rumors and ridicule. In fact, King Louis XV was forced to send agents at considerable expense to London and Amsterdam to buy up copies of existing pamphlets that detailed the sexual impotence of his grandson.

Without an heir, the security of Marie Antoinette's position at court was at stake, as was her future as queen. There was even talk of divorce for the "barren" Austrian princess. On her wedding night, King Louis XV had escorted the young couple to their room, as custom required, and the nuptial bed was blessed. However, their marriage would remain unconsummated for many years. The dauphine would suffer immensely five years later when the dauphin's nephew was born, an heir to the throne that would not be hers.

When their first child finally arrived in 1778, rumors circulated that the dauphin had agreed to a surgery to correct his deformity. Madame de Campan and Marie Antoinette's brother both insinuated that he had undergone the surgery, but historians still debate whether the future king submitted to such an operation. If the problem was indeed corrected without surgery, the daily procedures of stretching the prepuce would have been tedious and extremely painful. The surgery, according to medical journals of the time, only required one half-hour and hardly ever failed—though it was so painful that "frequently a strong-minded person would scream like a child."

As Marie Antoinette settled into and stretched her new role, Léonard saw his star on the rise. Since Léonard's encounter with Madame du Barry, his fame and fortune began to progress very rapidly. The favorite was more than pleased with his services, and she was determined to keep him at her fingertips.

Madame de Langeac was now entirely absorbed in her duties as lady-in-waiting to the Dauphine Marie Antoinette. She relented to having her hair dressed in the mixed society of the princess's morning court, composed of poets looking for pensions and lieutenants hoping for military appointments. As a consequence, Léonard now had all the time and leisure necessary to cultivate the protection of Madame du Barry. It was a productive arrangement, allowing him access to the dressing rooms of the most dignified ladies of the court of Versailles and other beauties who occupied the smaller apartments.

Léonard's talents had been praised to Marie Antoinette, but she had already become accustomed to the court hairdresser Larsenneur, the coiffeur of Louis XV's queen, Marie Leszczynska, who had died in 1768. Larsenneur was sent to Vienna on the 15th of October that year to dress the young dauphine's hair, receiving two thousand florins and the permission to dress the hair of other fine ladies in the Austrian capital. Arriving with the princess at the court of Versailles the following year, he remained in the princess's household as hairdresser for at least another three years—when a few choice words from Madame du Barry were soon able to change the princess's mind about the ageing Larsenneur.

It was in 1772, when Léonard's fate became irrevocably attached to the future queen. One day while walking in the park, Madame du Barry met Her Royal Highness, bestowing on her the most gracious and respectful compliments. Although Marie Antoinette was not fond of Madame du Barry and had only started speaking to her recently, she received the favorite with a kind smile on this occasion. Madame du Barry was delighted with the chance meeting, as well as the opportunity to speak to the princess about a matter that was "very important at her young age." She did not understand how the ladies, who had the honor of belonging to the princess's circle, and above all the Marquise de Langeac, could allow her to appear at court with a hairstyle that was both "antiquated and lacking harmony with such enchanting features."

This was not new. The ladies of the court had already encouraged Marie Antoinette to take Léonard under her wings, but she had grown too fond of Larsenneur to change hairdressers. Madame du Barry reasoned that the "true merit in the realm of taste was to be faithful only to its variableness." Understanding that variety was the spice of life at Versailles, the princess decided to take the countess's advice; she was already well aware of Léonard's success with his creations in the theater. She would retire the faithful Larsenneur with a generous pension, and take Léonard on as her new hairdresser; in fact, she wanted him to dress her hair that very evening.

Marie Antoinette might have made this impulsive switch—notwithstanding the woman who suggested it—for several reasons. Larsenneur had been brought to Austria by the dauphine's mother, the Empress of Austria, to style Marie Antoinette's hair in the French manner. Being satisfied with the hairdresser, the Empress sent Larsenneur back to France with her daughter to care for her hair at court. However, by this time Marie Antoinette was rebelling against the rigid court's rules, only to be reproached by her mother in letter after letter. Taking on Léonard would be another outlet for the princess's rebellious behavior.

The dauphine had also found another way to snub the king's favorite, Madame du Barry; she would simply deny her the services of the brilliant new hairdresser by taking him up for herself. The question then arises: Why would Madame du Barry even consider offering the dauphine her protégé? Despite the fact that the favorite was certainly concerned about her precedence at court and the king's continued favor, she may also have been thinking about her future. With the death of Louis XV, Marie Antoinette would become the Queen of France, and Madame du Barry's position at the court of Versailles would very well be endangered. Madame du Barry said that she was happy beyond expression that the princess would receive one of her protégés, adding that he was an excellent addition to her circle. The irony, of course, is that Marie Antoinette felt she was punishing Madame du Barry by taking Léonard, while Madame du Barry thought she was flattering the queen by giving him to her. The machinations of the French court often twisted back on itself in this manner, like a Möbius strip.

Nevertheless, the arrangement seemed to be advantageous to all parties involved—though, Léonard, now granted access to the most famous coif in France, certainly made out the handsomest.

The next day at noon, Madame de Langeac escorted Léonard to Versailles for an audience with Marie Antoinette. They were greeted by Madame Campan, now the first lady of the princess's bedchamber. Marie Antoinette was being dressed, when her sister-in-law, the Countess of Provence, accidentally disturbed the princess's hair.

"Oh, my dear sister," said Marie Antoinette laughingly, "my hair will have to be dressed anew."

Marie Antoinette abhorred the daily routines and was surely mocking Madame de Noailles. Before her hair had been arranged, her hands had been washed by the first lady-of-honor and then wiped dry by the lady of the bedchamber. Then her richly embroidered night-chemise was replaced with a simpler one to be worn during the day; the honor of presenting the new chemise was the privilege of Madame de Noailles.

Marie Antoinette, still giggling, threw herself into a chair before her mirror, and said: "I hope, madame, that etiquette does not require of the future Queen of France to appear before her court with disheveled hair. If I may be permitted to express a preference in the matter, I would like to have my hair in order."[9]

Moments later, Madame Campan entered and announced, "Your majesty, the hairdresser Léonard is in the outer room."

"Oh, go and call him, Madame de Campan," said the princess, as though Léonard's timely arrival were a coincidence. "And now, ladies," she continued, "you shall see one of the demi-gods; Léonard is called *le dieu des coiffures* [the god of hairdressing] in the world of fashion."

"Léonard!" cried Madame de Noailles. "And has your Royal Highness then forgotten that she is not permitted to be waited upon by any but womanly hands here?"

"*Not* permitted!" Marie Antoinette said. "We shall see whether the future Queen of France asks permission of her subjects to employ a male or female hairdresser!"

When the door opened, Madame de Campan entered the room with Léonard. "Now, ladies," continued Marie Antoinette, "if you will be so good as to await me in the reception room." When she saw Madame de Noailles about to open her prudish lips, she quickly added: "The mistress of ceremonies and the ladies of the bedchamber will remain here."

The princess seated herself, half reclining on a lounge, and cast that special look, a mix of grandeur and frivolity, that many authors of the time have often highlighted.

She smiled and quickly remarked that the hairdresser's reputation had preceded him there. She then asked a question that reveals that she was more aware of her standing in the court than others assumed: "Léonard, do you know that sometimes it is a very difficult task to uphold one's reputation?"

"I can at least assure Your Royal Highness," he replied, "that I shall strive to uphold mine!"

The end of autumn was approaching, and to go out without a hat would be risking catching a cold. Marie Antoinette loved her strolls in the open air of the gardens, but she loathed wearing bonnets, describing them as either too dressy or not enough so. Her reason may have been simply vanity, as she often removed them so that she might better be seen. Léonard became ecstatic with an idea: He would replace the bonnets with some odds and ends of chiffon arranged artfully in her hair.

"My dressing service!" the dauphine suddenly called out. Her page quickly left the room, and Madame de Langeac, the first chambermaid, and Léonard followed Marie Antoinette into her private dressing rooms. When Léonard first laid his hand on the dauphine's forehead, she surely felt a remarkable difference between the weight of his hand and that of the court hairdresser Larsenneur. Turning to the women in attendance, Léonard surprised them all by asking only for a simple piece of gauze.

When the styling was finished, Léonard noted in his journal that "Her Highness thought it was beautiful." She clapped her pretty hands together several times

MARIE ANTOINETTE
Archiduchesse d'Autriche,
REINE DE FRANCE,
Née à Vienne le 2 Novem. 1755.
Mariée à Versailles le 16 Mai 1770

Dauphine Marie Antoinette

as a sign of satisfaction and told Léonard that not only was he a man of talent but an artist. He need not worry about his future, because he now belonged to the dauphine; she promised to only loan him to her best friends (which, of course, did not include the king's mistress, who had brought Léonard to her in the first place).

That Léonard, a man, could be found in Marie Antoinette's private quarters was due to changes that she had made in her morning ritual, known as the *lever*. Upon awakening, the princess was routinely assisted out of bed. High-ranking noble ladies would select her clothing and then decide who would dress the princess. Her hair was brushed and arranged, and her makeup was meticulously applied.[10]

However, to simplify the ritual, she decided that she would first have her hair combed, and instead of being dressed by the noble ladies, she would lead her ladies-in-waiting to her private rooms. This annoyed the noble ladies immensely, who were left in the bedroom completely clad in their full court dress. Without these ladies gawking at her, she could then quietly get dressed and choose her own wardrobe and hairstyle with the help and advice of her new "artist."

She actually had no choice but to change the morning ritual. According to custom, Léonard would never have been allowed in her bedchamber. Custom also forbade any such underling with a post at court to exercise his "art" outside of the palace. However, fearing that Léonard's imagination might become "provincialized among the centenarians" of Versailles, Marie Antoinette later insisted that her favorite hairdresser should continue to look after the hair of the ladies of Paris as well. How the Countess de Noailles and other devotees to court etiquette must have shuddered! This only added to Léonard's fame—Parisian ladies would wait for hours in line to see the hairdresser of the Dauphine Marie Antoinette.

While the dauphine was congratulating Léonard (and he was pouring out his gratitude), the Dauphin Louis entered the dressing room with his brother, the Count of Provence. Léonard saw these two princes up close for the first time. So far he had only noticed the youngest brother, the Count of Artois, jumping over the flowerbeds in the gardens, crushing the flowers and angering the gardeners, who had no choice but to smile at him.

Louis had just turned seventeen. He was rather tall and slim with well-formed legs, short thighs, and a head that sunk between his shoulders. His features did not lack dignity, Léonard noted, but the habit of incessantly blinking tainted the royal prince's appearance. His manners were somewhat vulgar, the tone of his voice was short, and his elocution was common. Louis was brutally impulsive, but as soon as he had time to reflect on his actions, no one was more prompt to admit his wrongs and make amends. In time, age wrought notable changes in his temper; kindness, perhaps unfairly treated as weakness, would eventually become his dominant quality.

The Count of Provence was a year younger than his brother the dauphin. Already prematurely stout, he appeared to roll rather than walk. Even then one could have predicted that it would soon be necessary to lift this larger-than-life figure upon his horse with a hoist. Badly propped up on his legs, the count had attractive eyes, wit in his look, and malice in his smile. He was quite inarticulate, but he still carried a pretentious air. Marie Antoinette ran to meet the two brothers to show off her new hairstyle and to introduce her new hairdresser. Léonard respectfully bowed very low, but the dauphin insultingly remarked, "Ah, so this is the hairdresser?"

The dauphin said that he would rather see Léonard serve in the French Guards, being more honorable than using curling irons, and he could give the enemy a good *coup de peigne*, literally a "stroke of the comb," a good thrashing. The dauphin began to laugh at his own humorous jab.

Léonard was not amused, but he knew the game: The possibility of a post in the queen's household was perhaps at stake. Also, to win the future king's good graces, it was wise not to respond at all—at least not in the manner of a true Gascon. The count apologized for his brother's barbarian taste in fashion. Finding the princess's hairstyle rather charming, he congratulated Léonard for serving in her dressing room rather than the French Guards.

The piece of pink gauze placed in the dauphine's hair created quite a different sensation than the one caused by the fairy's hairstyle that had launched Léonard's career. This chiffon, mentioned in prose and in verse, was a lucky strike for the little minstrels of Paris. It gave rise to songs and jingles, and thus Léonard saw his glory shine with accolades from the poets. Hundreds of ladies from Paris and the court of Versailles would call upon Léonard at the same time, yet he was always kept at the dauphine's beckon. As was normal for her with all of her court, Her Royal Highness wanted to know Léonard's taste on all things pertaining to her *toilette*; she would often decide on the choice of her ribbons, flowers, feathers, and jewels only after having asked his opinion.

The young princess's infatuation crowned Léonard's reputation. Marquises, countesses, and duchesses all wanted him at any price, but he found it rather difficult to oblige any one of them, with Marie Antoinette sending for him around the clock. Moreover, he had been compelled to take a small apartment high up in the palace. Practically sequestered there, he was one step away from having the royal guard post a sentinel at his door to prevent him from going out without the dauphine's permission.

Perhaps the glory was too much, because Léonard would become weary of a fortune too exclusively dependent on Marie Antoinette's favor, which recent history had shown could be fickle. Though he had been appointed to the enviable position of *valet de chambre* to the princess, should he displease her but one time, he knew, he could very easily be reduced to nothing. "You must not load all your riches on a single vessel," he wrote in his journal. "Let us arrange to oblige the clientele which comes from all sides, and which I am unable at present to satisfy."

By this time, Léonard could not keep up with the demand for his presence in the salons and boudoirs of the noble ladies of Paris and Versailles; perhaps, too, he missed Frémont and his friends from the theater. After all, Frémont had played a major role in Léonard's rise to the top. Knowing that he could depend on his old friend, Léonard penned a letter:

My dear Frémont,
I am sinking under the burden of my laurels and of my reputation; if you do not come to my aid I am a crushed man. Hasten therefore; I am in a position to realize the promises I made to you last year at the Café Procope; come quickly, we shall share like brothers, glory, gold and other accessories; hasten, a hairdresser of my school cannot fail to reach, borne on the wings of my fortune, the summit of prosperity. I expect you for lunch tomorrow; I shall be at home at noon.

The next day, Frémont arrived at the château of Versailles at the appointed time. The pair then laid the foundations of their new arrangement, a kind of association by which Frémont would share Léonard's responsibilities as well as his wealth and fame. Friendship was their sole witness; nothing was written down, and their chivalrous contract, concluded only with a good lunch, was carried out with good faith.

Was this new association created to reward an old friend, or was there perhaps an ulterior motive, an attempt to solve an ongoing problem? It had been impossible for Léonard to take on the official title of "coiffeur" without having fulfilled the legal requirement of four years' apprenticeship (which he knew Frémont possessed) in addition to the payment of very hefty fees: forty livres for internship, three hundred livres for the title, and three thousand livres for the license.

Dining in the palace, Léonard and Frémont remained at the table for several hours. The dishes were prepared with finesse and served by his personal servant; the wines were exquisite. As preferred hairdresser to the dauphine and close friend of Madame du Barry, Léonard was on very good terms with those in charge of the kitchen and the cellars of Versailles.

"Happiness is seldom sober," said Léonard. "It becomes elated, and it almost always runs away beyond the limits of moderation." Neither he nor Frémont were given to drinking in excess, but that day they were so enthusiastic that both their heads were "fairly loaded with spirituous vapors." Raising his glass to his partner, Léonard toasted, "To the foremost and second hairdressers of the universe. France is the metropolis of the world, and Louis XV is the foremost monarch of Europe. I dress the hair of the foremost princess of his court, and you are my lieutenant!"

Léonard rambled on until a loud ring of the bell interrupted him. When his servant opened the door, it was one of the princess's grooms. All the furniture began to dance before his eyes as the valet spoke: "Madame the Dauphine requests the presence of Monsieur Léonard at once. Her Royal Highness is going to the opera this evening."

A lightning strike could not have startled him more. How could he arrange a state hairstyle for the opera in his condition? Léonard was tipsy "beyond that beginning of inebriation which, far from hindering the faculties, develops and lends them something like poetical inspiration."

Frémont, who shared Léonard's anxiety, advised him to down two or three cups of coffee, which he did. Feeling more stable on his legs and much clearer in his head, he was soon able to see the objects about him in their natural state. He then left Frémont, reminding him that their fortune was very well at stake and that the perilous adventure could very easily prove fatal to them and their dreams.

Léonard entered the dauphine's apartment with the assurance that a tipsy man never lacks, and it appeared that Her Highness did not notice his condition. The coffee had produced a rapid transformation, and the extreme redness of his complexion had faded away.

While Léonard slowly separated the princess's hair, attempting to conjure something magical, he no doubt was battling the thumping arteries of his temples. Her Highness, as if to excuse herself for the sudden call, said that she was initially not planning to leave her apartment that evening, but the royal prince of Sweden and his brother had unexpectedly arrived at Versailles. They were going to the opera that evening, and the King Louis XV sent word that it would please him to see her there as well. Obligated to honor the king's wishes, she would endure the terribly tiresome trip to Paris. The princess was likely exaggerating her dismay as it was well known that she had amorous feelings for the Swedish prince Fersen.

Léonard's panic gave way to inspiration, as he was already absorbed in an idea. He suggested that the princess wear white feathers in her hair for the opera. She would try it, she said, as long as the result was spectacular. Léonard said nothing more, only wrapping himself in his inspiration with comb in hand. Within an hour his flock of curls was able to hold three white ostrich plumes, set on the left side of her head and fastened in the middle of a rosette he had braided with her hair. A bow of pink ribbon, in the center of which was a large ruby, held the elaborate creation together.

This stunning work of art, which fully covered the high forehead of Marie Antoinette, became her wonderfully, but in an altogether different manner than the chiffon of his first masterpiece. It was no longer a coquettish expression that his work created—on the contrary, it enhanced all of the princess's majestic features. After Léonard rubbed his sleeve over the mirror, he held it up for Marie Antoinette to observe her new hairstyle. Léonard had found a way, through the princess's elaborate hairstyle, to signify her maturity and her raised status.

She examined it in silence. For a moment, from the wrinkled eyebrows, the princess appeared somewhat disappointed, saying, "My hairstyle is perfect, and it is admirably planned, but it is remarkably bold." However, this frown lasted only an instant, when, like a flash, her face lit up with delight: "Oh, Léonard, it must be over a yard high!"

Léonard admitted that the arrangement was daring, but he promised that there would be two hundred hairstyles higher than hers in Paris by the following evening. Though a foreign princess, Marie Antoinette was becoming more and more French by controlling fashion at the court of Versailles and in Parisian circles. Her subjects would throng to catch a glimpse of the elaborate hairstyles created by Léonard, and as he predicted, they soon spared no expense to imitate them.

When Léonard returned home that night, he found Frémont with his head resting on Léonard's bed. He woke his partner by shaking his shoulder; somewhat incoherent after awakening from a deep sleep, Frémont wanted to know if the intoxication had played any havoc with his royal duties. Were they to be sent to the Bastille?

Léonard admitted that his work would certainly have caused him to be hanged at the court of Louis XIV. Frémont was immediately alarmed, fearing that they both would be sent to the scaffold. When Léonard mentioned that the dauphine had a head more than forty inches long from the lower part of the chin to the top of her hair, Frémont cried out, "We are doomed!"

"No, say rather that we are rich!" Léonard bellowed, adding that they would be millionaires in less than two years; he had never seen anyone so enraptured with his work. If Frémont could be at the bottom of the grand staircase when the dauphine entered her carriage, he would be able to catch a glimpse of the concoction that he had just erected on Her Highness's head. By the next day every woman in Paris would want to copy that hairstyle, and he and Frémont alone would be capable of meeting the challenge.

Léonard told him not to lose a moment—fortune was right around the corner. Frémont was so keyed up that he jumped to grab his hat and, raising his arms high in the air, he shouted, "Léonard, I'm out the door!"

CHAPTER 4

Captivating a Queen and Her Subjects

Your majesty, there are no new fashions. Your majesty's word is necessary to create them. A queen does not follow the fashion. It follows her.

—ROSE BERTIN TO MARIE ANTOINETTE
VERSAILLES, 1772

October 1772
Versailles, France

Many foreign princesses throughout the House of Bourbon's history were known to be corpulent, ungraceful, and often less interesting than their servants. A princess in Louis XIV's court once said to her ladies, "Look at Madame the Dauphine; she is as ugly asleep as awake."[1] And when the Princess de Savoie first arrived at Louis XV's court, the king drily noted, "She is very ugly."[2] But Louis XV now had the beautiful Austrian princess Marie Antoinette adorning his court and he was ecstatic. The Parisians, too, were delirious whenever the dauphine visited the city; in response, the king ordered that the royal couple, whenever they attended the theater, receive all the tokens of deference that were shown to him. Cannon fire would echo from the Bastille to the Invalides, and Swiss Guards would be stationed at the theater entrance and below the box in which the couple were seated.

The theatergoers' delight was palpable when Louis and Marie Antoinette graced the royal boxes. The actors were especially indebted to the dauphine's presence. Theater etiquette had always forbidden applause at any performance attended by royalty—until the dauphine finally interceded. When she was seen giving the signal, the entire house would rise with enthusiasm. On the evening that Marie Antoinette wore Léonard's audacious masterpiece towering more than a yard high, people trampled over each other in the parterre, the rear section of the opera's main floor where spectators used to stand. Léonard, in hyperbolic Gascon fashion, reported that two ribs were fractured, three arms dislocated, and three ankles sprained. Whether there were indeed injuries to show for it, Léonard was indeed victorious—as he had expected—and one hundred francs quickly found their way into his pocket.

In order to circumvent all the regulations and expense of belonging to the wig-makers guild, Léonard started the *Académie de coiffure* with Frémont, soon to be located on the rue de la Chaussée-d'Antin. His school was destined for valets and chambermaids of the best families of the city, and was located at the entrance to an elegant area of Paris, not far from the grand manors of the famous actress Mademoi-selle Guimard and other aristocrats. All the grand ladies wished to have their hair dressed by the "*Académicien de coiffures et de modes,*" as he called himself. They would put themselves in his hands the evening (or even the morning of) a gala, sitting upright on a chair for hours, in order not to disarrange his splendid work, which was treated as art.[3]

Léonard's crafty idea of establishing a school worked, allowing him to send for his brothers Pierre and Jean-François from Pamiers, who would take up the comb as well; the three would create a virtual House of Léonard. To prosper from their brother's celebrity, Pierre and Jean-François also called themselves "Léonard." In what would later become a headache for historians, the three could only be distin-guished by using their Christian names or their positions at Versailles. The household of Marie Antoinette consisted of one *perruquier-baigneur-étuviste*, who was respon-sible for supplying all personal hygiene items and for managing the baths and toilette of the queen. The coveted post was customarily purchased, requiring an apprentice-ship and membership in the guild. Her household also included the premier coiffeur, Léonard, and two coiffeurs for daily services, his brother Jean-François and his cousin Villanou. The third Autié brother, Pierre, belonged to the household of the king's sister, Madame Élisabeth.[4]

According to *Léonard le Perruquier*, or *Léonard the Wigmaker*, a play presented much later in Paris in 1847, Léonard was actually married at this time, though his mem-oirs reveal very little about it.[5] Dressing in the secondhand clothing of the nobles and driving a six-in-hand carriage to his clients, Léonard was certainly concerned with his image; consequently, he undoubtedly preferred not to discuss his wife—the daughter of menial servants—in his journal. She was an embarrassing association he wanted to erase from his history like his decrepit room on the rue des Noyers from his early days in Paris. Ignoring her existence would not have been uncommon—marriage at the time was normally based on reasons far removed from love. A mar-riage of convenience often brought together a couple that was soon, if not from the outset, estranged. Emotion and affection were of little importance to a union; it was commonly accepted that married men kept a mistress and married women discreetly had a lover.

Léonard's wife was Marie-Louise Jacobie, the daughter of Jacques Malacrida, an assistant in the kitchens of Versailles.* Marrying the daughter of a king's servant might have been another of Léonard's tactics to help him secure a place in the royal household. The couple had shared interests—Marie Louise was also an actress—but it is doubtful that the relationship was an amorous one. It's also likely that after Léonard's initial successes, he might have thought it best to marry to fend off any whispering. Being a single man raised eyebrows in the eighteenth century, provoking questions about a man's sexuality or his impotence.

Marie-Louise would have married for different reasons. Noble women in eighteenth-century France could marry for love and pleasure, but women of lesser rank would have married to guarantee a household income. Marie-Louise would have married to ensure that there would be bread for her children, and Léonard had the means to provide for them. Although there was no marriage certificate recorded, church records show that a daughter, Marie-Anne Elisabeth, was born to Léonard Alexis Autié and Marie-Louise Jacobie Malacrida in 1781.[6]

"My happy presentiments were being realized," noted Léonard. "The pyramidal hairstyle of Marie Antoinette had created a furor at the opera!" A week after Léonard's triumphant acclaim for the queen's coiffure at the opera, an unknown lady arrived at his apartment at the palace of Versailles, asking to speak to him. It was a "young, pretty, and very fashionable woman" according to his servant, who had her wait in the antechamber. Léonard hastened to meet the unknown visitor, and he found a very charming woman with a plump and friendly face. His first inclination was that she might be seeking a favor for herself or for some relative—especially considering his newfound influence. And he was not exactly mistaken.

When the young lady sat near his warm hearth, she took the opportunity to display what he called the "prettiest foot in the world," and "a pretty foot always inclines a man to listen favorably to a woman,"[7] he later wrote. She immediately introduced herself as Mademoiselle Rose Bertin, a protégée of the Princess of Conti and the Duchess of Chartres. The princess and duchess had once promised to recommend her to Marie Antoinette as a talented milliner, a designer of women's hats and accessories. However, her patrons had still not done so, and she thought Léonard, highly regarded at the dauphine's toilette, might be able to help.

Léonard had often heard of Mademoiselle Bertin's talents as Madame du Barry's *couturier*, or fashion designer, having a luxurious boutique on the rue Saint-Honoré

---

* Marie-Louise was the second of three sisters, called the *Trois Grâces*. The oldest, Caroline, became known as the famous actress Carline of the *Comédie Italien* troupe; she was married to Nivelou, a dancer of the Opéra. The youngest sister became Madame Quincy. The sisters often appeared in the company of their cousin, Mademoiselle Duthé, the celebrated French courtesan.

and importing exquisite laces and textiles from abroad. He replied that he would be more than happy to recommend her to the dauphine. Léonard's motives were not entirely selfless. He knew all too well of the short-lived and fickle vogues of the royal court; Mademoiselle Rose's support might someday be beneficial and Léonard, aware of the milliner's talent and taste, was wisely playing the odds.

Mademoiselle Bertin, uneasy with a prolonged unchaperoned visit in a gentleman's room, thanked him in advance and Léonard courteously led her to the stairway. Although he may have had doubts about actually helping her, an opportunity presented itself that very evening: Marie Antoinette asked him for one of his chiffon hairstyles, which gave her, as she said, a coquettish face.

Léonard suggested that it would be best if the dauphine ordered an exquisite variety of fabrics for this sort of headdress. He had new creations in mind that would require linen and muslin embroidered in white, in assorted colors, and some in silver and gold. He also needed beautiful lace, such as that from Valenciennes or Malines; for furnishing all these, he could think of only one person.

"Mademoiselle Rose Bertin!" Marie Antoinette said. "You do well to mention her; I now recall that Madame the Duchess of Chartres has spoken of her." The princess then turned to Madame de Noailles, telling her to have word sent to Mademoiselle Rose; she was to present herself at Versailles as soon as possible. She told Léonard that she expected him to be present when the milliner arrived.

Mademoiselle Rose arrived within the hour and was ushered in according to the palace's ways and customs of etiquette—Léonard kept in the background as much as he could. Four royal lackeys followed the young milliner, laden with boxes.

"Mademoiselle," said Marie Antoinette, "have you brought me the latest fashions?"

"No, your majesty," replied Mademoiselle Rose. "I bring the materials wherewith to fill your majesty's orders."

"Were you not told to bring your samples of fashions?" asked Marie Antoinette, with surprise.

"Your majesty, there are no new fashions," said Bertin. "Your majesty's word is necessary to create them. A queen does not follow the fashion, it follows her."[8] We cannot know how much Marie Antoinette took these words to heart, but clearly, the young milliner had a deep understanding of the dauphine's influence in Paris. Mademoiselle Rose, having noticed Léonard in a corner of the dressing room, smiled at him graciously. The following week she supplied more than twenty thousand francs' worth of fabric and accessories to the court—the milliner had thus secured an important role at the court of Marie Antoinette, and her name would soon be no less popular than Léonard's.

The influence of the popular dauphine was known to secure the fame and fortune of many budding artists. "The dauphine's youth," wrote a courtier, "her face, her

Mademoiselle Rose Bertin

figure, seduced all hearts and called forth enthusiasm."[9] The princess was indeed the idol of the nation, and her influence was so far reaching; both Léonard and Mademoiselle Rose were almost magically transformed into celebrities overnight.

Mademoiselle Rose was ever conscious of the extreme distance that separated her from the royals. She had been sent to Paris in 1760 at the very young age of sixteen to follow in the footsteps of her parents. She worked in a milliner shop, the Trait Galant, where her talents were well publicized, allowing her to open her own shop, the Grand Mogul, in 1770.[10]

In March 1772, Mademoiselle Rose was introduced to the Dauphin Louis's cousin, the Duke of Chartres (later the Duke of Orléans), who became obsessed with the young beauty. He told her that if he would be allowed to replace his present mistress with her, she could have a beautifully furnished house, horses, carriages, and diamonds. The proud milliner declined, replying that she "preferred her virtue" to his lavish way of life. What began innocently enough led to a terrifying period of harassment and humiliation that would follow Mademoiselle Rose into the dauphine's court.

Léonard would soon encounter this abominable *prince du sang*, or "prince of the blood," under the most alarming circumstances.[11] A prince of the blood was traditionally a king's son, uncle, nephew, or cousin—all descending from the same monarch. The Duke of Chartres was from the house of Orléans, and thus not a member of the Bourbon king's immediate family. But descending from Louis XIV, the duke was in line for the throne should the Dauphin Louis and his brothers have no heirs and the Bourbon line die out. His rank was the highest held at court after the immediate family of the king. Likely it was for this reason that the duke continuously slandered the Bourbons and hated Marie Antoinette. Although talk that the duke was plotting to dethrone the king was just rumor, it was certain that he was the king's enemy, and he later became a leading anti-royalist.[12] He would one day even vote for his cousin's death at Louis XVI's trial.

A known womanizer with many illegitimate children, the duke could not accept Rose's rejection, and he continued to pursue her. The young milliner was soon not able to take a step without meeting the prince or one of his emissaries. The situation became intolerable when the Duchess of Chartres became Rose's patroness, calling for her on a daily basis. The duke never failed to be in his wife's chambers when Mademoiselle Rose visited, secretly whispering propositions that she pretended not to hear and quickly withdrawing her hand every time he tried to take it. For Mademoiselle Rose, it was a nearly impossible bind.

By chance (or perhaps providence) one evening, Mademoiselle Rose had just entered the parlor of her patron, Madame the Countess d'Usson, when the Duke of Chartres was announced. The prince was seated, but he pretended not to notice Mademoiselle Bertin—which was his game in such gatherings. Seeing her chance, the milliner remained in her armchair, refusing to rise—an outright insult to the duke in a world of carefully delineated hierarchies.

Shocked at Rose's boldness in snubbing the royal prince, Madame d'Usson made a sign for her to rise. When Rose refused, the countess began to cough softly,

Monsieur the Duke of Chartres and his family

and then more loudly. But Rose would still not move. Finally, becoming impatient, Madame d'Usson chastised the milliner, asking her if she had forgotten that she was in the presence of His Royal Highness.

"No, madame," she said, "assuredly I do not forget it."

"And how is it that you thus act?" asked Madame d'Usson.

"Ah! Madame the Countess does not know that if I were willing, I should be the Duchess of Chartres this evening." The young prince immediately changed color and did not reply.

"Yes, madame," continued Mademoiselle Rose, "I have been offered all that may tempt a poor girl, and because I have refused, they have threatened to kidnap me. Thus, ladies, if you are ever short of any pretty bonnets, if none of your lovely gowns are ready, and you are told that poor Rose has disappeared, you will need to ask His Royal Highness for her."

"What do you say to that, Monseigneur?" asked the countess.

"Faith, countess," replied the duke, fully recovered from the blow. "There is nothing else to do when it is a question of conquering a rebellious beauty; one has one's honor to uphold."

Mademoiselle Rose made a low bow to the duke, who said in a low voice, "You are a veritable serpent, madame."

The virtuous, and now victorious, milliner then took leave of Madame d'Usson and left the room. Mademoiselle Rose was confident that she would never be tormented again.

It is undeniable that Marie Antoinette, from the time of her arrival in France, was frivolous, especially forgetful of her rank as dauphine and the future queen. From the very day that she arrived at Versailles, her lady-in-waiting complained that she had begun "to rid herself of every circumstance that imposed any restraint upon her." She would descend the stairs without any assistance from an attendant, or she would "run the streets of Versailles" on foot, accompanied by only one or two ladies of her court, her usher left walking a distance behind. There were magnificent balls given in the palace that Marie Antoinette loved to attend, but she would not leave until six o'clock in the morning. She would then hear mass and go to bed, sleeping until two o'clock in the afternoon, thus missing her afternoon lessons in singing or the harpsichord.

And though it was not proper for princesses to go horseback riding, the dauphine was adamant about taking up "such violent exercise." The king gave in, but he did not consent to horses—she could ride only donkeys. One afternoon the princess, while riding with her ladies in the forest nearby, slipped from her saddle and fell to the ground, all the while doing her best to keep from laughing. The attendants could not help the princess up, because there were no rules of etiquette to observe. Thus, she was left sitting on the grass. Embracing the lack of court precedence for riding donkeys, Marie Antoinette continued to ride them, but she longed more and more for an actual horse.[13] The dauphin's spinster aunts despised Marie Antoinette but, whether trying to please the princess or from a more treacherous motive, they arranged for a horse to be in the forest for the princess to switch with the donkey. When Marie Antoinette's mother, the Empress of Austria, heard the news in Vienna, she was flabbergasted and immediately wrote her daughter, chastising her: "Riding spoils the complexion and in the end your figure will suffer and will appear fuller." Quite incredibly, exercise was considered to *cause* portliness at the time. To make matters worse, it appears that the princess rode astride, straddling the saddle, which was unbecoming of any lady—much less a future queen.

Léonard, having lived many years at Versailles, cut a very different portrait of the princess than her harsher critics. He viewed her as a young lady in a foreign court and easily swayed by those in her intimate circle, especially the deceitful aunts and in-laws. Aware of the constant rumors, the indifference of a husband who lived only for the hunt and his workshop, and the rigid rules of etiquette, Léonard admired her freedom and *joie de vivre*. He delighted whenever he heard the dauphine laugh in her chambers—a laugh that was "not forced and as hearty as at the home of a bourgeois."

During the first years she spent in France, the dauphine saw only women in her private circles, except for the dauphin and his brothers, who attended her court regularly. The Dauphin Louis usually fell asleep; his brother, the Count of Provence, recited verse or tried to improvise some; and his youngest brother, the Count of Artois, was but a noisy and teasing schoolboy. He spent the evening tickling his sister-in-law's ladies, and he would challenge her pages to wrestling and gymnastic games. Whenever he defeated them, he would merrily, but condescendingly, kick them.

In 1772, when the Count of Artois reached his fifteenth year, he was tall and blessed with a handsome face. Reports claim he was quite the ladies' man, and he was not at all shy about praising the beauty of his sister-in-law, Marie Antoinette. Léonard admitted that the princess, married to a cold and serious husband, could not remain indifferent to the charming count. Though he chose to turn a blind eye to insinuations about the queen's fidelity, it was quite clear that something existed between Marie Antoinette and her brother-in-law.

The count would practice driving a light carriage, called a *phaeton*, and although Marie Antoinette had very little confidence in her driver, she would always join him for the thrilling escapade. By slipping past the guards at the gates, they could also entertain themselves in donkey races, gambling at cards, and midnight walks in the gardens of Versailles. Soon there was another pastime that he was about to introduce to her—the masquerade ball.

Léonard happened to be in Marie Antoinette's dressing room one afternoon when the Count of Artois boisterously entered her room.

"My beautiful little sister-in-law," he said, "I must tell you of one of my jaunts of early in the week. And all of you must promise not to mention it to the dauphin or my brother."

Marie Antoinette promised; she was anxious to hear about this new adventure. When he told her that he had been to the most exotic masquerade ball ever, the dauphine was elated. She couldn't know what one would be like outside of the court of Versailles; her husband had always refused to hear about such outlandish events, much less agree to take her to one.

The count held the princess's attention as he described the costumes and the women's disguises. There were Dianas, Venuses, shepherdesses, and black dominos with bright bouquets, brilliant-colored ribbons, glistening spangles, and waving plumes. Indeed, the most fashionable masquerade balls were those at the Grand Opéra, where only the ladies were masked. Here, the ladies were the aggressors, and

The Count of Artois, Charles-Philippe de France

gentlemen were not allowed the first word. Although most of the ladies were from the best of families, they were permitted to "knock off their fetters" at the gala occasions. An enthusiast of the masked balls wrote:

> *The hot houses pour out their treasures into the lobbies, amidst the blushing roses and dahlias, gallant gentlemen and ladies whisper their loves in each other's ears, or repose about in groves that are full of ravishment. There is besides, the emotion, the excitement of curiosity, of mystery, of adventure which lends many new attractions to a woman.*[14]

Marie Antoinette was ecstatic and promptly asked her lady-in-waiting, Madame de Misery, to run an errand for her. The prim and proper servant immediately left; she would certainly frown on such intrigues and frivolities. As soon as Marie Antoinette could speak freely, she told the count that she wanted a masquerade ball "before a week's time."

"Here, Léonard will help you," she said. "He is clever and ingenious; he will make arrangements with Mademoiselle Bertin for my costume, and she should secretly meet me at the Tuileries palace for my disguise."

The Count of Artois was delighted, though worried that his brother would object. "But he goes to bed at nine o'clock!" replied the princess.

Her brother-in-law promised to organize the masquerade ball, but only if Léonard was willing to assist him. Léonard complied, promising a ball before the end of the week, and knowing well that the Count of Artois would have very little at all to do with the project. With the help of the famous dancer Dauberval, Léonard was able to arrange the event for the following Saturday. No members of the court were allowed to attend, fearing that their secret escapade would be discovered by the dauphin and the royal family.

Léonard also came to an understanding with Mademoiselle Bertin as to the costumes of the dauphine, who was to appear first as a gray domino and then as a Swiss peasant girl. It was agreed that these masquerade outfits would be brought early, on the day of the ball, to an apartment at the Tuileries which was to be prepared in great haste.

On Saturday evening the dauphin, who had come to his wife's apartment after supper, pulled up an armchair to relax near the fire. Marie Antoinette trembled with anxiety, but her fears were soon quieted. Her husband whistled softly for half an hour near the hearth, finally yawned, wished her goodnight, and withdrew to his chambers.

At a quarter to midnight, Marie Antoinette, Madame de Langeac, the Count of Artois, and Léonard left the château through a little door opening onto the terrace. When they reached the apartments of the Tuileries palace, Mademoiselle Bertin was waiting for them with two of her assistants, adding the finishing touches to

Gala ball, late eighteenth century

the elaborate costumes. Then Dauberval received the three anonymous masqueraders when they arrived at the ball; however, he did not announce them, having been told not to reveal their names. Such secrecy excited the curiosity of the crowd and, from that instant, the masqueraders were watched and studied with their every movement.

Marie Antoinette and the Count of Artois were overjoyed with the ball. The domino costume disguised the dauphine well; however, there were several other masqueraders who were well familiar with the gestures and manners of the Marquise de Langeac. One masquerader in particular, disguised as a magician, confirmed her identity, and thus easily discovered the identities of the other guests. When the duchess informed the count that a certain magician had taken Marie Antoinette by the hand and escorted her off to another salon, he began frantically searching for his sister-in-law, but to no avail.

In an adjoining salon, Her Royal Highness discovered that the magician knew very well to whom he spoke. Fortunately, Léonard entered the room right as the magician was putting his arm about her slender waist and making a most passionate declaration of love. Léonard was about to confront the insolent magician, when he

Shepherdess, coachman, and harlequin costumes
(BIBLIOTHÈQUE NATIONALE DE FRANCE)

saw two of the magician's accomplices come out from behind a curtain with clubs in their hands. In Léonard's version, he managed to take one of the clubs away from them, and gave them both a good thrashing. We can only assume what really happened in the salon.

Léonard then turned to the magician, who succeeded in jumping out a window (but not before he had felt the swing of the knotty pine stick two or three times). The encounter with the magician was kept quiet, but Léonard discovered that the magician was none other than the Duke of Chartres. Léonard then felt he had at the very least avenged Mademoiselle Rose Bertin for the insulting pursuits that she had endured. Léonard later shuddered to think what might have happened had he not entered the salon when he did. The event could be read as a moment of bravery and selflessness on the hairdresser's part—but attacking the duke and his men would certainly not gain him any favors at court.

The masquerade ball was only one of Marie Antoinette's favorite pastimes; she also cherished concerts, opera, and the theater. As a child in Vienna she had played the harpsichord with Mozart, and had received lessons from the composer Gluck. She had also shown a lively taste for the stage, organizing and presenting small plays in her apartment—until the old king finally put an end to them.

Once the princess first discovered the theater in Paris, she attended it frequently, and French actresses soon appreciated the new patronage of the dauphine. The beautiful Sophie Arnould, who had been the idol of the theater for more than twenty years, found that she had lost her power of holding the audiences enthralled, and she was relentlessly hissed. Marie Antoinette attempted to stem the tide by applauding the singer, but whenever the princess did not attend, the audience would return to hissing.

At the beginning of 1773, a new actress, Mademoiselle Rancourt, created a great sensation at the Théâtre Français, where she had just made her debut and was, according to the press, as "bright as a comet." The Marquise de Langeac also spoke highly of her. After seeing the play, Marie Antoinette continually spoke of nothing but Mademoiselle Rancourt for several days. She eventually ordered Léonard to bring the actress to Versailles. The lovely debutante withdrew after less than an hour's audience with the princess, but she did leave with fifty gold coins in her purse.

Unfortunately, the new "comet" would cause Marquise de Langeac to fall from Marie Antoinette's grace. The dauphine became so interested in Mademoiselle Rancourt, beyond simply admiring her unusual talent, that she frequently invited her to Versailles, flattered her, paid her debts, and overwhelmed her with tokens of affection. The Marquise de Langeac, who at that time was first in favor with Marie Antoinette, became inflamed with jealousy at the sight of the actress. The marquise's tears and reproaches only made the dauphine dismiss her more quickly.

Amazed by Mademoiselle Rancourt's popularity in the press, Léonard thought, "Why should I not invent a headdress *à la comète?*" He had no idea how to create it, but when he accidentally spoke of it to the dauphine, Her Royal Highness commanded him to try it at once. Although he felt that it was a complete disappointment when finished, the headdress, a confused combination of fire-colored ribbons entangled in her locks of hair, pleased the princess so immensely that she appeared that very evening at the theater in it. Murmurs were heard circulating from box to box:

> *"It is a headdress à la comète!"*
> *"What an artist that Léonard is!"*
> *"Doesn't it look as if he had studied it for a week at the observatory?"*
> *"It is scrupulously excellent!"*

Léonard hadn't seen the comet of 1773 at all. After his sensation appeared at the theater, there were scarves, ribbons, fans, carriages, and even jewelry *à la comète* in the shops of Paris. Confectioners turned the comet into preserves and jellies, and pastry cooks molded Léonard's newest design into cakes and tarts.

Léonard's secret to getting this trend to spread was actually a simple one: He had planted accomplices in the theater, all raving about Madame the Dauphine's newest masterpiece *à la comète*—created by her brilliant hairdresser.

The Dauphine Marie Antoinette
(BIBLIOTHÈQUE NATIONALE DE FRANCE)

Léonard was well aware of the way fashion spread through Paris, and sometimes the salesman took it upon himself to puff up the artist.

By the winter of 1774, Marie Antoinette had acquired a taste for extravagant fêtes and masquerade balls, and no one danced with greater grace than the Austrian princess. At first, unmarried women were not admitted to her balls at Versailles. Among the gentlemen most in vogue at these royal soirées was the Count of Artois, but the king's other brother, the Count of Provence, hardly ever attended—except to serve as a wallflower with his wife. They did, however, make great wallflowers. Their corpulence was developing so rapidly that they very often presented themselves sideways at court, in order to fit through the doors. The Count of Provence did enliven these dances with his witty conversations. His wife appeared "busy enough breathing and digesting under the pressure of her corset."

At one of these balls Marie Antoinette looked out and noticed that very few people in her circle were wearing the latest fashions from Paris. She asked Léonard the next morning if it would be possible to revive the fashion periodical

Journal des Dames, January 1774

Journal des Dames (which had already been resurrected unsuccessfully several times in the past). "It is an institution wholly French which one is astonished not to find in Paris," she said.

Savvy enough to know it was in his best interest to be associated with a journal that would endorse his creations, he volunteered to take on the task; the princess pledged to provide the funds to back the venture.

Promising to have the journal published within two weeks, but also burdened with a busy schedule, Léonard spoke to Mademoiselle Bertin about finding a

Rose Bertin's *ques-a-co*

managing editor. She recommended the financially ruined Baroness de Prinzen, who could hardly lend anything more than her name to the journal. They made her an offer, and she eagerly accepted the management of the *Journal des Dames*. Léonard asked for permission from Marie Antoinette to dedicate the journal to her; she graciously accepted, and the editors devoted their time to flattering the princess—as well as the creations of her celebrated hairdresser.

The *ques-a-co*, meaning "what is it?," was one of Mademoiselle Bertin's inventions and the first hairstyle that erupted in the pages of the *Journal des Dames*; it later became an immeasurable success in the fashionable world. It was composed of three feathers that ladies wore on the back of the head, creating a design resembling a question mark. The new style was copied by all the royal princesses, especially Madame du Barry.

Léonard was very fond of Mademoiselle Bertin, often commenting that their fortunes "trudged along hand in hand like two good sisters." Their services were indeed complementary, but Léonard was bothered and burdened by jealousy; the glory of her *ques-a-co*, which the milliner had created on her own, gnawed at him. In fact, Mademoiselle Bertin's laurels and praise were beginning to prevent Léonard from sleeping at night. He needed just one more of those grand ideas, one that would overthrow all existing vogues—not only to win back the favor of the dauphine, and to assuage his bitterness at Mademoiselle Rose, but to keep his name on the tongues of Paris.

CHAPTER 5

"Le Pouf Sentimental"

"I myself had been frightened by the shamelessness of my conception; but soon the folly of the period got the better of mine. One saw in the puffs the strangest things that fancy could imagine."

—Léonard Autié
Versailles, 1774

April 1774
Versailles, France

After many sleepless nights, Léonard finally came up with a new sensation: the *pouf sentimental*. It was the spirit of rivalry with Mademoiselle Rose that brought these headdresses to such monstrous heights, both literally and figuratively. The pouf was first worn by Madame the Duchess of Chartres in the month of April 1774. The duchess had always boldly accepted all that the most eccentric fashions of Paris had to offer, and the sentimental pouf was quite eccentric—to say the least.

The duchess's pouf was composed of fourteen yards of gauze and numerous plumes waving at the top of a tower. Léonard employed two waxen figures as ornaments, representing the little Duke of Beaujolais (later King Louis Philippe) in his nurse's arms. Beside them he placed a parrot pecking at a plate of cherries, and reclining at the nurse's feet, he put the waxen figure of a little African boy of whom the duchess was very fond. On different parts of the hairpieces were the initials of the Duke of Chartres, of Penthièvre, and of Orléans, formed with the hair of those princes—the husband, father, and father-in-law of the duchess.

The pouf was quite unprecedented; never had anyone dared to create such a hodgepodge. Even Léonard was a bit frightened to show the absurd conception at first, but like most of Léonard's creations, it caught on. Soon afterward one could find the strangest things in the poufs of Paris. Frivolous women covered their heads with butterflies, sentimental women nestled swarms of Cupids in their hair, and the wives of officers wore squadrons perched on their heads. Melancholic women went so far as to put crematory urns in their headdresses.[1]

And the hairstyles continued to rise in height. In February 1776, the queen, going to a ball given by the Duchess of Orléans, had plumes so high that they had to be removed from her coiffure to get into her carriage. She had to leave them behind when she returned to Versailles. The next popular pouf, the *hérisson*, or the hedgehog, was Léonard's concoction of unpowdered hair curled to the tips and rising in tiers, leaving several strands of curls falling on the neck. The hair on the forehead was held up in a high and very large clump with hairpins. The entire bouffant style was supported by a ribbon that encircled the entire pouf.

Pouf hairstyles worn by Marie Antoinette
(BIBLIOTHÈQUE NATIONALE DE FRANCE)

Léonard continued to invent a number of new styles, each more extravagant than the next. Some were so high that it appeared that a "woman's head was in the middle of her body."[2] One of Léonard's creations, the zephyr, was a moving garden of brightly colored flowers, which caused everyone to talk in raptures about the hairdresser's achievements.

The theater of Paris was a source for innovation and inspiration in hairdressing. When Gluck's opera *Iphigenia in Tauris* was performed in Paris, the lugubrious coiffure *à l'Iphigenie* was born. The hair was adorned with a wreath of black flowers, surmounted by a silver crescent, and a long white veil flowing behind. Due to the increase in poufs worn in the theater, spectators complained of not being able to see above the towering obstructions. Consequently, the director of the opera made it a rule, enforced by the police, that only poufs of moderate height could be worn.

Marie Antoinette's hedgehog pouf
(BIBLIOTHÈQUE NATIONALE DE FRANCE)

The coiffure *à la Belle-Poule* consisted of a ship sailing on a sea of thick, wavy hair. It was invented after the naval battle in which the frigate *La Belle Poule* was victorious. The ship itself, with its masts, rigging, and guns, was imitated in miniature in the pouf. This elaborate creation, a celebration of sorts, was an overnight success.

Marie Antoinette's
coiffure à la Zephyr, 1776
(BIBLIOTHÈQUE NATIONALE DE FRANCE)

One of Léonard's favorite stories described an evening at the opera when, forgetting the height of Léonard's pouf, the Duchess of Chartres leaned forward to speak to the Duke of Penthièvre—her headdress becoming entangled in the ornaments of a girandole, a decorative candlestick. When resuming her upright position, the girandole remained firm but it drew out a long piece of the headdress's gauze and displaced the parrot and the cherries. Luckily, they fell on the duke, who caught them, preventing them from falling to the seats below, and thus saving Gluck's opera and his daughter from becoming an "object of mirth."

Such merriment and frivolity was cut short in May 1774. The unexpected death of King Louis XV momentarily diverted everyone's attention from the balls, the operas, and Léonard's illustrious creations.

While a solemn occasion, Louis XV's death was not free from court intrigue and political maneuvering. As the king lay in his bed at the Petit Trianon with a high fever, Madame du Barry and her followers took the king's illness lightly, calling it indigestion and advising against moving him to his chambers at the grand château. The favorite remained as calm as possible at the king's bedside and barred any audience with him; she was going to care for him herself. She also had an ulterior motive; she needed to keep him from becoming alarmed at his condition and asking for a confessor. The favorite would be sacrificed and banned from court if the king were to obtain absolution for his sins, of which she was a notable one.[3]

For Madame du Barry, the confessor was a real scarecrow; she trembled at the sight of any confessor but her own. The king's reign was thus ending with a battle

The coiffure *à Belle-Poule*
(BIBLIOTHÈQUE NATIONALE DE FRANCE)

between the Du Barry party and her enemies. By prolonging the king's sacramental ceremony as long as possible (and against the wishes of the royal family), the favorite was hoping for a miracle to save the king—and herself.

Not daring to come to the favorite's Petit Trianon, the royal family sent their doctor, who advised that it would be best for the king to recuperate at Versailles.

Duchess of Chartres
(BIBLIOTHÈQUE NATIONALE DE FRANCE)

The king agreed over the objections of Madame du Barry. For several days the doctors were puzzled by the king's illness, and he was bled on several occasions. When the king's doctor gave the king a drink of water, he noticed a rash in his mouth. It was smallpox, and only those who had already had the disease stayed by the king's side. Madame du Barry had never had smallpox, which was never more prevalent than toward the end of the eighteenth century. Symptoms included a high fever, abdominal pain, and lesions; the resulting encephalitis and extensive bleeding usually caused death. The king's smallpox might have been contagious at the onset of his fever, but it would have been most contagious when his rash began to appear. Nevertheless, the favorite courageously stayed near the king, which speaks to both her loyalty perhaps, and to the fear with which she spent those final days.

When the king decided to call his confessor, he first called for Madame du Barry. "I am obligated to God and to my people; it is necessary for you to leave," the king said, wishing to avoid any and all scandal in his final days. The next morning, the pale but calm mistress left the château, to the merriment of her enemies. The king then begged his noble-hearted daughters to leave him; for the first time in their lives, they disobeyed him.

At one o'clock in the afternoon on the 9th of May, the king's door was opened and his valet announced, "Messieurs, the King Louis XV is dead." At once there was a great uproar as the courtiers awaiting the news fled the king's antechamber. As was

France in tears, leaning on the medallion of Louis XV
(BIBLIOTHÈQUE NATIONALE DE FRANCE)

tradition, they rushed headlong to greet their new monarch and shouted, "Vive le roi!"

King Louis XVI and Queen Marie Antoinette were saddened by the king's death, of course, but also quite frightened by their new responsibility. They fell on their knees, praying: "Oh, God, guide us and protect us; we are too young to reign!" Future events and history itself would prove this decidedly to be the case.

The new King Louis XVI and Queen Marie Antoinette immediately withdrew to Choisy in mourning with the princes and the princesses, and it was decided that Madame du Barry should be politely exiled to the convent of Pont-aux-Dames. The new royals also lost no time in banning Du Barry's supporters from court.

Granting mistresses a special status at court had become an institution at Louis XV's court—despite the courtesans' backgrounds. "Louis XV required the salt of scandal to season his dull appetite," wrote a historian in the next century.[4] But at the moment of the king's death, only flagrant hypocrisy reigned as the court wiped the royal slate clean. Although many courtiers had mistresses themselves, they too disavowed any knowledge of the king's adulterous affair.

On the 14th of May, Marie Antoinette wrote her mother, "The creature has been placed in a convent, and all who bear this scandalous name have been driven from the Court."[5] And a letter was sent to the favorite's family informing them that the court was henceforth also forbidden ground. Madame du Barry, the king's favorite mistress,

Happier days at Madame du Barry's Château Louveciennes, 1771

the one who had fatefully introduced Léonard to Marie Antoinette, remained at the convent for two years until retiring to her Château Louveciennes.

The change of the king's ministry was completed by August, which caused a type of mild coup d'état. Something no one had suspected before also became known. Word was out that Marie Antoinette exercised enormous power over her husband's feeble mind.

At a time when reform was needed for his poor subjects, Louis XVI did not trust his ministers. Scolded by his wife and courtiers for his stinginess and called on by the clergy and nobility to prevent any change to feudal institutions, the king felt obliged to dismiss his ministers. History shows that the king was far too weak to halt the monarchy's tumble.

Louis XVI thought little of government—domestic troubles had already rendered the duties of his reign too wearisome. For over four years His Majesty had refused to listen to the rumors that came to him regarding Marie Antoinette's frivolities. Although he didn't approve of her "childish acts," it had never occurred to him to doubt her virtue. In August 1774, however, the king's confidence at last began to ebb. Libelous pamphlets about the queen's nocturnal strolls with the ladies and lords of her private circle had become too venomous to His Majesty's new throne.[6]

The new king chastised Marie Antoinette about the accusations, almost disregarding whether or not they were true. In fact, this seemed to be beside the point; the king knew that perception was what kept everything together in his court. Louis ordered that the author of the scathing pamphlets be found, and the ill-advised poet was thrown in the Bastille at the king's request. But that first blot on the reputation of Marie Antoinette would never fade away.

During the time of this conjugal storm, Léonard was dressing Marie Antoinette's hair when she received the following note from Louis XVI:

Madame, I am now in a position to satisfy a wish which you have made known to me; I beg you to accept Little Trianon. This beautiful place has always been the abode of the favorites of Kings; herefore, it must be yours.[7]

When Marie Antoinette first took possession of the Petit Trianon, she called it her "Little Vienna" and she spent much time there alone, personally giving permission to courtiers to visit her gardens as little favors. However, when she received a request to visit "Little Vienna" from a prominent member of court, she was offended. Perhaps she was afraid that the public would doubt where her loyalty lay. Nevertheless, the court member was denied access to Trianon then and for some time afterward. Marie Antoinette adored Trianon and she would sometimes spend months at a time there, only receiving her closest friends and never observing the etiquette of Versailles—one

Le Petit Trianon

can assume this was one of her favorite aspects of the château. Whenever she entered her salon, her ladies never left their needlework or the harpsichord to recognize the queen; nor did men interrupt their game of billiards or cards. The lavish embellishments of the queen's hideaway and the elaborate galas were costly; eventually the queen was reproached for aggravating the treasury's shortfall. Meanwhile, the people of France were becoming hungrier and more destitute. "Madame Deficit," as the queen was nicknamed, was unwittingly conjuring a monstrous storm on the horizon.

The queen had sacrificed her popularity in Paris for her seclusion at the Petit Trianon. She paid a visit to Paris on a whim and soon learned of this trade-off. The queen returned quickly to Versailles in tears, asking everyone, "But what did I do to them?" Thinking it was her seclusion (and not her spending) that angered the public, she decided to purchase the château of St. Cloud where she could mingle with her people on Sunday afternoons, reconciling with them and regaining the love from them that she experienced as the new dauphine.[8] Of course, the purchase of St. Cloud only enraged her destitute subjects; a second château was nothing but fuel on the raging fire. Revolution was already stirring in France's heart.

On the 11th of June 1775, Léonard and Mademoiselle Bertin were called to escort the queen to the city of Rheims for the royal coronation. This occasion, too, was marked with scandal. Much was written about the apartment constructed for the

Coronation portrait of Louis XVI
(BIBLIOTHÈQUE NATIONALE DE FRANCE)

Coronation of Louis XVI, Rheims Cathedral, June 11, 1775
(BIBLIOTHÈQUE NATIONALE DE FRANCE)

queen in the interior of the cathedral of Rheims. Her chambers erected in the church contrasted sharply with its sanctity. There was a boudoir, a voluptuously decorated bedchamber, and a dressing room with all its accessories. Léonard could not help but note that a guardroom had also been erected under the Gothic arches "where no less swearing was done than in that of Versailles."[9]

The coronation took place with all the pomp that was given a king at the time in France. Louis XVI was still quite popular; in the town of Rheims, where almost all of the kings of France had been crowned, the people came out enthusiastically for him. He, too, was overcome with emotion, enjoying his walks in the midst of the crowds that pressed around him. In the middle of the choir of the cathedral at Rheims, he put his hand up to his head at the moment when the crown was being placed upon it, saying, "It pinches me." The king could not know how prescient this comment would be.[10]

The luxury of Louis XVI's coronation was also seen as something of an insult to the French people. The queen wrote to her mother, Empress Maria Theresa, "It is at once amazing and gratifying to be so well received, in spite of the dearness of bread." At the time of the "flour wars," an uprising caused by the ever-increasing price of bread, rioters talked of going to "shake up" the queen—and this a full fourteen years before the Revolution. Rumors flourished that the queen was wasting precious flour to powder her elaborate poufs at a time when bread was becoming scarcer and scarcer. The rumbles—of stomachs and of bitterness—were already audible.

When the court returned to Versailles, the queen made important changes in her household. Her Majesty first established the post of lady superintendent for Madame the Princesse de Lamballe, a faithful ally who would remain devoted to the queen for the rest of her life. Her Majesty also rid herself of Madame de Misery, who was not only too formal and unbending in her dated habits, she also lacked the slightest taste for dress. In Madame Campan, the queen found a more kindly advisor who understood her tastes—as well as her whims.

Madame Campan helped change the queen's daily routine—the imposing etiquette of the former court gave way to elegance and frivolity. The new superintendent, always careful to anticipate the queen's wishes, never considered the price of things. Thanks to her numerous innovations, which Léonard and Mademoiselle Bertin seconded heartily, Her Majesty's expenses soon knew no limit. The queen became worried that the tremendous increase in the royal wardrobe would be too great a burden for Mademoiselle Bertin. She decided she required an extra milliner, who would soon become more of a rival to Mademoiselle Bertin than a collaborator.

Léonard remained the sovereign of the empire of hairdressing. He relegated his secondary duties to his prime minister, Frémont, who managed the *Académie de coiffure*. Over the years, Léonard had always been responsive to the queen's slightest requests, loyal and committed to Her Majesty no matter the issue. Even as things started to unravel for her, Léonard remained steadfastly loyal to the queen, guarding all the secrets and fears that she had shared with him. In turn, the queen always showed her hairdresser the utmost trust, confiding in him at a time when courtiers were increasingly turning against her. The hairdresser's loyalty was rewarded in kind. Unlike Rose Bertin's situation, the queen agreed with Léonard that the throne of hairdressing was too narrow to be shared. He would have it all to himself.

PART TWO

The Queen's Confidant

CHAPTER 6

A Hairdresser's Gossip

"You see, ladies, Her Majesty suffers everything from me, everything absolutely, since we have shared the same bed."
—Léonard to Marie Antoinette's Ladies-in-Waiting
Versailles, 1779

October 1775
Versailles, France

Gossip is a centuries-old offshoot of hairdressing, and Léonard surely got an earful from the courtiers who devoted much of their time to rumor-mongering at Versailles. Even under the reign of the past king, Louis XV, Madame du Barry's jealousy of Marie Antoinette and her influence had always been a constant source of whispering. Madame du Barry criticized Marie Antoinette's manners, her youth, her naiveté, and her accent; but it was Marie's irreverence toward proper appearance that bothered Madame du Barry the most. The princess's attendance at court in simple attire was described as "a relaxation of the royal dignity" and "a considerable injury to the respect due to her rank."[1]

Popular hair colors at the time were black, brown, and blonde; red hair was often dyed black. Marie Antoinette's hair was a peculiarly beautiful soft shade of blonde, but there was a slight red tint to her hair, especially when she was younger. In turn, Madame du Barry always referred to the dauphine as "la petite rousse"—carrot-top—behind her back. Gossip in the new reign, fed by jealousy and hatred of the foreign and irreverent queen, would not be as harmless as Madame du Barry's whisperings. In fact, the whispers would gather into a deafening roar, and lay the groundwork for revolution.

While Léonard detailed many sordid stories about Marie Antoinette in his memoirs, he simultaneously (and sometimes, contradictorily) argued that most accusations could not have been true. Having spent much of his time with Her Majesty as her personal valet and hairdresser, he was certainly in a position to know what was real and what was rumor. But Léonard likely turned a blind eye to the queen's indiscretions, if they existed, for fear of endangering his own standing. He may also have had such high regard for Her Majesty that he could not validate any story that would tarnish her name. He would not have been the only one to paint Marie Antoinette with such a brush.

One such story was the queen's relationship with the young Duke of Lauzun, agreed to be one of the most handsome gentlemen of the queen's court.[2] When the duke first appeared at the court of Versailles in 1775, after his successful diplomatic mission to Russia, his good looks, his graceful manners, and his reputation at the court of Catherine II—Catherine the Great—attracted the attention of all the courtiers. All the ladies wished to meet him, and the queen seemed the most eager. She asked one of her favorites, Madame de Guéménée, to introduce him to her circle as soon as possible.

Duke of Lauzun

The duke was brought to court, and the queen received him with such marked enthusiasm and compliments that the courtiers spoke of nothing but the queen's effusiveness the following day. A few days later, when the duke arrived late, Marie Antoinette cried out, "Here he is, at last!" The queen's inappropriate fawning again spread throughout the palace. At a time when rumors and counter rumors floated rampantly about the halls of Versailles, the inexperienced monarch was surrounded by courtiers who dwelt upon her every caprice. At times the queen hardly knew which way to turn from the invectives, though her lofty spirit sustained her in public. In her boudoir, however, she often wept irrepressibly.[3]

The Duke of Lauzun was the darling of the court, known to be witty and chivalrous as well. Léonard was present one day when the duke made an appearance at Madame de Guéménée's salon in a uniform decorated with a magnificent plume of white heron's feathers. When the queen purportedly admired the plume, he offered it to her through the Princesse de Guéménée's good graces. Afterward, the queen was embarrassed for accepting the present, but she had not dared refuse it, for fear of disappointing the duke. She wore the plume on only one occasion, letting the duke see her adorned with his gift, as a matter of *politesse*. In his memoirs Lauzun tells a different story, claiming that Madame de Guéménée, after speaking softly with Marie Antoinette, approached him and asked, "Are you very attached to the plume of feathers that you are wearing? The queen would die to have it—would you refuse her?"

The art of flirtation depended on this back and forth dance with the gift—right beneath the eyes of the court. The slightest snub or gesture spoke volumes, only fanning court intrigues and petty jealousies. With court etiquette forbidding him to present the gift in public, Lauzun sent the feathers to Madame de Guéménée the next morning. When the queen wore the plume of feathers later that evening, he overheard various courtiers remarking how indecent it was for the queen to wear such a sign of her affection for him in public. Lauzun soon became known as Marie Antoinette's favorite, as he himself confirmed in his memoirs, but whether or not this was just court rumor or Lauzun's own vanity, history cannot say. We do know that though he had often spoken of returning to Saint Petersburg and the court of Empress Catherine II, suddenly, and without explanation, he changed his mind. Such an unprovoked decision sent the court reeling—they whispered that only the queen could have influenced him to pass on Catherine II's offer to claim the highest rank in the Russian army.

This episode took place before the king and queen's coronation in June of 1775. Before going to Rheims for the ceremony, the queen visited Madame de Guéménée at her residence in Auteuil on several occasions. Lauzun was there at each of those visits, and Her Majesty was determined to have the duke accompany the court to Rheims for the regal occasion. Lauzun politely refused, claiming that he had been ordered to rejoin and command the French Royal Legion. All the queen's efforts to change his mind were in vain—but it would not be Her Majesty's last word.

When Léonard reached the queen's dressing room the next day, she hardly let him enter before telling him to run to the Biron residence to tell the Duke of Lauzun that she forbid him to leave Versailles, and that she wished to see him at her circle that very evening. Léonard obeyed the queen, but the duke seemed annoyed by the sudden request. Léonard heard him murmur, "This persistence is tyrannical." Then, rather bluntly, he added, "Tell Her Majesty that I shall comply."

That evening, as the duke paid his respects to the queen at one of the gaming tables where the Baron of Viomenil was playing, Her Majesty said, "Baron, you are in charge of the movement of the troops. Therefore, you must order the Royal Legion near Versailles, so that Monsieur Lauzun will not be far from us." This was an obvious break from protocol; such a command would have customarily been given by the king. Even more bizarre, here was a military order being given for no other purpose than to keep the queen's favorite nearby.

Yet the baron was all too aware of the queen's influence over her husband, and he replied that he would obey. Most surprised, however, were the ladies and gentlemen of the court who crowded Marie Antoinette's apartments. At Versailles the next day, the duke's favor with the queen made such a great clamor in the galleries that the echo finally reached Louis XVI's ears. Léonard later heard through the palace grapevine that Lauzun would find himself behind the great iron doors of the Bastille if he did not leave the court at once.

Whether rumored or real, the queen's attention toward Lauzun had only encouraged the scathing reports of her enemies. Léonard, however, who did not pass a day without seeing Marie Antoinette, affirmed that there was nothing whatsoever inappropriate in the queen's relationship with the Duke of Lauzun. Because Lauzun was known as the darling of society and the ornament of the French court, many of Léonard's contemporaries thought otherwise. After all, Lauzun was a soldier, an accomplished gentleman, and the queen's favorite. Léonard may have had his reasons for defending the queen; not only was he grateful to her for his fame and fortune, but his memoirs were written years later, while he was in exile with, and under the protection of, the Royalist Party.[4]

When the duke's father died, everyone assumed that the duke would inherit his father's important post as colonel of the regiment of the French Guards. The queen, however, procured it for the Duke of Châtelet, and from that day forward there was no more conjecture about their relationship. The Duke of Lauzun, with one swoop, became a vicious enemy of the queen. The queen's impulsivity took many forms, and her whims seemed to blow with the wind.

Beginning in 1776 a flurry of scandalous pamphlets circulated in Paris—moving their target from the former king's mistress to the vulnerable new queen. While the *Journal des Dames* made Marie Antoinette the queen of fashion, these libelous pamphlets also turned her into a monster and a criminal—accusing her of adultery, of sexual deviance, of having orgies, and of wasting flour on her hair while her subjects were starving. The scathing verses mentioned not only the Duke of Lauzun, but also the Counts of Coigny, of Vaudreuil, and of Bezenval. The Count of Coigny was especially singled out for being Marie Antoinette's lover and the future father of her first son:

> *Nothing can undo Coigny's work,*
> *The boyfriend's caresses and his obscene hand,*
> *Despite nature's offense of the work,*
> *At Louis's expense arrives a fat dauphin,*
> *Just after nine months from the time*
> *When Coigny dove into the royal clam.[5]*

The Duchess of Polignac

Each of the four favorites alternated in the queen's good graces and favors, but during the first months of this year the malicious chronicle also added a fifth name to those of the four noblemen—Monsieur Dillon. The ladies of the court had nicknamed him *le beau Dillon,* or the handsome Dillon.

Édouard Dillon was a member of Madame de Polignac's circle, and one afternoon while he was rehearsing the quadrille dance for the queen's next ball, he suddenly turned pale and fainted. He was carried to a sofa, and Marie Antoinette, imprudently, placed her hand on his heart to see if it was still beating. When he regained consciousness, Dillon apologized—he had left Paris without having breakfast. The queen ordered him some soup, and all of the courtiers, perhaps jealous, insisted that he was surely intimate with her. The gossip escalated when Dillon was seen on a later occasion in the queen's royal coach. What spectators did not know, however, was that he had fallen from his horse while hunting and had broken his arm. Since her carriage was the only vehicle on the spot, the queen ordered him to take it home, and she returned later in the king's coach.

Their Majesties asked to be present at the first dressing of the gentleman's injury, where the tearful Marie Antoinette seemed devastated by the accident. But it was rumored that the queen, accompanied by only one of her ladies and wrapped in a large cloak, had also later secretly visited the handsome Dillon. This act of kindness appeared to all the courtiers as overstepping the bounds of ordinary compassion.

Pamphlet depicting the queen's rumored promiscuity
(BIBLIOTHÈQUE NATIONALE DE FRANCE)

Léonard recalled that the *beau Dillon* could only have been the queen's favorite—if he ever actually was a favorite—for a very short period of time, because Madame Gabrielle de Polignac had just arrived at court, a beautiful and charismatic new courtier who would soon win all of Marie Antoinette's affection and attention. Madame de Lamballe and Madame de Guéménée, whom the queen had preferred to all the ladies of the court, suddenly lost a good part of Her Majesty's good graces.

The queen now spoke tirelessly of Madame Gabrielle de Polignac, consulting only her about the day's wardrobe and toilette. Although the entire Polignac family benefited greatly from the queen's favor, the court became outraged by the family's increasing wealth and lavish lifestyle. Gabrielle's husband was given the title of "Duke of Polignac," thus making her the "Duchess of Polignac"—which only intimidated the courtiers even more. The queen opened the court coffers to this new favorite; it was said that not even Louis XIV's Madame de Maintenon, nor Louis XV's Madame de Pompadour, cost as much as this court favorite.

Obscene pamphlets circulated widely, claiming that the duchess was the queen's lover. The message of one of the pamphlets, *The Historical Essay on the Life of Marie Antoinette of Austria, Queen of France*, was either the duchess had corrupted the queen, or the queen was so hungry for love that she wanted the duchess "as a lover wants his mistress." Despite the fact that these claims were unfounded, rumors of the queen's sexual relations with lovers of both sexes did immeasurable damage to her reign and to the prestige of the French monarchy.

The queen became so overwhelmed with anxiety that she cancelled invitations to parties at Trianon and avoided the theater and all public places. It was a vicious circle; the royal family was separating itself from its courtiers and subjects and, at the same time, losing the influence that a monarch so crucially needed at court. Eventually the queen only entertained strangers and family at her retreat at Trianon, and when she was chastised for it, she sighed, "You are right, but they ask nothing of me." Outside the Trianon's walls, songs and pamphlets continued to damage the queen's character. This isolation from the French people only increased the queen's vulnerability, at the same time tarnishing the monarchy's legitimacy. A perfect storm was rising outside of the world of Versailles.

Léonard, for one, constantly downplayed the queen's irreverence. While others accused the queen of meddling in public affairs, he believed she had no taste whatsoever for them and he often noted a tone of gaiety that was natural to the queen. Léonard's wittiness and his own irreverence brought him favor with the queen, allowing him to address Her Majesty with a marked lack of ceremony—informality that often shocked courtiers and other servants.

Toward the end of April 1778, the queen entered the king's study one morning.

"I come to ask justice of one of your subjects, who has violently insulted me," said the queen.

"What are you telling me, madame?" the king asked. "That is impossible."

"Sire, to tell the truth, I have been struck!" she said.

"Nonsense!" said the king. "You are jesting!"

"Not at all, sire," said the queen. "Someone has been audacious enough to kick me in the stomach."

Louis XVI, finally understanding, expressed his delight. The couple had not been able to consummate their marriage for eight years. Rumor and pamphlets claimed that the king was impotent, and that his Austrian-born queen had been taking on lovers to give France an heir to the throne.[6] Such rumors not only cast doubt on the legitimacy of the queen's children, but they were also grounds for repudiation, thus endangering Marie Antoinette's title. Moreover, these rumors jeopardized the Franco-Austrian alliance—the goal of the royal couple's match in the first place. As soon as news of the pregnancy reached the Hôtel de Ville in Paris, the mayor and the aldermen made the trip to Versailles with majestic pomp, bringing the royal couple customary gifts.

Louis would have surely been thrilled—and relieved; for years his impotence had been questioned and subjected to unforgiving ridicule. Timid and awkward from his youth, the years without fathering a child could only have aggrandized his sense of inferiority. Perhaps the guilt alone had often allowed him to overlook the often absurd and unpredictable whims of his wife.

The queen sent joyous dispatches off to all the courts of Europe and all of her royal relatives. Her close confidant, the Princesse de Lamballe, wrote:

> Such also was the exulting feeling of Marie Antoinette when she no longer doubted of her wished-for pregnancy. The idea of becoming a mother filled her soul with an exuberant delight, which made the very pavement on which she trod vibrate with the words "I shall be a mother! I shall be a mother!"[7]

Now came Marie Antoinette's triumph; her satirists and the malevolent pamphleteers were silenced. The months of pregnancy passed quickly, highlighted with splendid fêtes, balls, and entertainments as magnificent and luxurious as those of the great Louis XIV.

In the final weeks of her pregnancy, the queen kept to her bed, and Léonard continued to dress her hair; this task was performed daily, but not without some difficulty. "There is nothing harder than dressing the hair of a person in bed," he noted. In fact, he was compelled to lie down beside the queen to care for her hair.

The child, Marie-Thérèse, named for Marie Antoinette's mother, was born on the 19th of December 1778. According to tradition, Marie Antoinette had given birth in front of the entire court. The queen knew that she had disappointed France by not giving her subjects an heir to the throne, but she wrote her mother, the Empress of Austria: "I did not give the king a dauphin, but my poor little daughter will not be less adored; a son would not have belonged to me, but she will always be by my side. She will help me live, console me in my despair, and we will be happy together."[8]

The Empress rejoiced at the birth of the new princess, but especially because she had given birth at all; it meant that there was still hope for her to produce a dauphin. As the months rolled by, the Empress reproached Marie Antoinette for not using her conjugal nights wisely. Finally, in 1780, the queen was pregnant again. Unfortunately, the Empress would die that year—never experiencing the joy of having a grandson who would be king of France.

As early as 1779, the news of the Petit Trianon, Marie's private château on the grounds of Versailles, had begun to spread about Paris and provoke harsh criticism. The château and adjoining gardens had been a gift to Marie Antoinette from the king, and no cost was spared to suit the queen's taste. She was the sole mistress of the Petit Trianon, and no one, including the king, could visit the storybook manor and lush gardens without her invitation.[9] The people saw the queen's embellishments to the Petit Trianon as the cause of the treasury's deficit; the press wrote of "the millions sunk at Trianon."[10] While the people could not afford soap, the princely guests were entertained at the Trianon on such a scale that the washing for a single day included over four thousand pieces. While the people struggled to put food on the table, the "comedy, supper, and illumination" continued as normal.[11]

Any criticism, however, fell upon deaf ears. Trianon might have been on an island for all its connection to daily life in France. Marie Antoinette spent her time preparing for plays that she and her favorites would perform at the château. The Count of Artois was the only man allowed to participate, and the audience normally consisted of the king, the Monsieur, and the rest of the royal family. The queen's ladies and their children also attended, totaling about forty spectators. The queen herself, shuttered from the cries of her people, was content to reply to any criticism: "I have already made my determination with respect to Trianon. I hold no court here; I live like a private person."

Toward the end of February, the Count of Artois would secretly leave the grand château in the evenings and scurry to the Petit Trianon, followed by a single servant. The prince usually returned between midnight and one o'clock, and courtiers noticed that he always looked somewhat fatigued on his return from these early morning excursions.

The Trianon Gardens
(BIBLIOTHÈQUE NATIONALE DE FRANCE)

The king heard rumors of his young brother's nocturnal excursions to Trianon, and he finally ordered one of his valets to follow the prince. Three days later, the valet entered His Majesty's chamber beaming that he knew everything. The Count of Artois did not go to the Trianon every evening to see the queen, but rather to "practice on a tightrope." The king doubled over with laughter as the valet described the Count of Artois, dressed in white trousers, a sweater, a pink belt, and a small cap with feathers balancing a pole in his hand. He was apparently practicing for a small skit to be presented during one of the queen's soirées for her private circle. Léonard wrote of other baffling escapades at the Trianon, but the count's tightrope walking episode remained the most bizarre and unexpected.

Across the ocean, the revolutionary spirit had taken hold in the British colonies and the news had been followed closely throughout Europe. Léonard only mentioned the American War of Independence once in his memoirs. And when he did, it was in the context of his art. His newest headdress, *aux insurgents*—which he invented toward the end of 1780 and named for the revolutionaries across the Atlantic—became vogue at Versailles and in Paris. Ben Franklin's visit to France had caught the imagination of the court and Léonard's creation was a celebration of what the American represented. Léonard was unwittingly promoting the abolition of privileges that he currently enjoyed by promoting the budding cause of independence. It would soon come down and crush them all. At the time, the court lived in a decidedly narrow world, failing to recognize the dangers of the changing tides. In fact, Léonard considered this year the zenith of his glory—like the rest of the court, he was all too blind to the fact that revolution was not a harmless and passing fashion. It was a very real, and decidedly bloody, ordeal.

It was during the queen's second pregnancy in 1781, when Léonard found Her Majesty in such good humor that he risked some of the more risqué topics during her toilette. Madame Campan signaled him with her eyes to put a stop to it several times, but Marie Antoinette, who laughed until she had tears rolling down her cheeks, said to him: "Continue, Léonard, continue. This is all very amusing!"

"You see, ladies," he said, "Her Majesty allows me everything, absolutely everything . . . we have even shared the same bed."

"What's that?" exclaimed Marie Antoinette, who ceased laughing for a moment, still suspecting that there was some witty answer to follow.

"Yes, madame," Léonard said. "Her Majesty will be pleased to recall that, when confined to her bed waiting for the new princess, I shared it daily to dress her hair."

"That is true, ladies, Léonard is right," said the queen bursting into laughter.

Emboldened, Léonard continued, "And I hope that Your Majesty will soon permit me to lie by her side again."

"Certainly!" said the queen, laughing even more loudly.

Although Léonard was implying that he was hoping for another prince or princess, this strange talk was repeated throughout the palace galleries and the Parisian salons. Noble ladies were certain that nothing could be in better taste than to "suffer from Léonard all the liberties which might come to his mind."

By the time Queen Marie Antoinette had given France its first dauphin, Louis Joseph, on the 22nd of October 1781, she was threatened by the increasing loss of her hair. Her lovely locks and her exotic hairstyles had always been the topic of the liveliest conversations; even the color of her hair had become fashionable, called *cheveux de la reine*. At the first indication of this catastrophe, Léonard began to tremble. This was his life's work and it was in danger of vanishing quite suddenly. When he returned home that evening, he could not sleep, tossing and turning with nightmares about his fate. Along with the hair of Marie Antoinette, Léonard would lose his power, that supremacy enabling him to open up the hearts of the ladies of Paris and the court—as well as their purses. Léonard had no choice but to plan for this inevitability. He did more than this—he turned it into a trend.

en Fichu

à la Douce Raillerie

à la Grecque

à la Junon

en Echelle

à la Distinction

à la Zéphire

Bonnet à l'Argus

en Rouleaux

Petite Palissade

à la Janot

Dormeuse

à la Harpie

à la Belle Poule

à la Reine

Bonnet à la Candeur

le Parterre Galant

Baigneuse

le Bandeau d'Amour

Baigneuse

Coiffures during the reign of Marie Antoinette

"Madame," Léonard said to the queen shortly after the birth of the dauphin, "the high headdress is becoming very common; first the bourgeoisie copied it, and now the common people of Paris are wearing it."

The queen was perplexed, telling Léonard that she was saddened to hear such news, because these hairstyles had always been so becoming to her. Léonard replied that any hairstyle would complement Her Majesty's beauty, but she could no longer wear one that the *grisettes*, the flirtatious working ladies of Paris, were wearing.

He added that he had carefully planned a "total revolution" in Her Majesty's hairstyle. He had her portrait drawn with the new arrangement, a style that would certainly make the queen look six or seven years younger. The queen received the news favorably until she noticed that her hair would be cut to just a few inches long. Léonard quickly replied that if the queen would consent to his *coiffure à l'enfant*, the new style would surely meet with the same enthusiasm as her previous coiffures. Without using the scissors, he warned, her hair would completely fall out within two weeks. Terribly frightened, Marie Antoinette finally allowed Léonard to cut her long locks and begged him not to cut them too short.

The queen's beautiful hair fell under Léonard's scissors, and within two weeks, all the ladies of the court had their hair dressed *à l'enfant*. And again, the hairdresser with the magic comb shined—the new coiffure spread throughout Paris and the provinces. This sudden change in fashion from the towering poufs to the short-cropped coifs created a new era in hairdressing. New styles were created for short hair, including the *au plaisir des dames* (the ladies' pleasure), *à la paresseuse* (the idle), and *à l'urgence* (the urgent).[12]

The slanders, the epigrams, and the songs against Queen Marie Antoinette knew no more bounds by the end of 1781. Each was injurious to Her Majesty's reputation, and the authors could never be discovered. Up to the end of the year, the chronicles had only mentioned the Counts of Coigny, of Vaudreuil, of Lauzun, of Bezenval, and of Dillon, but now more names were added to the damning list of favorites—including all those on the Civil List, the list of personnel on the royal payroll. But Léonard, in his sixteen or seventeen years of service to the queen, had entered Her Majesty's apartments at all hours and hardly ever lost sight of her:

> *I did not happen to see even the appearance of one wrongful act. I am well authorized, it seems to me, to firmly believe that Marie Antoinette was innocent, at least of the majority of the faults with which her life has been charged and her memory tarnished.*

Léonard did admit, however, that Marie Antoinette was partially responsible for all the attacks against her character:

Marie Antoinette's *coiffure à l'enfant*
(BIBLIOTHÈQUE NATIONALE DE FRANCE)

But, unfortunately, too disdainful of the changes of opinion with regard to her, the princess was not sufficiently careful of her fame; contenting herself with despising her enemies, she was never on her guard against appearances which could give them weapons to use against her.

Léonard's good friend, the milliner Rose Bertin, was herself not free from spiteful conversations. Toward the end of 1781, Léonard doubted whether she would ever be admitted to the queen's toilette again.

Marie-Thérèse, Marie Antoinette, and Dauphin Louis
(BIBLIOTHÈQUE NATIONALE DE FRANCE)

Mademoiselle Bertin's head milliner, Julie Picot, was very clever, perhaps too clever, taking the addresses of her mistress's wealthy customers, and secretly calling on them. While offering them her services, she made uncomplimentary remarks about Mademoiselle Bertin. The ladies in turn left Mademoiselle Bertin to employ Julie. Mademoiselle Picot had herself personally revealed all of this to Léonard.

Mademoiselle Bertin had certainly profited from her frequent trips to court, acquiring not only wealth and prestige, but fine manners as well. On Easter day, the 15th of April 1781, on a visit to see the queen, she met Julie Picot in one of the galleries at Versailles. Furious that her former assistant had frequented the queen's apartments, Mademoiselle Rose was unable to control her anger. She approached her rival, and spat in her face. Mademoiselle Picot, robust and wanton, was about to slap her ex-mistress when some bodyguards patrolling about the gallery put a stop to the quarrel.[13]

When the guards made their report to the palace superintendent, Mademoiselle Bertin was fined twenty francs and other costs for the benefit of the poor. The punishment was rather light, according to Léonard, when compared with the severity of an insult committed in the royal chamber. Marie Antoinette fortunately interceded to lessen the severity of the punishment.

Marie Antoinette *à la rose*
(BIBLIOTHÈQUE NATIONALE DE FRANCE)

The queen always trusted both Mademoiselle Bertin and Léonard's tastes, but Her Majesty added Mademoiselle Montansier and Mademoiselle Guimard to her renowned committee of advisers soon after the "spit affair." The influence of the musician and actress did not affect the reputation of her famed milliner and hairdresser. In fact, Léonard and Rose prospered from the arrangement. Were the new advisers to suggest new ideas and designs, Léonard and Rose would be quickly called in to make them a reality—at any cost.

In 1782, Léonard and Rose Bertin introduced the queen (and the public) to the work of Ventzel, who was first to introduce the fashion of artificial flowers, invented in the convents of Italy. This allowed the designers to substitute natural flowers, widely used until this time, with artificial ones. The Gascon noted that this new vogue of artificial flowers became so popular that twenty rival houses started to make the most of it.

The new trend had an important impact on French fashion—diamonds and pearls were neglected, and jewels even lost their value. Women tried to make themselves look younger by crowning themselves with roses and by covering their clothes with garlands of brilliant colors. Nymphs everywhere were decked with flowers, and the fragrant signs of spring prevailed as winter arrived. These young ladies were admitted to the queen's gala events, and the Duke of Chartres created an open space for them to showcase their fashions year-round in the garden of his Palais Royal—only increasing the demand for Léonard's creations and putting him in a lucrative position to take advantage of the new vogue. Queen Marie Antoinette now passed her happiest hours as a shepherdess at the Petit Trianon, replacing the brilliant adornments to her hair with colorful flowers, garlands, and feathers. She devoted herself to embellishing the Petit Trianon, needlework, and educating her children.

But court tradition had always dictated that the noble courtiers educate the royal children. The queen's popularity had long been on the wane and, although it was somewhat revived with the birth of her children, the queen further alienated the courtiers vying for the coveted post. Having already been shut out from the queen's private court at Trianon, resentment soon turned to revenge in the form of malicious rumor and defamation.

The storm outside Marie Antoinette's door only intensified while her seclusion continued; she busied herself designing the hameau, a model hamlet in the garden of the Petit Trianon. The hamlet, constructed in 1783, was a fairy-tale village with lakes, a stream with a mill for grinding grain, a farmhouse with cottages, and dozens of gardens.

The hamlet had the added effect of abandoning the last bit of supporters she may have had. Now no one was on her side. The public continued to condemn her isolation and wastefulness, while the court felt, by playing the simple milkmaid and ignoring the grand palace of Versailles, that she was stripping the monarchy of its dignity.

CHAPTER 7

The Queen's Temperament

"I shall soon be compelled to have the controller's permission in order to buy an undergarment."

—Marie Antoinette
Versailles, 1788

December 1784
Versailles, France

Since the beginning of the royal couple's reign, it had been no secret that Louis XVI's aloofness allowed his wife the queen to get her way. In fact, without the king's silence on certain matters and general weakness of disposition, Marie Antoinette would likely have ruled in a much different mode.

Once, while Léonard was alone with the queen in her boudoir—the queen seated on a sofa, practicing her harp—Calonne, the controller-general, was announced. She had summoned Calonne to tell him about her "whims and fancies" during her latest pregnancy.[1] The official rightly guessed that she must have accumulated some debts, and when he asked her for the amount, she replied, "Not very great, about nine hundred thousand francs at the most."

Léonard noted that the queen played a few extra notes on the harp—likely to give the official an opportunity to get over the shock of the "not very great" amount (almost three million in today's US dollars[2]). Stammering, Calonne informed the queen that, while he was always at Her Majesty's service, it would be practically impossible for him to draw nine hundred thousand francs from the state treasury at that time.[3]

"But, I can wait!" the queen replied. "There is no hurry—provided that the check can be signed within a week. That is all I ask. You will agree that I am being very reasonable, and I hope tomorrow at the council meeting you will not fail to tell the king."

The minister did indeed speak to Louis XVI before the council about the queen's financial predicament, and the king considered it very wise of his controller-general to mention the matter. He also heartily congratulated him for the firmness he had shown the queen on such an awkward occasion.

And before the end of the week, the sum of nine hundred thousand francs was granted to Her Majesty.

On another occasion soon after, Léonard was announced to Her Majesty before the ladies-in-waiting had arrived at the toilette. As he entered her salon, she immediately called out to him, asking if he was going to bring her the new novel, *Les liaisons dangereuses* (*The Dangerous Liaisons*). He told her that he had read the book, and that it was creating quite a sensation in Paris, but he could not dare bring such a provocative novel to the Queen of France.[4]

The queen responded by quoting from "Épitre à Margot," a poem written by the same scandalous author, Choderlos de Laclos, which had harshly scorned her adversary, Madame du Barry.[5] Anxious to read the book, she insisted that Léonard bring it to her. Unsurprisingly, it was on her dressing table the very next day.

Louis XVI did not always approve of the queen's taste in literature. When the king detected a subversive slant in the satire on the aristocracy in *Le Mariage de Figaro* by Beaumarchais, he immediately banned the play.[6] But Beaumarchais had already received the queen's protection, and with her support the play was eventually presented.

The immense success of Beaumarchais's comedy, which called the king and queen *"lions et tigres"*[7] (lions and tigers) among other things, "disquieted [Louis XVI] as a king, and scandalized him as a Christian."

From his card table, the king wrote an order for the arrest of Beaumarchais; he ordered that the fifty-three-year-old man be taken to the prison of St. Lazare, a place usually reserved for young vagabonds. He was released soon after, and the king would even "seize with pleasure occasions to confer on him marks of his good will."

Not only was the *Le Marriage de Figaro* an immediate success, but the royal court later played the great playwright's *Le Barbier de Séville* at the small theater at Trianon, with Marie Antoinette playing the character of Rosine and the Count of Artois (later Charles X) as Figaro.[8] The Beaumarchais fiasco was soon forgotten, but a new embarrassment was about to make the headlines of the French newspapers. It was a scandal that would shake the palace and repeatedly test Léonard's allegiance to his queen.

The scandalous "Affair of the Necklace" created a tremendous sensation in 1784, subjecting Queen Marie Antoinette's character to disgrace and humiliation—the fact that she was set up, and entirely innocent, was treated as beside the point. The scheme was all the doing of Madame de la Motte, formerly known as Jeanne de Valois, an illegitimate descendant of King Henry II not recognized at court.[9]

Madame de la Motte befriended the Cardinal Prince Louis de Rohan, the French ambassador to Vienna when Marie Antoinette was a child. The cardinal's arrogance had so disgusted the Empress that she had him removed. The Empress feared the cardinal's influence over her daughter, and later warned Marie Antoinette about ever receiving him. As queen, Marie Antoinette banned the cardinal from her court.

At the time, Madame de la Motte was living near the palace of Versailles, amid all the gossip surrounding the queen's affairs, when the outline of a scheme struck her. She was aware that the queen's court jeweler, Boehmer, had once created jewelry for Louis XV, and for years the jeweler had been collecting and arranging stones for his masterpiece, a necklace with row upon row of diamond tassels.

Boehmer had tried, but failed, to sell his creation in many European courts. When it was presented to King Louis XVI, the king admired it so much that he wished to purchase it for the queen, but she deemed it too expensive and she already had too many beautiful diamonds.[10]

Madame de la Motte had deceitfully told Cardinal de Rohan of the queen's shortage of funds, of the difficulties meeting her charitable duties, and of her secret desire for the famous necklace, which in her version, the king would not allow her to purchase. She hinted that it might be possible for the cardinal to finally win the queen's favor if he assisted her in the matter. She also

Madame Jeanne de la Motte
(BIBLIOTHÈQUE NATIONALE DE FRANCE)

produced written notes from the queen, acknowledging the cardinal's devotion to Her Royal Majesty and authorizing him to purchase the diamond necklace *for* her.

These notes were signed "Marie Antoinette de France," a signature that the cardinal should have known was fraudulent, as it was never used by the queen. (The phrase "de France" belonged only to the children, and not to the wife, of the sovereign king.[11])

Madame de la Motte also told the cardinal that a private rendezvous with the queen would be arranged for him one evening in the park of Versailles. Monsieur de la Motte had earlier noticed a pretty young lady in the park of the Palais-Royal,

Mademoiselle d'Oliva, who resembled Her Majesty. When the bawdy young lady was informed that the queen wished her to play a role, she soon accepted the part along with a small payment.

Mademoiselle d'Oliva arrived at the appointed hour on the night of the 28th of July 1784, having rehearsed what to say. Cardinal de Rohan was told he could freely express his wishes to Her Majesty and, as a sign of his graciousness, the queen would present him with a rose and a small box containing her portrait.

When prompted by Madame de la Motte, the cardinal hurried to the spot, where he could barely perceive a tall lady in white, with chestnut hair, blue eyes, and hair dressed *à la Léonard*. He fell to his knees out of respect, and the royal impersonator recited her lines and gave him the box. Before the cardinal could utter a word, La Motte appeared at his side, whispering, "Someone is coming." The lady in white dropped a rose, saying, "You know what that means," and vanished. The cardinal, in turn, immediately fled the scene to keep from being detected.

Mademoiselle d'Oliva
(BIBLIOTHÈQUE NATIONALE DE FRANCE)

When Boehmer received the message from the cardinal that he might sell his necklace to the queen, the jeweler drew up his terms—1.6 million livres (approximately eight million dollars) to be paid in five equal installments over a year and a half—to which he and the cardinal affixed their signatures. The necklace was then delivered to the cardinal who, in turn, entrusted it to Madame de la Motte, though it was not passed to the queen. It was instead broken down into pieces and sent abroad to England. While the cardinal waited to receive a kind word from the queen, Madame de la Motte's husband was selling diamonds to jewelers on New Bond Street in London.

When the day arrived for the first installment of the loan for the necklace, there was no payment forthcoming. The cardinal and Boehmer felt they had been betrayed;

Boehmer took it upon himself to appeal to Her Majesty for payment. When the queen said the whole enterprise must have been a mistake, the man left the palace trembling.

On the 15th of August, Cardinal de Rohan was at the palace of Versailles to celebrate mass when, suddenly, he was summoned to the king's cabinet where the king and queen were waiting.

"Monseigneur Cardinal, you purchased the diamonds from Boehmer?" asked the king.

"Yes, sire," he said.

"What did you do with them?" he asked.

"I believed they were given to the queen," he said.

"Who authorized this commission?" asked the king.

"A lady named Madame the Countess de la Motte-Valois, who gave me a letter from the queen, and I genuinely believed it to be the queen's wishes."

Marie Antoinette angrily interrupted, "How, Monsiegneur, could you ever have believed that I would select a man, a man to whom I have not spoken for eight years, to negotiate this with such a woman as Madame de la Motte?"[12]

The cardinal had no answer.

Baron de Breteuil, the old rival of Cardinal de Rohan at the embassy in Vienna, followed him as he left the king's chambers. While the crowd in the gallery stood aghast, the baron summoned the officer on guard, and said to the cardinal, "Monseigneur, you are arrested."

The cardinal was arrested and taken to the Bastille. More arrests followed, including those of Madame de la Motte and the impersonator of the queen, Mademoiselle d'Oliva.

Marie Antoinette wept inconsolably over the scandal. Although the court was able to prove it was forgery, every other court in Europe was buzzing with the story. The queen had made enemies, if not of the Church itself, the great houses of Rohan, Soubise, Guéménée, Marsan, and a number of other former allies.

Madame de la Motte was sentenced to be whipped, branded, and imprisoned for life. The man who actually forged the queen's handwriting, Villette de Retaux, was exiled. When caught selling some of the smaller stones, he fingered Madame de la Motte, the person who had entrusted him with the diamonds to sell. The Cardinal de Rohan, however, was fully acquitted.[13]

Madame de la Motte endured the branding by a red-hot iron, with the letter V for *voleuse* (thief) on each shoulder, though not without a struggle; she screamed and "bit like a wild cat." She cursed the queen and, although she was gagged, her words spread through Paris like a fire.[14] A few months later, Madame de la Motte

Boehmer's diamond
necklace

escaped from prison. There were rumors that she had been scapegoated because she had a claim to the House of Valois, another royal lineage. She was more than likely allowed to escape to join her husband in England and stop his incessant attacks on the queen there.[15]

Léonard remarked that, despite the damage the Affair of the Necklace caused to the queen's reputation, the fame of misfortune also has its advantages. Mademoiselle d'Oliva, the harlot who had impersonated the queen, had a number of admirers. Upon her release from the Bastille, she was sought after by the wealthiest libertines of the court—all waging bets who would become her protector. Now a celebrity, she was also the star of the pamphlets flourishing in Paris at the time—at the queen's expense.

The Queen: It suits you well, you vile wench,
                           For playing the role of Queen!

Mlle d'Oliva: And why not, my Sovereign,
                           You so often play mine![16]

It was impossible that the Necklace Affair should pass through the city of fashion without leaving any traces. Léonard announced the introduction of the hat *cardinal sur paille*, a straw hat edged in flame-colored ribbon—a rather bad allusion to the Cardinal Rohan's ruin. The red represented the color of the cardinal's cloak; the straw represented that on which the cardinal would lie—on the floor of the Bastille.

But Léonard was soon more interested in another matter, one that would raise suspicions of a completely different nature.

There appeared at Versailles a foreign colonel who surpassed all the court's cavaliers with his noble demeanor and Apollo-like appearance: Monsieur the Count Axel von Fersen. All the women adored him, and all the gentlemen were jealous of the response he caused. Although Léonard exaggerated when he said that the colonel "had a duel every day," when the colonel did have a duel, he was always the victor. (Despite the efforts of the king and the Church to ban duels in the eighteenth century, duels were common well into the nineteenth century.) It appeared that the colonel only accepted a duel when his honor was at stake. Wounding his adversary, he would later coldly remark, "I am sorry, monsieur, to have been compelled to fight with you; I never intended to win the woman with whom you are in love."

The count, who was also colonel of the regiment of the Royal Swedish Army, did not, in fact, love any of the women of the court; the brilliant officer was obsessed with a lady of more exalted rank: the queen herself.

Once admitted to the queen's circle, Fersen had such self-control that nothing in his behavior, actions, or speech ever betrayed his secret. And Marie Antoinette, captivated by the charisma of the Swedish officer, could not help but love him. Her looks, and even her words, had been so encouraging that the colonel confessed to her that she alone filled his mind with thoughts with a love, albeit a "hopeless" one.

The queen's warm response was difficult to conceal from the courtiers. She even sent him a note that opened the secret doors of the Petit Trianon to him. Despite these rather telling details, Léonard insisted that nothing dishonorable occurred between the two.

Axel von Fersen

The royal family also suffered personal tragedies around this time. In 1787, Marie Antoinette's younger daughter, Sophie-Béatrix, died shortly before her first birthday. The queen was profoundly grieved, shutting herself up at the Petit Trianon without her court, alone with the king and his sister. "Come," she wrote to her sister-in-law, "we shall weep over the death of my poor little angel. I have need of your heart to console mine."

When some of her intimate friends, to soften her grief, reminded her of the princess's young age, the queen replied, "Do you forget that she would have been a friend?" And Marie Antoinette never had a greater need of a friend than at this point. Having been assailed as a woman, as a friend, and as a mother, she began to accept her unfortunate destiny, sighing "Ah, there is no more happiness for me, since they have made me a politician!"[17]

The queen always had found time for her children. She went to see them at all hours of the day and night. Once, when she had unexpectedly gone to visit her younger son, she found that some leeches had been applied without forewarning her; she fainted from the fright. Soon afterward, the court physicians informed the family that the Dauphin Louis-Joseph was now terminally ill; the child's condition had been deteriorating rapidly and his spine seemed to be diseased. Marie Antoinette's only hope of saving him rested on the fact that his father had also been sickly at the same age. She was anguished, but she was also relieved that her younger son, Louis Charles, was strong and healthy—"a true peasant child," she would say with a forced smile.[18]

To add to Marie Antoinette's troubles, Léonard found that Mademoiselle Bertin had dangerously extended herself with expenditures beyond her means. Bertin's frequent trips to Versailles, her zeal to please the queen, her lack of business savvy, and the misfortune of losing the patronage of many titled ladies to Mademoiselle Picot forced her to file for bankruptcy with liabilities of more than two million francs.[19]

The main cause was Bertin's constant attendance on the queen and the prolonged, frequent stays that she made at Versailles. These trips compelled her to leave her business in the hands of young women who were either too frivolous or too busy with their love affairs to properly attend to their duties. Her business suffered enormously as a result. Léonard was crushed when, a few days after her financial calamity, she presented herself at the palace to work with Her Majesty; her admission was refused at the gates.

Two hundred thousand francs could have set Mademoiselle Bertin afloat, and Léonard claimed that he would have been more than happy to loan them, had he not started to invest all of his capital in a new enterprise six months earlier. Knowing that the king's brother, the Count of Provence, was a great lover of Italian music, Léonard decided to create a theater devoted particularly to performers from Italy. The king had granted his brother the privilege to open a theater. However, it was necessary to build it, and the Count of Provence did not wish to furnish the required funds for such an enormous construction project.

Léonard committed himself entirely to his new enterprise, a theater that he would build almost entirely at his own expense. He noted, "I would have helped with all my heart, because I had a great liking for this traveling companion of my fortune." The queen only added to the milliner's discredit and dishonor by dismissing her. Léonard claimed to be saddened by the end of Rose Bertin's seventeen years at the court. However, his memoir is mostly silent on the matter—it's not unlikely that he was jealous of Mademoiselle Bertin's increasing influence in the court, saw it as a threat to his own, and was glad to solely occupy a unique position again.

If Louis XVI's aloofness was to blame for Marie Antoinette's frivolity at the beginning of his reign, he made the more damaging mistake toward the end of the 1780s of taking her advice on *political* matters—which proved disastrous. Despite the queen's intervention, Léonard avowed, it might just have been too little and too late:

> *She had conceived the idea to stop the chariot of the Revolution, and unfortunately this reflection, this experience, born but late of her mistakes and of the misfortunes it had brought her, were too feeble resources to control the events which were dragging the monarchy with them.*

Inefficient taxation and costly foreign wars (including financing the colonies' uprising in the American Revolution) had dire consequences for the monarchy. King Louis XVI summoned a meeting of the nobility to discuss the situation, but "The Assembly of Notables," as it was called, was unable to rectify the government's financial crisis. The assembly did, however, divert attention away from the queen's long succession of intrigues, and, although the assembly was later criticized, it did propose cost-cutting projects for the court in an effort to curb its outlandish expenditures.

The queen had already ordered various reforms in her household, and she gave daily orders to those monitoring her expenses to reduce them as much as they could, even if they had to cut back on "necessities." For one thing, Marie Antoinette made changes with regard to gambling at court, declaring that no more than twelve francs should be played at backgammon in her circle. Taking this reform lightly, the Monsieurs de Belzunce, de Vaudreuil, and de Talmont continued to play their former stakes; the king soon banned all three from court and exiled them to military regiments for disobeying the new limits.

The Assembly of Notables insulted the queen and her cost-saving projects with the following back-handed comment: "We must congratulate the Queen for showing

Assembly of Notables, 1787
(BIBLIOTHÈQUE NATIONALE DE FRANCE)

herself today such as should be the august wife of the King and the mother of the Dauphin."

"I shall soon be compelled to have the controller's permission in order to buy an undergarment,"[20] she replied.

It soon appeared that the queen was not serious about complying with all of the reforms that she had promised, despite the assembly's recommendations. During the assembly deliberations, Marie Antoinette was all the while busily approving plans for a grand *fête* costing more than five hundred thousand francs to be given at Fontainebleau.

The people increasingly blamed the queen for the country's worsened finances. They were so wrought up against her during these hectic times that she felt imprisoned at the Trianon, not daring to leave her beloved retreat. The hatred that the Parisians had for Her Majesty was so vicious that the lieutenant of police cautioned the Minister of Paris against letting the queen visit the capital at all. The minister, not daring to convey this warning directly to the already fragile queen, informed the king who then indelicately stormed into his wife's apartment and exclaimed: "Madame, I forbid you to go to Paris until further order!"

Up to this point, the economies recommended by the Notables had been the subject of ridicule among the princes of the court, but on the 13th of August 1788 the king ordered that the regulations regarding the economies be published and posted in his palace. In spite of the king's new efforts, virulent placards were posted in Paris, Versailles, and even on the trees of the road leading to the royal palace. Members of Parliament even posted placards on the walls—all directed against the queen, "the invisible power hidden behind the curtain."

Although the measures to cut expenses were well received (especially cutting income to the likes of the favorite Polignac and her family), they were thought grossly insufficient. More important, the king's minister Brienne made out like a bandit in the shuffle—he received an estate that earned over nine hundred thousand francs from just cutting wood. The parliament was angry because he owed his ascent to Marie Antoinette's patronage. In fact, she guaranteed his spot on the king's council. In response to the king's decrees, Parliament itself dared to declare: "Such measures, Sire, do not spring from your heart; such examples are not according to the principles of your Majesty: they come from another source."[21] The other source was only digging a deeper hole for herself.

It was in the midst of all these troubles that the unforgiving winter of 1788–1789 set in, only adding fuel to the revolutionary fire. Léonard was well aware of the problems at hand:

> Add misery to any political oppression, and you will soon have a revolution. That which perhaps contributed a great deal to the breaking out of ours, was the luxury which the nobles displayed at the very time when the people were overwhelmed with calamities, under the influence of the cold gone down to seventeen degrees.

Whether deliberate or not, Léonard was not referring to the luxury of his coiffures, but the luxury of gliding in the streets in magnificent sleighs. The court nobles, princes, and princesses—wrapped in fur-lined velvet cloaks ornamented with gold braid—had recently been helping the queen revive memories of her childhood sleigh rides in Vienna.

Madame Campan, the queen's first chambermaid, wrote in her memoirs that the jingly bells and pompoms decorating the horses' harnesses, the elegance and whiteness of their plumes, the varied shapes of the carriages, and the gold with which they were all trimmed, made these parties a "delight for any eye."[22] But when the parties extended as far as the Champs-Élysées in Paris, the queen's enemies took the opportunity of accusing Her Majesty of traveling through the boulevards of Paris in a sleigh. The timing of these winter follies—while the poorest subjects froze to death on the streets—obviously increased the already fomenting resentment; Marie Antoinette wisely put an end to the amusements.

The accusations, scathing rumors, and the scandals were finally taking a toll on the queen. Léonard wrote, "At times deep sighs escaped Her Majesty, sighs full of painful recollections and even of regrets." She often repeated, "Ah, if only I had known . . . how thoughtless is youth!"

Then, as if to escape from this internal torture, Marie Antoinette would say to her hairdresser, "Léonard, tell me some story, some anecdote."

Her eyes seemed to add, "That I may be rid of my gloomy thoughts."

CHAPTER 8

The Monsieur's Theater

"How can a very Christian prince permit actors to present their works of the devil in his noble name?"

—*JOURNAL DE PARIS*
FEBRUARY 1789

October 1787
Versailles, France

The pampered courtiers at Versailles took advantage of their station by accepting gifts and titles—in their minds, it was their due. Even Léonard was said to have put on the airs of a marquis. Besides charging ten louis (about eight hundred dollars) for creating a new hairstyle, he received three louis per month from his clientele for two visits per week. For comparison, a Parisian manufacturer paid his workers from thirty to fifty sous (cents) per day; whereas Léonard received ten louis, or four thousand sous, for each new hairstyle. The hairdresser's earnings were extraordinary, considering that bread cost from four to five sous per loaf at the time. By the onset of the Revolution, the same manufacturer would cut his workers' wages to fifteen sous per day, and bread prices would almost double to eight sous per loaf. Parisians also had to pay rent and higher taxes, as well as supplement their bread with wine and meat. When asked about the workers' welfare, a factory owner simply replied, "Bread is too good for them."[1] They soon drove him out of the neighborhood.

For the most part, Léonard sent his assistant, the *beau Julien* (handsome Julien) as he was called, for his regular customers. Julien was not quite as imposing as Léonard, but he too was soon pampered and indulged by the noble clients. Even Queen Marie Antoinette would remark about the hairdressers' borrowed status, often saying, "Do not meddle with *our nobility*."[2]

The Chevalier de Boufflers, a world traveler, recounts when the Italian Prince Lanti sent for Léonard during his Paris visit. The famous hairdresser arrived so well dressed, with his sword on his side, that the prince mistook him for a noble. When the prince asked Léonard to be seated, Léonard replied that he did not deserve such an honor; he only came to dress hair.[3]

"Ah, you are Léonard!" said the prince.

"Yes, your highness, at your service," said Léonard.

As the prince waited for Léonard to begin arranging his hair, he was taken aback when the hairdresser said, "My prince, I am only the *physionomiste*, please allow me to call my assistant."

Julien arrived and turned the prince's head back and forth at Léonard's command. Léonard then blurted out, "Chestnut-shaped face, Julien. Style this gentleman's hair *à la châtaigne!*" He then bowed and promptly took his leave.

The Chevalier de Boufflers noted that the easily angered Prince Lanti had once thrown a similar fool out his window at home in Italy. In this case, however, the prince relented, knowing that the renowned hairdresser was protected by the queen—he accepted the chestnut face remark without comment.

Léonard was still associated, albeit in name only, with the *Académie de coiffure*, the successful venture that he had opened a decade earlier. The academy, originally created for valets and chambermaids of noble families, was situated on the corner of the rue de la Chaussée-d'Antin at the entrance to an elegant district of Paris, and it included a perfume boutique.[4] The academy generated a profit from the beginning, selling 4,063 livres, or about sixteen thousand dollars, of beauty products to Queen

IV. — Mémoire des coiffures et fournitures faites à Mᵐᵉ la duchesse de Châtillon (pour la princesse de Tarente), par Léonard Autry (coiffeur de Marie-Antoinette); savoir :

Le 2 juillet 1781. — Fourni deux boucles..	6 liv.
Deux peignes à queue......................	4 liv. 16 s.
Deux peignes à deux fins..................	8 liv.
Deux peignes à démesler	18 liv.
Le 10 dudit. — Une coiffure pour le mariage.	48 liv.
Fourni un paquet d'épingles..............	7 liv.
Sept petites boucles à 40 s. pièce..........	14 liv.
Un chignon à l'enfant.....................	12 liv.
Le 11 dudit. — Une coiffure de lendemain.	24 liv.
Le 12. — Une coiffure....................	6 liv.
Le 17. — Une coiffure....	6 liv.
Le 19. — Une coiffure........	6 liv.
Le 22. — Une coiffure de présentation.....	72 liv.
Fourni trois plus à 10 liv. pièce..........	30 liv.
Pour avoir arrangé les diamants et fournitures................................	9 liv.
Total	294 liv. 16 s.

Cost of Léonard's services

Académie de coiffure on the rue de Chaussée-d'Antin, 1788

Marie Antoinette alone in 1787. This receipt [pictured] for 294 livres (twelve hundred dollars), recorded a noble client's bill for one month of supplies and services.

This receipt to Madame the Duchess of Chatillon for the Princess of Tarente included *boucles* (curls), *peignes* (combs), *coiffure* (hairdressing), *épingles* (hair pins), and *plumes* (feathers).[5] The prices for hairdressing ranged from six livres, for daily maintenance, to nine livres for arranging jewels in the hair, twelve livres for children, forty-eight livres for a wedding hairstyle, and seventy-two livres for a style appropriate for special events and galas.

The rue de la Chaussée-d'Antin was also known to be one of the livelier streets of Paris, and even Dickens later wrote that the street was always very animated: "The crowd both of carriages and of foot passengers was as thick here as in nearly any other street of the capital."[6] The *Académie de coiffure* was located near the Hôtel de Montmorency and the residence of the star ballerina of the Opéra, Mademoiselle Guimard. The mademoiselle's mansion was decorated with paintings by Fragonard and housed a theater that accommodated up to five hundred spectators. The academy's studio was situated in the warehouse of the French guards. The king's guardsmen, while on horseback, could watch the instructors hovering over the students, each busily combing and dandifying the wigs in front of them.

Having already made his fortune, Léonard had mostly abandoned his career as hairdresser in 1787, leaving behind the curling papers, his homemade pomade, and the powder that had made him so famous. Although he was no longer dressing the queen's hair on a daily basis, Léonard was still known as the *Coiffeur de la Reine* (Hairdresser to the Queen). He was still summoned by the queen for galas, balls, and other special occasions to dress her hair, but it was his youngest brother, Jean-François, who now attended to Her Majesty's everyday needs. Jean-François also took over Léonard's role as director of the academy, with Frémont as manager.

Léonard's brother, Jean-François Autié

Leaving his residence at the palace of Versailles in February 1788, Léonard set about to find his new career in the theater. Queen Marie Antoinette encouraged Léonard in his new direction, having given him her permission and best wishes; she was very fond of Italian opera, and her lady-in-waiting Madame Campan remarked that it had only been brought to Paris "to please the queen."[7] The queen was a patron of Mademoiselle Montansier, director of the theatre at Versailles, and Jacques de Visme, head of the Royal Academy of Music, both enthusiasts of the opera of Piccinni and Sachini.

A notice on the 17th of June 1788 in the press confirmed that the queen's hairdresser was indeed serious about honoring his queen with a permanent venue for the Italian theater: "The gentleman Léonard Autié (Coiffeur to the Queen) proposes to present a production at the Tuileries."[8]

But Léonard did not proceed with his new theater without unforeseen difficulties. Château workers housed near the theater had to be relocated; the odors from their kitchens filled the theater in the evenings. Some of the workers, especially the smiths, protested when they had to stop all work for the performances due to the noise. Léonard immediately began consultations with the château's building superintendents.[9]

One week after Léonard's notice, King Louis XVI formally accepted Léonard's request to open the Théâtre de Monsieur in the Tuileries Palace, but only until a new theater could be built.[10] Unfortunately, Léonard could not open the theater without the Monsieur's formal consent and protection. The king had wanted to tear down the theater, but Léonard had already begun negotiations with the building

Théâtre de Monsieur, Tuileries Palace (front, left)

superintendents for plans to enlarge the venue with an additional level of loges. The Monsieur interceded on behalf of Léonard's committee and his renovation plans were accepted. Within a very short time, Léonard had shown himself to be an astute entrepreneur. His theater would produce forty-one pieces at its venue in the Tuileries in the chaotic and historic year of 1789.

When Léonard finally received permission from the Monsieur to open a theater uniquely devoted to performers from Italy, the king acquiesced. Léonard would still be obligated to build the new venue at his own expense—neither the king nor the prince wished to furnish the required funding for such elaborate construction. The Monsieur would only pay for his own loge and annual subscription. He also refused to be involved in the management of the theater, his protection and patronage being in name only.

Léonard could not forget to pay tribute to Marie Antoinette for her influence in the king's decision—proof of the monarchy's trust and faith in the royal hair-dresser. Plans for Queen Marie Antoinette's loge were prepared, including a small salon, wardrobe, guardroom for six of the queen's guards, and an antechamber for four valets. This enormous expense was also borne by Léonard. Although Léonard had become quite wealthy since his arrival on foot from the south of France some twenty years earlier, he still needed financial assistance for the incredibly expensive

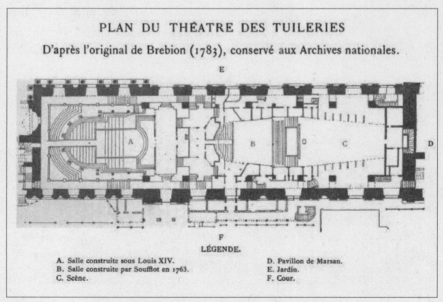

PLAN DU THÉATRE DES TUILERIES

D'après l'original de Brebion (1783), conservé aux Archives nationales.

LÉGENDE.

A. Salle construite sous Louis XIV.
B. Salle construite par Soufflot en 1763.
C. Scène.
D. Pavillon de Marsan.
E. Jardin.
F. Cour.

Floor plan of the Théâtre de Monsieur

Giovanni Battista Viotti
(BIBLIOTHÈQUE NATIONALE DE FRANCE)

undertaking. To make up any shortfall, he was forced to start a company and, with the involvement and name of the Monsieur, many nobles and aristocrats became shareholders. Moreover, to put together a theater worthy of the illustrious hairdresser's imagination, another one hundred thousand livres were raised by a partnership with the Demoiselle Montansier, a loyal customer of his perfume boutique and a protégée of the queen. At this time she was also the director of the Theatre of Versailles.

Favorite: The Count Decazes
(BIBLIOTHÈQUE NATIONALE DE FRANCE)

Léonard soon found himself unable to work with Montansier due to incompatible artistic visions. Léonard felt that his associate was too "provincial" while the master of the towering pouf had grander expectations; he ambitiously wanted to present a number of genres in his new venue, including French opera, Italian opera, and vaudeville. Montansier's emphasis on producing Italian works only and the need for a permanent Italian troupe was most likely the root of the disagreement. Léonard, on the other hand, would only require a visiting Italian troupe several months at a time, using Parisian amateurs for his vaudeville and parodies. Montansier argued that she could not, in such an arrangement, create a reputable Italian theater comparable to that in other capitals of Europe.

To find a partner who shared his ideas, and to buy out Demoiselle Montansier, Léonard approached Il Signor Viotti, the famed violinist, to take her place. Viotti was unfortunately short on funds, but Léonard succeeded in persuading Montansier to accept forty thousand of the original one hundred thousand livres she had invested, also promising an annuity of twenty thousand livres for life. Accepting Léonard's offer, she returned to her duties at the Theatre of Versailles, but she would later open her own theater in Paris to compete with the Théâtre de Monsieur. The sophisticated entrepreneur would also resurface some forty years later—only to complicate the financial situation of the aging hairdresser.

The honor of being the royal patron of the theater traditionally rested upon the shoulders of the oldest brother, the Monsieur, of the reigning king. When Louis XVI's younger brother, the Count of Artois, showed interest in opening a theater in the Marais district, he was criticized by other theaters already patronized by Monsieur the Count of Provence. The Monsieur, in turn, was criticized by many nobles for opening a theater in his royal name, especially at a time when a revolutionary fever was finding its outlet in pamphlets and the press in Paris. With respect to morals, one brochure asked, "How can a very Christian prince permit actors to present their works of the devil in his noble name?"

Léonard was aware of the Monsieur's distaste for the theater. In fact, the Monsieur had always refused his wife permission to participate in (or even attend) the queen's plays at the Petit Trianon. But Léonard was determined to have complete and active patronage of the prince, and the crafty "marquis" concocted a plan to ensure it.

The Monsieur had no children, and no one thought he had it in him to ever have any. Some whispered that it was his wife's fault; the foul-smelling princess Marie-Josephine, with the unplucked eyebrows, preferred to sleep alone.[11] Some whispered that the Monsieur was simply not fond of women, which led members of the court to question his sexuality. The writer D'Arnault revealed in his memoirs that "Courting ladies only for the sake of courting showed that his tastes were more *Socratic* than *Platonic*."[12]

More damning, D'Arnault wrote that the Monsieur would only take on a mistress in title, as an object of conspicuous consumption—"as one would spend for a prize horse, but a horse that would never be mounted."

Monsieur clearly was close with some handsome men of his entourage. One *éphèbe* (Adonis) was the Duke of Avaray, the son of the king's master of wardrobe, better known as the Monsieur's "intimate" favorite at court. Although the Monsieur strictly observed the rules of court etiquette at Versailles and his residence at the Luxembourg Palace, he would always overlook the young favorite's breaches of tradition, especially on

Louise-Marie-Joséphine de Savoie

Théâtre de Monsieur, formerly Salle de Machines, Tuileries Palace

those occasions when he appeared at court in his dressing gown. Upon the death of the Duke of Avaray, the Count Decazes became the next favorite.

Léonard knew that the prince needed a mistress (or one for show) to drown out the villainous whispers. The prince's wife, Madame Louise-Marie-Joséphine de Savoie, had even chosen one of her ladies-in-waiting, Anne de Caumont-la-Force, to play the part of the mistress but the court was not convinced. Anne was known to be a virtuous and extremely spiritual woman, and as chaste as the Monsieur himself.

Madame de Savoie was not much help in upholding the prince's reputation. She was known to be rather intelligent and graceful, but also was extraordinarily ugly. She had lived very happily with her husband during the first years of their marriage, but after his attachment to his favorites, he scarcely ever saw her. She consoled herself with "the intimacy of her ladies in waiting and, it was said, by drinking to such an extent that the consequences were obvious in public."[13]

Her tumultuous, physical relationship with Madame de Gourbillon was well-known in royal circles, but revolutionary gazettes had also written that the king and queen turned a blind eye to the "unnatural" relationship.[14] In any event, the royal couple remained childless; the rumors spread, and the enemies of the crown used the situation to their advantage.

When Léonard discovered that the Monsieur was an admirer and generous patron of the Demoiselle Marianna Limpérani, a beautiful and young Italian singer, he requested the honor to dress her hair. The demoiselle was flattered by his attention, unaware that Léonard planned on using her for a plot to win over the Monsieur.

When Léonard later recruited the demoiselle to join the troupe at his new theater, she asked her patron for permission, but the Monsieur resisted. Marianna cried, the prince hesitated, and then she threatened to end their quasi-relationship. This would have been disastrous for the Monsieur. He had just reinforced his affair with the young singer by offering her a small hotel on the beautiful rue de la Chaussée-d'Antin. Any further scandal caused by the singer would only add to the rumor and contempt at court; his reputation with the theater-going public would be threatened as well. To Léonard's delight, the Monsieur finally gave in.

Marianna Limpérani later would play leading roles at the Théâtre de Monsieur, and the *Mercure de France* would praise her for her graceful singing and her charming voice. Léonard's ruse was successful, and the Monsieur's presence at the theater—to pay tribute to his protégée's talents—enhanced the theater's popularity and its ticket sales.

Queen Marie Antoinette at Café du Théâtre
(BIBLIOTHÈQUE NATIONALE DE FRANCE)

The Monsieur's renewed interest in the theater was a blessing in more ways than one. The king's Council of Ministers assured the shareholders of Léonard's company the privilege of using the Tuileries theater for at least thirty years. When, on the 26th of January 1789, the Théâtre de Monsieur opened, four shareholders were designated by the Monsieur to observe and control all operations for the grand venture. At least an additional 250,000 livres were spent to decorate and luxuriously furnish the new theater.

A weather delay forced the Théâtre de Monsieur to open three weeks later than planned, but the first performances of *Le Vicendi Amoroso* (*Vicissitudes of Love*) and *La Serva Padrona (The Servant Turned Mistress)* received rave reviews in the papers. The

Théâtre de Monsieur: Queen Marie-Antoinette's loge (lower left)
(BIBLIOTHÈQUE NATIONALE DE FRANCE)

BIENFAISANCE.

Hier nous avons reçu des Muſiciens du Théâtre de MONSIEUR 300 livres, provenant d'une gratification extraordinaire qu'ils n'ont pas voulu ſe partager & qu'ils ont préféré d'abandonner aux Pauvres, à la diſpoſition de la Société Philantropique.

Goodwill: *"Yesterday, the Journal received three hundred livres from the musicians at the Théâtre de Monsieur, coming from an extraordinary gift which they wished not to share, preferring to give it to the poor, at the disposition of the Philanthropic Society."*

Monsieur was especially pleased when Mademoiselle Limpérani was singled out for her duo in *Le Vicendi Amoroso*.

Though the theater received very good reviews, there was constant infighting and jealousy between the French troupe and the Italian troupe of actors. Taking in more receipts at the door than the French, the Italians would boast, "It is we who feed them."[15] The status of French actors was lower in respect to other European actors; in fact, French actors had been excommunicated "by the mere fact that they were stage-players." But the Italian actors, even though they did not attend mass on a regular basis, were not excommunicated, a source of constant conflict.

Some incidents at the theater revealed the storm brewing outside its walls. During *Le Roi Théodore* (King Theodore) the audience reacted fervently when the penniless king asked how he could fill the coffers of the treasury with more gold. A spectator in the audience cried out, "Assemble the Notables!" and the interruption lingered with applause—Louis XVI himself had refused to convene a session of the notables and the Estates-General for needed reforms. News of the political comment resulted in full houses at the Théâtre de Monsieur for the following performances. Ironically, the royals were unknowingly funding such political fervor.

By May, though things seemed to run smoothly, Léonard was already ruined financially. The skyrocketing expenses of the theater, including that of the queen's loge and the failure to work with the Demoiselle Montansier, were insurmountable. The new venture itself had also fallen upon hard times. Not only did the theater have to be closed for the Easter holidays, but by July, the performances would soon be interrupted again by bigger events—historical changes—that were far out of his control.

PART THREE

The Clouds of Revolution

(BIBLIOTHÈQUE NATIONALE DE FRANCE)

CHAPTER 9

The Fatal Banquet

"Come, dress my hair, Léonard. I must go like an actress and exhibit myself to a public that may hiss at me."

—QUEEN MARIE ANTOINETTE TO LÉONARD
CHÂTEAU DE VERSAILLES

May 1789
Versailles, France

France's financial situation had been deteriorating considerably since the previous August. By May 1789, Louis XVI had no choice but to summon the Estates-General, a body of representatives from the clergy, nobility, and common people. One hundred and seventy-five years had elapsed since the last meeting of the Estates-General, which occurred during the reign of Louis XIII. It was not unprecedented, but certainly an indication of a rumbling shift. The monarchy was showing signs of buckling from its own weakness.

All the members had gathered near the court by the end of April for the opening of the Assembly set for the 5th of May 1789. The king decided that there should be a procession to celebrate the occasion, and that all the princes and the princesses should participate—on foot. The queen, who planned to wear a state gown, sent for Léonard two days before the event. Her Majesty was very pale, and she told Léonard she was ill and that the upcoming ceremony was annoying her terribly.

"Ah, Léonard, I sometimes have sad thoughts followed by gloomy premonitions," she said.

Léonard, either refusing to acknowledge the growing gloom or pretending for the queen's sake, asked Her Majesty to banish such thoughts. "The clouds will again pass away and fair weather will return," he said.

"I doubt it," said the queen shaking her head, "fair weather on the throne is forgetting all the cares which cruelly pay for sovereign grandeur; as soon as one is aware

Marie Antoinette's portrait
(BIBLIOTHÈQUE NATIONALE DE FRANCE)

of them, it is no longer possible to get rid of them. Come, dress my hair, Léonard. I must go like an actress and exhibit myself to a public that may hiss at me."

Léonard noted a significant transformation in the queen on that day; she seemed sadly changed not only in features, but in her entire person. The queen's bosom had sunken, and her arms had become frail and thin. After she complained of extreme weakness that morning at her toilette, Madame de Polignac and Léonard begged her not to take part in the procession. Madame de Campan offered to explain the circumstances to the king and to obtain his consent for the queen to be excused from taking part in the ceremony.

"You do not know what you are about to solicit," replied Marie Antoinette. "It is now too late and not to take part in it would be, for me, a crime."

The queen may have felt obligated to accompany her husband to the assembly where he would face representatives of all the social classes of France; there were members of the clergy without a living, doctors and lawyers without patients and clients, and nobles who had been expelled from their ranks for want of character. Or perhaps, having played an enormous role in the selection and removal of the king's ministers of state, Marie Antoinette may have wanted her regal presence felt. She was no longer the frivolous young princess flittering from gambling tables to masquerade balls; she was now Queen of France, mother of the Dauphin, and a blameless wife in a shamelessly immoral court. Whether it was true or not, this was how she was perceived in the other courts of Europe.[1]

The queen had become so increasingly forlorn that all those who had approached her in the past two years "could not notice in her a single trait of that frivolity of which she had been accused in the past." However, she persisted and took part in the long promenade, leaning on the arm of the Duchess of Polignac for support. Léonard was astonished by the strange sight of the long line of deputies leading the king and queen through the streets and crossroads. The representatives of the nobility were clad in cloaks ornamented with gold, the members of the clergy in their clerical gowns, and commoners dressed like theater ushers. All of the princes following the royal couple wore clothes of the Middle Ages with eighteenth-century headdresses, while the princesses swept the dust with their long trains. This would be the last occasion on which the queen would appear in the regal magnificence of her state gown and jewels.

Léonard was struck with sadness as the king passed before his subjects who filled the streets and the windows—only a mournful silence greeted His Majesty. Murmurs and insults, many of them violent, erupted whenever Marie Antoinette appeared. Some working class women treacherously praised the queen's enemy: "The Duke of Orléans forever!"[2]

Slipping through the crowd and following her closely, Léonard did not lose sight of the queen. Léonard remained apprehensive along the hostile route—he remained devoted to his queen. Hardly able to stand upright, she was leaning on the arms of her friends, Mesdames de Polignac and de Lamballe. Near the middle of the rue du Reservoir, the queen staggered and almost fainted but the queen's favorites struggled to support her. When their strength was about to fail them, two of the bodyguards standing in front of the crowd sprang to help. The Queen of France narrowly missed being sprawled on the dirty pavement in front of the hostile crowd.

Straightening herself, Marie Antoinette said to the two soldiers, "It is nothing, gentlemen; return to your ranks." Then, in a lower tone to her friends, she added: "Be without anxiety henceforth, courage and indignation have given me back my energy. The daughter of Maria Theresa will find strength to go through with this horrible situation."

From that moment, Léonard noticed that Marie Antoinette appeared to be fully recovered; she proceeded to walk upright, a natural smile upon her face. However, she regretted that she had not been able to command more presence of mind in front of her subjects. When the king was greeted at the assembly, he acknowledged his attachment and respect for the queen and he was applauded. But the queen, keeping her head high, was well aware that the applause was in fact homage rendered to the king, and to the king alone.

The Estates-General had a separate assembly for each of its three estates; the First Estate was comprised of the clergy, the Second Estate the nobility, and the Third Estate the peasants, farmers, and bourgeoisie. But the Third Estate was thought, though incorrectly, the only estate required to pay taxes at the time, and on the 17th of June, the members of the Third Estate boldly declared themselves the National Assembly, an assembly of the people and *not* of the Estates-General. When the news of the historic debut of this national representation reached King Louis XVI's ears, he was holding court at Marly, where Their Majesties were mourning the death of their young son.[3] Louis-Joseph-Xavier François, heir to the throne of France, had died on the 4th of June 1789, suffering from rickets, which affected his spine, and other ailments.

Within two hours of the seven-year-old's death, the oncoming Revolution began to exhibit its total disregard for the monarchy, even on a solemn occasion. A deputation of the Third Estate wished to see the king on business, and insisted on being received at once. But Louis XVI was shut up alone, mourning in his private apartment. At first the king declined to see them, but at last, he yielded. As he admitted the intruders, he asked pathetically, "Are there, then, no fathers amongst them?"[4] Thinking of the starving children of the kingdom, the intruders might have asked the same question of the monarch. When the queen heard of the daring act of the representatives, proclaiming themselves to be the National Assembly, she suspended her maternal grief and hastened to the king's apartment in her night-robe. Louis XVI was still in bed; his face was inflamed, his eyes swollen and filled with tears.

Léonard was in a neighboring room, eavesdropping on the royals' conversation. The queen's influence over the king had only gotten more pronounced over the years. Although amiable and kindhearted, the vacillating monarch realized his weakness

Dauphin Louis-Joseph with his sister Marie-Thérèse
(BIBLIOTHÈQUE NATIONALE DE FRANCE)

when coming to decisions. And unlike her mother, the queen had been too frivolous for too long in her reign to learn the politics of governing in his place. "Sire," said the queen, "it is not by tears that you will dominate this vulgar, national herd. It is energy that you require, and I have come to inspire you with my own."

"Well, what can I do, madame, against the deputies? Is not the entire nation behind them?"

"There is a way open to you; throw yourself in the arms of your Parliament. Order the mighty of your kingdom, your nobility, to gather around the throne; and by royal decree, which the Parliament will undoubtedly register, dissolve the Estates-General without considering the title of National Assembly which they have adopted."

"Ah, madame," said the king, sitting up in bed, "your advice seems rather good. In truth, considering this assembly simply as Estates-General, I have the right to dissolve it."

"After all, what matters is the title!" resumed the queen excitedly. "Estates-General or National Assembly, these people must not continue to assemble against your will."

"Then, madame, this is settled," replied the king. "I am going to call my Parliament of Paris along with the peers of my kingdom and we shall come to a decision."

Léonard did not describe the failed attempts by the court to disperse the so-called representatives of the nation and "check the growing evil," as he called it. The plan suggested by the courtiers was to initiate the ancient practice of holding a *séance* (session) *royale*, and the 22nd of June was appointed for that purpose. Heralds were sent through the streets of Versailles on Saturday proclaiming that the king had resolved to hold a royal session in the Estates-General on Monday.

It was the king's intention that no person should be admitted into the halls, and that the assembly's sittings should be suspended until after the king's session. The members of the National Assembly, however, did not comply. Their mandate was to settle the constitution of the kingdom, to bring about public order, and to support the true principles of the monarchy; nothing would prevent them from continuing their deliberations to complete their work. Location was not going to dictate whether or not the National Assembly would convene:

> *Resolve, that all the members of this assembly shall instantly take a solemn oath, not to separate finally, but to meet wherever circumstances may make it requisite, until the constitution of the kingdom, and the regeneration of public order, shall be established, and firmly settled upon solid foundations; and that after this oath shall have been taken by all the members, they shall all, individually, by their signatures, confirm their immoveable resolution."5*

Having been locked out of the Estates-General, the assembly members convened inside a tennis court near the Palace of Versailles. All but one of the members took the oath, which became forever known as the *Serment du jeu du paume*—the Tennis Court Oath.

Queen Marie Antoinette had been sleeping at her Petit Trianon for some days afterward when Léonard arrived early to dress her hair. The queen had just received a letter from London that Calonne, the former controller-general, was going to publish some damaging statements that would mention her having sent large sums of money to her brother, the Emperor Joseph in Austria. After finishing the letter, the queen jumped out of bed, exclaiming, "Quick, let me be dressed, and see that a coach leaves this minute—this second—to notify Madame de Lamballe that I shall be with her in a quarter of an hour."

When she approached her hairdresser, she said, "You will not dress my hair this morning, Léonard, but will wait for me at Trianon. I shall perhaps have some orders to give you in the course of the day."

Léonard had just learned about Calonne's threat from Madame Campan. She also informed him that Madame de La Motte, who was serving a life sentence at Salpêtrière, the prostitutes' prison, had managed to escape during the night. A rumor was also circulating that the escape had taken place with the king's consent.

Madame de La Motte had been imprisoned for her role in the Necklace Affair. Despite La Motte's public trial and conviction, the French still blamed the queen for the expense incurred for the diamonds. La Motte was flogged, branded on both shoulders for being a thief, and imprisoned for life. She insulted the queen while the first part of her sentence was carried out. Although she was then gagged, enough had been heard to cause irreversible damage to the queen's reputation.[6]

La Motte's husband, who had escaped to England, had recently threatened to publish a pamphlet compromising the queen even further—if his wife were not immediately set free. Madame de La Motte was thus permitted to escape, disguised as a boy, and made her way to England.

The queen sent the Princesse de Lamballe to London to enter into negotiations with Calonne. She also instructed the princess to find the fugitive La Motte, most likely to silence her. According to Léonard, Marie Antoinette appeared to have recovered some peace of mind after her friend's departure for England, but within a week she evidently became as upset as she had been. The queen received no one and locked herself up almost all day, alone in her apartment, and several times he noticed that she had wept.

When Léonard found the queen more agitated than usual one morning, he heard her murmur, quite distinctly, this broken sentence:

"Attachment, doubtless—I cannot doubt it—a thousand proofs, but no intelligence—a silly frankness. What I needed was some prudent person, cunning even . . ."

Then, suddenly raising her voice, the queen asked, "Léonard, are you man enough to go to London?"

"To London and anywhere, madame, for Your Majesty's service," replied Léonard.

"I know it. Well, I wish to entrust you with a mission, a delicate one," said the queen. "Do you understand, Léonard?"

"Your Majesty may be pleased to recall that I know how to conduct affairs with some ability," said Léonard.

"I am going to think over the one for which I shall require a clever person," she said. "Be ready to start off." Then, suddenly correcting herself, the queen continued, "But no, it is impossible. Susceptibilities would be aroused, she would feel humiliated, and there would be endless jeremiads."

The Princesse de Lamballe

"I am much grieved to be unable to serve Your Majesty on this occasion," Léonard said.

"No, you will not go," said the queen. "I am sorry, let us drop the subject."

Léonard guessed that the queen had at first intended to send him to London to assist the Princesse de Lamballe with her secret missions; perhaps she changed her mind when she thought that the princess might be humiliated by the intervention of a "mere" hairdresser. Considering the queen's dependence upon Léonard by this point, it is most probable that she could not part with her confidant during such a delicate time. She had few friends at court by then, and Léonard could always lend an ear to the queen's woes.

Léonard did his best to entertain the sad queen by telling her the latest gossip of the capital city and other curious anecdotes that he had heard in noble circles. Princesse de Lamballe eventually returned from London without having succeeded in her negotiations. This failure then prompted the queen to send the Duchess of Polignac to England to purchase the silence of the infamous La Motte with a large sum of money, though she was not much more successful. In fact, the bribe was a waste of money; although one edition of the slanderous pamphlet was burned, a second was published some time later. Evidence of an alleged intrigue between the queen and the Cardinal de Rohan had never existed—other than in the minds of Marie Antoinette's enemies—until La Motte's stories were made public.[7]

The queen fell prey to rumors, scandal sheets, and the daily insults of the Parisians. She retreated to the Petit Trianon, which was no longer a place of enjoyment, but a kind of hermitage where Her Majesty led a sorrowful, solitary existence. Marie Antoinette feared the winds of contempt might blow fresh accusations and slurs in her direction.

And the winds did blow. The exiled and disgraced Controller-General Calonne wrote from Holland that he alone was not responsible for a deficit of millions. Calonne's policy of disguising economic distress with his profuse expenditures only magnified the country's deficit.[8] But he mentioned such names as the Polignacs, the Coignys, the Dillons, the Bezenvals, and many others found in the state ledgers alongside large sums of money, insinuating that the queen had squandered state funds on court favorites. Even Calonne, a royalist, knew which way the winds blew; he refused to take all the blame for the alarming state of finances that had led to his dismissal.

Moreover, when the queen sent the Duchess de Polignac to England, little did she know that the duchess was accompanied by a number of gentlemen, devoted favorites of the Trianon; all appeared to have made the queen's mission nothing but a pleasurable getaway to the British Isles at the expense of the people.

Léonard did his best to amuse Her Majesty, but he could hardly bring a smile to her pale lips. Anecdotes and pleasantries that would have once made his queen laugh produced no light in the queen. Though he continued to try.

On the 11th of July 1789, the king, persuaded by the queen, banished his minister of finance, Necker, who was popular with the French commoners. News of Necker's dismissal reached Paris the following afternoon, and crowds began gathering throughout the city, including more than ten thousand at the Palais Royal. Léonard witnessed the demonstrations, along with the closing of the politically charged theaters.

Public outrage at the minister's dismissal, along with the concentration of the king's army in Paris, escalated when the new minister, the Baron of Breteuil, was given the post; the unpopular Breteuil was better known for his connections with the police, who were even more unpopular with the Parisians. By the 14th of July, thousands of armed rioters were parading in the streets, spreading rumors that the queen was going to blow the Assembly up with gunpowder. The king's orders seemed to backfire: Because the troops were ordered to avoid bloodshed at all costs, the crowds grew bolder and began to set fire to houses and to attack the armories.

When the mob thought itself strong enough for any exploit, it stormed the Bastille, a prison that housed only eight prisoners at the time. The strong and well-armored fortress of former times was regarded with pride by the citizens of Paris, but this day, as a state prison, it was only a symbol of despotism and barbarity. Its entire garrison of little more than a hundred soldiers was inadequate to hold off the siege. The walls were scaled and the gates assailed; thousands of angry rioters forced their way in the prison, murdering the warden, Governor de Launay. They cut off his hands and his head, stuck them on a pike, and paraded them through the city streets as trophies of their conquest.[9]

The next day Léonard hastened to Versailles to inform the queen about the fall of the Bastille. When Léonard arrived, however, he heard military bands in all the quarters of Versailles, in the courts of the château, and in the park; he also saw all the guards dressed in parade uniform. He could not fathom this scene with the frightful events that were taking place in the capital. All the ladies of the court were oblivious, clamoring for his services, even the king's aunts—whose hair he rarely dressed.

Fall of the Bastille, 14th of July 1789

Léonard was shocked by the merriness with which Her Majesty received his solemn report. The fall of the Bastille may have finally opened Léonard's eyes, but the queen and her circle remained in the dark. Fifteen miles from the riots of Paris, a false sense of security prevailed at Versailles. The queen's jovial mood baffled him.

"You are surprised at my good humor, Léonard, but rest assured, great things are happening," said the queen. "The Parliament of Paris has come back to us, and we are going to have in our grasp the power which we have been lacking since 1786."

"But, madame, all of Paris is in arms," said Léonard.

"Oh, but troops are coming to us from all over!" interrupted the queen.

At that moment the general of the King's Army, Baron de Bezenval, entered the queen's apartment. The queen rushed to meet him. "Is it not true, my dear baron, that our affairs are getting on nicely? I have given orders to all our ladies to make themselves even more beautiful than yesterday, to encourage, by their kind attention, the brave soldiers supporting us."

"Madame," said the baron gravely, "has the prince, Her Majesty's husband, promised you to be sincere?"

The general had been an eyewitness to the uprising; in fact, he had found himself face to face with it. He clearly saw the emptiness of the court's hopes. The queen was virtually the last one clinging to the hope of restoring the splendor of the court and the glory to the reign.

Once Baron de Bezenval left the room, Marie Antoinette merrily asked Léonard to make her very beautiful. The short-sighted king, who did not recognize Léonard when he first entered the queen's apartment, looked at him with blinking eyes.

"It is Léonard," the queen said to him.

"Ah, good, I can then speak in his presence—he is with us," said the king.

Léonard bowed respectfully, and he prepared to dress the queen's hair.

"Madame, we must change our plans, and we must appease those people," said the king. "We are not now strong enough to master them."

"Who told you that, sire?" asked the queen.

"A man whom I know to be sincerely attached to the monarchy and to my person," said the king.

"But who is he, I pray!" said the queen, stamping her foot in a manner which showed her impatience. "Who is he?"

"It is the Duke de La Rochefoucauld, who sought me out during the night and gave me a true picture . . . a true one, do you hear, madame, of what is going on in Paris?"

The Duke de La Rochefoucauld-Liancourt had warned the king of the state of affairs in Paris, meeting the king's query, "*Une revolte?*" with the answer that would become part of legend: "*Non, sire, c'est une révolution.*"

"Ah, I see!" exclaimed Marie Antoinette, "The duke quite naturally proposes that you give back the power to Necker, thereby *insulting me* with his and his family's triumph."

"That is not the question, madame; it is only suggested that I reinstate Necker to his post of controller-general, and that, in fact, is the only thing to do for that National Assembly, if we do not wish the state coffers to remain empty."

"What else, monsieur?" asked the queen.

"He begged, in the name of your own safety, that I appear tomorrow at the National Assembly—alone," said the king. "That, madame, is what Monsieur de La Rochefoucauld said to me."

"And what use do you expect to make of such brilliant advice?" asked Marie Antoinette in an ironic tone.

"I wish to carry it out, at least for the present," said the king.

"And so you surrender the monarchy to rebels!" cried the queen. Escaping from Léonard's hands, she rose with petulance and began to walk excitedly about the room.

"Well," continued Louis XVI, "what project, what plan, not deceptive illusions, do you offer me to replace that of La Rochefoucauld! When one wishes to oppose a revolution, it does not suffice to listen to blind animosity. There are required, not only troops to combat it, but principles to quiet it."

Léonard noted that the queen, in a confused and somewhat disconnected manner, began to explain a plan to remove the National Assembly, and march the army against the population of Paris. It was all that Marie Antoinette was able to offer as a counter to the measured counsels of La Rochefoucauld.[10]

The king shrugged his shoulders, rose from his seat, and left the room without saying a word. That same evening, the queen heard that Louis XVI had agreed to appear at the National Assembly—without her.

In his memoirs Léonard did not presume to write the history of the Revolution. He had always shown a very limited, narrow view of the events outside the palace, culminating in the violent days of July 1789. However, the hairdresser did recognize that the reconciliation between the throne and the French people could have been possible on the 15th of July—the day after the riot at the Bastille prison—had King Louis XVI not allowed himself to be deluded with the hope of once again seizing absolute rule.

Louis XVI had misjudged the impact of the changing times and the people's will. The abolition of rights, titles, prerogatives, and privileges soon followed. Freedom of the press and religious opinions were new decrees declared permanent by the new National Assembly. Finally in August, and perhaps most significantly as far as history is concerned, the National Assembly proclaimed the *Declaration of the*

Baker François is hanged for the scarcity of bread
(BIBLIOTHÈQUE NATIONALE DE FRANCE)

Rights of Man and Citizen—a document giving the people a claim to universal human rights—and the king accepted it.

Despite these developments and the appointment of committees of subsistence, there was still a shortage of food. An order was issued in Paris that corn could not exceed a maximum price, causing dealers to become disinclined to sell, and only further exasperating the people. The situation turned dangerous enough that the presence of National Guards soon became necessary in the markets to protect the dealers from violence.

Léonard reported that the bakers' shops were assailed from morning until night, and the bakers were abused, ill-treated, and threatened with hanging, as if they were the cause of the people's hunger. A wave of paranoia was soon added to this explosive concoction. When, by a mixture of rye and millet and other cheap cereals with the wheat, the bread became dark in color, a rumor spread that the aristocrats were trying to poison the people. This rumor gained traction among the people and a mob would end up hanging the mayor of St. Denis for permitting such bread to be sold.

As autumn approached, the court answered the uprisings by ordering the Regiment of Flanders, a regular infantry regiment of the king's army, to take up quarters at Versailles, which they did on the 23rd of September. Despite the court's good intentions, the people were deeply suspicious of the long train of wagons and tumbrils, carts generally known for carrying prisoners to the scaffold, that had accompanied the troops. They also didn't trust the supposed fanatic royalists comprising the Flanders regiment. In fact, rampant orators in Paris claimed the people would be murdered in their beds by the military amassing in Versailles.[11]

The court, once again, did not help defusing such rumors. The royal bodyguards and the courtiers, from the moment that the regiment of Flanders arrived, paid unusual attention to its officers, not only presenting them at the king's morning ceremony, but also introducing them to the queen in her drawing room and sparing no expense in wining and dining them.

The royal bodyguards thought it only right to invite the Flanders regiment to a dinner, and the palace opera house was chosen for the grand banquet. The cost of the feast, some thirty livres a head, was not an amazingly extravagant sum for a public dinner in ordinary times, but these were not ordinary times. The court knew perfectly well that the time was ill chosen for such a feast but went ahead with it anyway. The beauties of the court wore their most elegant dresses and their brightest jewels. Military bands played and the feast was prepared by Harmes, the most famous caterer of the day. But as the banquet went on, it began to change in character.

There were toasts after toasts, and a number of common soldiers who had been admitted into the amphitheater were summoned by the captain of the bodyguards to

The fatal banquet
(BIBLIOTHÈQUE NATIONALE DE FRANCE)

come onto the stage, where they were supplied generously with wine. "Faces began to flush a foolish red, tongues to grow somewhat incoherently eloquent. The health of the queen was proposed and drunk to in a rapture."[12]

Suddenly, the doors of the great hall were thrown open, and, to the amazement and enchantment of the guests, the queen appeared before them with the dauphin by her side and the king behind her. The queen moved among the enraptured guests, maintaining a gracious smile.

In a moment more than two hundred swords waved in the air, shouts of "Long live the queen! Long live the king!" roared throughout the hall, and the ladies leaned out of their boxes and applauded. Moments later the royal party reached the door again and vanished as suddenly as it had appeared.

But the enthusiasm did not die away with their departure. The banquet was followed by other dinners on the 2nd and 3rd of October. Sunday, the 4th of October, was a very uneasy day in Paris. Tidings of the banquets and rumors of drunken orgies at Versailles were the talk of the city. Thousands of hungry people were saying, "We are starving, but yonder at the king's palace, there is plenty to spare."

Léonard wrote that hunger and anger worked together, and finally one heard the first cries, "Bread, bread! To Versailles, to Versailles!" and soon thereafter eighty thousand Parisians began the inevitable fifteen-mile march to the royal palace.[13]

It was seldom that Léonard happened to sleep at the château of Versailles, because he knew when the queen, the princesses, and some of the noble ladies of the court wanted their hair dressed. He also had plenty of time to perform the few court duties he had retained since he had acquired his wealth, which permitted him to pursue interests in other great enterprises, such as the Théâtre de Monsieur. But Léonard had seen, on the 6th of October, the shocking gatherings in the capital, and he was well aware that they were on their way to Versailles.

The royal hairdresser hurried to Versailles in the evening to warn the queen of the crisis and to tell her that she must take precautions for her personal safety—though he would keep from her the horrific threats he had heard repeated. He reached the château rather late in the evening. It was impossible for him to see Her Majesty, who had been in conference with the king since that morning.

The Duke of Guiche, the captain of the King's Guards, informed Léonard about the weak defense of the château; he also discovered that, in spite of the growing number of angry crowds surrounding the palace, the king had refused to admit Monsieur de Lafayette, who had raced to Versailles with the Paris National Guard, to defend the royal family if the need arose. This distrust, the result of the queen's dislike for the officer, grieved Léonard immensely. The palace grounds were in serious peril.

Preoccupied with a need to protect the queen, *his* queen, Léonard resolved not to go to bed. Instead, he read near his fire and waited. At the gates of the château,

Women's march on Versailles
(BIBLIOTHÈQUE NATIONALE DE FRANCE)

the clamors of the hostile throngs camped there, the great glow of their raging fires, and the cries of "Vive la Nation!" (to which a few faithful bodyguards weakly replied "Vive le roi!") shook the night.

Léonard heard the clock strike three. Tired of sitting, he had begun walking through his two rooms; when he neared the door leading outside, he heard a number of voices whispering in the hall. He placed his ear to the thin panels of the door, and he distinctly heard the noise of many muffled footsteps.

The mysterious way in which they were speaking and walking made Léonard suspicious; they either belonged to the outside bands or there was treason among the servants of the court. Léonard threw the door open. The hall was now deserted and silent, and the conspirators had disappeared. Candle in hand, he went to the end of the hall, and saw a strange sight —a door wide open leading to the main hallway. It was something he had never seen in his eighteen years living at the château.

Fearing that Parisian insurgents might have penetrated the château, Léonard returned to his room and retrieved his pistols. He made his way toward the queen's apartments by a secret entrance. Chambermaids and servants of the wardrobe were fleeing, crying that the brigands were in the château, that the bodyguards posted at the main door of the queen's apartments were being massacred, and that Her Majesty had perhaps already fallen under the blade of the assassins.

Léonard pressed forward, brushing aside everything in his passage. By the light of a flickering lamp, he saw a woman almost nude, her hair disheveled, walking bare-footed. At the sight of his pistols Her Majesty mistook him for one of the brigands and uttered a fearful cry.

"Be reassured, madame, I am Léonard!" said the Gascon.

"Ah, my friend, save me!" cried Marie Antoinette, throwing herself into his arms and clinging to him. "The bodyguards have been killed," she continued in a broken voice, "my door was opened, and I saw horrible faces."

"They will no longer be able to reach you, madame," he said. "I will look after Your Majesty's safety."

Léonard took off his coat and threw it over the queen's naked shoulders. After putting his shoes on her feet, Léonard scurried the queen to the king's apartment. Lafayette and his principal officers had just entered the chambers to save the royal family, despite His Majesty's refusal to give him permission to do so. Léonard noted that the sovereign's shamed face was sufficient enough revenge for the general.

Léonard more than likely witnessed the March on Versailles, led by angry fishwives with axes and pikes in their hands. He also more than likely witnessed the royal family being forcefully escorted to the capital by the mob that sang "We are bring-ing back the baker, the baker's wife, and the baker's boy." But it was doubtful that the boastful Gascon actually valiantly *saved* the queen—as he described. Other ver-sions of the queen's escape through the secret passageways of Versailles, including the eyewitness accounts of Madame de Campan and other maids and valets, have never divulged Léonard's role in the escape, nor have they ever mentioned his presence.

He might not have sacrificed his life in this way, but Léonard would indeed pay a price for his closeness with the royal family. The location of his Théâtre de Monsieur, in a wing of the Tuileries, would soon become problematic for his theater troupe. The name of the theater alone aroused the indignation of the revolutionaries who rejected all things aristocratic or affiliated with the crown. Léonard would be forced to find another location, and name, for his new venue, the Théâtre Feydeau (not to be con-fused with the nineteenth-century dramaturge of the same name).

The following day, when the royal family settled in under prison-like conditions at the Tuileries Palace in Paris, Léonard took on the dangerous role of messenger and secret liaison between the royal family and their supporters in Paris; they were all shocked by the conditions of the dilapidated palace.

"Everything is very ugly here, mamma," said the young Dauphin Louis Charles.

"My son," replied the queen, "Louis XIV lodged here, and found it comfort-able. We should not be more fastidious than he." And turning to the ladies who had accompanied her, she said with a sad smile, as if to excuse the destitution of the palace, "You know that I did not expect to come here."[14]

CHAPTER 10

The Flight of the Royal Family

"And do not forget, Léonard, that a King of France can make a noble of a messenger who serves him to his satisfaction."

—KING LOUIS XVI TO LÉONARD
TUILERIES PALACE, JUNE 1791

December 1791
Paris, France

Shortly after one o'clock in the afternoon on the 6th of October, Louis XVI, his queen, his sister, and his children were taken from the extravagant palace of Versailles in the royal carriage. They were escorted to Paris by thousands of drunken, ragged *poissardes* (market fishwives) and angry Parisians, spurred on by hunger and destitution. Ladies of the bedchamber, royal valets, and palace servants followed in court carriages while a hundred deputies and the bulk of the Parisian army closed the procession.[1]

The poissardes surrounded the royal carriage as they walked, singing about the baker, his wife, and his son. In the midst of this enraged throng of market women, the heads of two murdered bodyguards were carried on pikes. The brutes, who made trophies of them, conceived the horrid idea of forcing a wigmaker of Sèvres to dress them up, and powder their bloody locks. Madame de Campan reported that the wigmaker "died as a consequence of the shock it gave him."[2]

Léonard witnessed the court of Versailles establish itself at its new disheveled residence in the Tuileries Palace. He saw a red-eyed Queen Marie Antoinette seated near a smoky hearth in which flames had not appeared for many years. He watched her chambermaids nailing strips of cloth to the doors of her apartment to prevent the chilled winds from blowing through the cracks.

Léonard understood the public's grievances but his heart still broke for the royal family that had treated him so well and had been so instrumental in him making his way in Paris. Like many royal servants, he was likely torn between the republican ideas of equality and his loyalty to his masters. Like many servants, he was also dependent on his masters for his livelihood, which made the choice somewhat easier, the inner conflict less pronounced.

Léonard agreed to return to Versailles to gather together a number of objects for Her Majesty. His orders were to look up everything and read everything and, because Her Majesty knew him to be forgetful, she told him to take *everything*. When he reached Petit Trianon, only a small number of servants still remained; he was overcome by the silence at the once grandiloquent château, as well as the traces of a frantic, harried departure.

The queen's apartment had been frozen in time since her nocturnal flight. Léonard saw the dress which Her Majesty had worn on the evening of the 5th of October, the silk stockings which she had taken off before going to bed, and under Her Majesty's bed, the slippers which she had no time to put on. The queen had apparently escaped the assassin's dagger by only a few moments. Léonard first gathered up the queen's items that he knew had memories attached to them. After reading through her papers (the contents of which he would take to the grave), he collected her portraits and jewelry.

Léonard could not help but stop in the middle of that immense courtyard before leaving. He knew that he might never again return to the palace, where nobility once wore his own towering masterpieces. The courtiers that once filled the galleries at all hours were now gone. There were no sentinels in the guard houses and sentry boxes; the courtyard was now a deserted space, somber and silent. There was nothing but ghosts.

When he arrived back at the Tuileries, he found Marie Antoinette pacing in her room. "At last, here you are!" she said, running to meet him. "And you have everything?"

"All that I could find, madame," said Léonard.

"Let us see, let us see," said the queen.

Léonard laid out all that he had found before Her Majesty's eyes. After examining the objects agitatedly for a few moments, an expression of serenity finally appeared on the queen's face, and she said, "Good, Léonard, all is here."

"How happy I am, madame, to have been so favored by destiny, as to be able to satisfy your wishes!"

"They are more than satisfied," said the queen. "Here are jewels I never expected to see again after the invasion of those brigands."

But Léonard considered it quite natural that the men who had broken into Her Majesty's apartments that morning did not take any diamonds. The assassins of the 6th of October were not prompted by petty theft; it was vengeance alone that drew them to the queen's quarters.

Palace of the Tuileries, Place Carrousel

While the royal family faced a grim situation, Léonard did his best to keep his own family together. The royal hairdresser had welcomed his third daughter, Fanny, to the world a year earlier, but it appeared that the family line of the eldest Autié was about to come to an end. But on the 27th of November 1790, during the troubled debates in the Assembly, Léonard's wife brought a son, soon baptized Auguste-Marie, to the world. This would be the last child that Marie-Louise would give Léonard; the marriage would only last another year.

The world outside the Autié's door was also in turmoil. By the end of 1790, King Louis and Marie Antoinette understood the absolute necessity of winning over certain deputies in the National Assembly who waged a persistent war on the court, especially the moderate revolutionary Count Honoré de Mirabeau. It was rumored that Mirabeau, a star of the Assembly, sought to undermine the throne only to erect on its ruins the throne of Philippe of the House of Orléans, the king's cousin.

The queen had received bits of information through Léonard and others regarding the admission of Mirabeau into the Duke of Orléans' circle. If the rumors of placing the king's cousin on the throne were true, the monarchy would need a new strategy to win the famous minister's favor. The queen charged Léonard with the mission of casting more light on these mysterious meetings.

Léonard quickly learned that as soon as the Count de Mirabeau had finished his thunderous remarks in the assembly, he always hurriedly ate dinner and then set off for one of two isolated houses, one located in the Faubourg Saint-Antoine and the other in Belleville. He also learned, with the help of his agents, that the Duke of Orléans went in the same direction as that taken by Mirabeau every evening for a secret rendezvous.

Léonard began his own work in secret, starting out by trying to get the prince's or Mirabeau's servants to talk. He succeeded in entering the mysterious houses under various pretexts and disguises, and was able to lure the servants to a neighboring tavern. All that he gleaned at first was an "awful disgust for the atrocious beverages" which he was compelled to swallow—almost as liberally as he bought them—to keep from raising the servants' suspicions.

Léonard had enticed a tall and stout servant of Mirabeau to an inn one evening; he had been watching the man for a long time, aware that he was well liked by his master (and better informed about Mirabeau's private life than his comrades). The trusted lackey was fond of drink, and Léonard succeeded in getting him tipsy; unfortunately, the scamp was able to keep his wits about him.

In spite of the man's intoxicated state, Léonard's frequent and insidious questions excited the lackey's suspicions, and he took Léonard exactly for what he was: an inept secret agent. Before Léonard had time to explain or was able to bribe the man into silence, the brute struck Léonard's left eye, a blow which, in typical over-dramatic fashion, caused him to "unseasonably behold the most beautiful display of fireworks ever beheld by mortal man." Though Léonard's first attempt at espionage was an unmitigated, and embarrassing, disaster, he would have another chance to prove himself soon enough.

Duke of Orléans, Louis Philippe II
(BIBLIOTHÈQUE NATIONALE DE FRANCE)

Mirabeau was a revolutionary, but he had studied England's political history and favored the creation of a constitutional monarchy, not a republic. When he was informed of the king's idea to escape across the border to rally support of allies and retake the throne, he was enraged. He had recommended a public departure in the light of day, with the king appealing to his subjects "without begging for outside support." Under no circumstances would he be the accomplice to anything resembling an escape; if such an escape were attempted, he swore to "denounce the monarch himself."[3]

Honoré Mirabeau

At the same time, there was also talk of an Orléans conspiracy, the popular overthrow of Louis so that the Duke of Orléans could step in and take the throne. Fearing the worst, General Lafayette wished to break off the intimacy between the Duke of Orléans and Mirabeau. He also alerted the king and queen to the intrigues of the duke and his designs for the throne.

In the middle of the year 1790, with the aid of an actress from Monsieur's theater, Léonard learned that Mirabeau was waiting for an opportune moment to abandon the Duke of Orléans—a piece of highly precious information for the court. Mirabeau was becoming increasingly alarmed with the duke's radical opinions; he also realized that he was risking his head in such a treacherous game. Queen Marie Antoinette was extremely pleased to learn of Mirabeau's possible turn. "That man is ours! Leave him to me!" she exclaimed.

"Let us," continued the queen, "let us, without loss of time, put the irons in the fire to secure Mirabeau. No matter what price he may set on his conscience, it will be cheap if we succeed in taking him from the Duke of Orléans, and I count on you to make the first attempt toward that end."

"Your Majesty knows my devotion," said Léonard, "but do you not think, madame, that the names of Mirabeau and Léonard are rather a jarring juxtaposition?"

"Why so?" asked the queen. "Mirabeau will not consider it extraordinary that, in a confidential mission, we should make use of a person who deserves more confidence than all the statesmen by whom we are surrounded."

"I never had, nor shall I ever have, the thought of refusing to obey Your Majesty! What must I say to that haughty orator?" said Léonard.

"Nothing directly from me, and less from the king," said the queen. "It is possible that we might fail with a man so difficult to handle, and we must risk as little as possible."

"I think that I understand Your Majesty's intentions," said Léonard. "I am thus supposed to have heard from reliable sources that the king regrets being deprived of the assistance of Monsieur de Mirabeau; that daily His Majesty speaks with admiration of the talent which he displays in the assembly, and that more than once he has repeated that only through Monsieur de Mirabeau could the monarchy form a strong and lasting agreement with the revolutionaries."

"Do not forget to add that the king's opinions are the more believable as they are shared by the queen," said the queen. "For you know, Léonard, that all the oppositions of the court to the measures dictated by the assembly's patriotism, are always thought to come from me."

Léonard promised the queen that he should see Mirabeau the following morning; he knew the statesman spent most of his nights drinking and eating with courtesans, and that he remained in bed all morning. It was, in fact, in bed that he received the deputies, the magistrates, and especially the women who wished to speak to him.

Léonard went about his way on that beautiful summer morning, weaving and reweaving his speech in advance; he would have to be as subtle as possible to fulfill his mission without exposing the queen to the disgrace of a refusal. He needed to pull off the trick—as Albert Camus would describe it centuries later—of getting a "yes" without asking a question. He followed the rue de la Chaussée-d'Antin for about a third of its length, watching for a modest-looking house with a courtyard gate and two horse's heads sculpted on the house's façade. Léonard was neither confident nor apprehensive; over the years he had gained experience in coming into contact with such erudite personages. He compared his dexterity to that of a musician, being able to play upon his imagination and wit as a musician would play upon his fiddle or flute. Léonard was insecure about his long-windedness in the presence of a man like Mirabeau, whose eloquence roared loud as thunder and flowed swift as a torrent.[4]

In front of Mirabeau's house on the Chaussée-d'Antin, Léonard rang the little brass bell. He wrote that he could hear his heart palpitate, his temples throbbed enough to raise his hat, and his legs trembled beneath him. When the door opened, Mirabeau's servant told Léonard that he would be admitted at once; his master's habit was not to keep the patriots waiting whenever he could help it. The servant added that it was also not the custom to ask the names of the persons who were being received—all Frenchmen being equal before Mirabeau's eyes.

The deputy's bedroom door opened, and Léonard saw his large pimpled face, crowned by a handkerchief, resting on a rather natty pillow. His courage almost abandoned him when he heard the famous Mirabeau speak, "What do you wish, sir?"

"Monsieur Count de . . ." said Léonard.

"My name is Mirabeau; omit the titles," interrupted the minister.

"Monsieur," said Léonard, "I come to you because I know that the constitutional monarchy must recognize in you its most sincere as well as most eloquent supporter."

"Oh!" said Mirabeau with some surprise. "Be kind enough to take a seat, monsieur, and inform me to whom I have the honor of speaking."

"Monsieur," he replied, "I am Léonard."

"Léonard, the poet?" he asked.

"No, monsieur," said Léonard.

"Ah! I see, Léonard the . . ." and Mirabeau, drawing his two bare and muscular arms from under the covers, imitated the action of curling a lock of hair.

"Exactly," replied Léonard with a rather forced smile, but blushing.

"Well, Monsieur Léonard," said Mirabeau, "the queen had beautiful hair ten years ago."

"Yes, monsieur," he replied, somewhat dismayed. It seemed that Mirabeau could not conceive that Léonard might be part of an important mission. Léonard persisted, "The queen had beautiful hair ten years ago, and I was kept rather busy taking care of it. But that beautiful hair is beginning to turn gray. I thought that, at a time where the distinction of professions has disappeared in the eyes of the law, I could exercise my share of the rights of men by coming to speak with the deputy of the nation who has shown himself the most ardent promoter of these rights."

"Fine, Monsieur Léonard!" said the minister. "I should have suspected by your accent that I had to deal with a man of parts. I am listening."

"You readily understand, monsieur," said Léonard, "that I have continued relations with persons attached to the court. I may even tell you that these relations are such that reports of the most intimate conferences have sometimes reached me."

"Ah! The devil!" said Mirabeau.

"To such an extent, monsieur," continued Léonard, "and I know from an excellent source, that you are often mentioned by the king and even by the queen."

"I am mentioned? And what do they say of me?" asked Mirabeau, who eagerly raised himself up on his elbow.

"Many complimentary things," said Léonard.

"You don't say so!" said the minister. "That astonishes me."

"That's because you are not acquainted with the present mind of the court," said Léonard.

"Which is . . . ?" asked Mirabeau.

"In a state of awe and admiration of Monsieur Mirabeau," said Léonard. He was well aware of how flattery could knock down one's natural defenses.

"Monsieur Léonard," said Mirabeau, looking in his eyes, "have you been sent here by the queen?" He sat straight up in his bed.

"The queen is totally unacquainted with my visit of this day, Monsieur Mirabeau," said Léonard, "but I am quite certain that Her Majesty would attach great value to your accession to the interests of the court."

"What's that you are saying, monsieur? Have I ever shown myself opposed to the court's interests?" asked the minister. "I have only attacked the court in its mistaken policies and when its awkward changes tended to destroy the monarchy itself. Thus you will readily comprehend that, standing on this conservative principle of the rights of the crown, I shall never refuse to come to an understanding with the sovereign; I have not deserted him, it is he who has left me."

Mirabeau's uncompromising speech proved to Léonard that the great orator took him for what he really was—an agent of the queen. The deputy added, "I desire that the king and queen should know that I am, and always shall be, their most faithful servant."

The queen was delighted when told of Mirabeau's intentions. Her Majesty considered, from the circumstantial details, that she could now make an appointment with the great minister. Léonard was sent to Mirabeau the following day to arrange it.

The first interview between Mirabeau and the queen took place at nine o'clock that evening in the garden of the Tuileries under the tall chestnut trees. This rendezvous was well documented, found in many memoirs of the time. However, Léonard warned that many falsehoods were woven into the stories of the historic meeting. In some, Mirabeau was a sort of sentimental lover; in others, the statesman was carried away by his feelings to the extent of asking Her Majesty for a kiss. "Nothing of all this is true," noted Léonard.

Mirabeau also met with Louis XVI, proposing measures to assist the king in controlling the Revolution without changing its principles. He also expressly urged the king *not* to leave France. It was possible that Mirabeau suggested Montmédy as a suitable place for refuge, but Léonard insisted that Mirabeau never for a moment approved of any escape across the border. This minister hated emigration, considering it downright cowardice; from a monarch, he would have considered it a crime.

Despite Mirabeau's efforts, and the initial charade, it was not long before he noticed that the king and queen would never follow the path of salvation that he had opened to them. Louis simply refused to give up his idea of absolute power. Léonard's view was more nuanced: He was adamant that Louis XVI and Marie Antoinette never openly attacked the new order of things, but "their inert resistance," he explained, "led them, by an incline steeper and steeper, to the precipice which was to swallow them." History would perhaps agree with Léonard's assessment; the king, other than using his veto, did not contemplate any resistance. He also refused to enlist the assistance of neighboring monarchs, who might have been rewarded with land holdings and gold for their help. But Louis was also worried about civil war; bringing foreign troops onto French soil would have further alienated him from his people.

Louis XVI's inability to respond to revolutionary demands upended the royal family from Versailles to the Tuileries. From that point on, the king seemed to have become emotionally paralyzed, leaving most important decisions to his politically untrained queen. When, on the 17th of April 1791, the royal family was prevented from leaving for a visit to the château of Saint-Cloud, it was evident that they were now prisoners in the Tuileries. The queen immediately began discussing secret plans with her Swedish admirer, Count Axel von Fersen. Counseled by the queen and others, Louis finally committed himself and his family to the only choice left, which would prove disastrous: an escape from the capital.

On the 12th of June 1791, around ten o'clock at night, Léonard opened a note which had just been delivered to him in his bedroom:

> *Monsieur Léonard is requested to come to the Tuileries at once. He will present himself at the little door opening on the passage leading to the Feuillants; the doorkeeper*

Parent will let him in. At the door situated at the foot of the Pavillon de Flore, on the side of the garden, a footman will wait for M. Léonard and will lead him to the place where he will be received. No delay.

Once inside the Tuileries, Léonard was led through the dark and deserted apartments to the queen's bedchamber, where he found the king, the queen, and the dauphin's sister, Madame Élisabeth.

The king was seated on a small sofa; bloated as usual after his gigantic meal, he had taken off his collar. Nevertheless, his face appeared more animated than normal. The queen and Madame Élisabeth were seated in armchairs on each side of the sofa. Louis XVI eyed Léonard.

"It is long, Léonard . . ." said His Majesty with a softness of voice which, for some years, had been his habit. "Yes, it is very long since your zeal and faithfulness have been known to us, and you have therefore seen that, on several occasions, our confidence has rewarded your devotion."

"Sire," Léonard replied bowing, "I am overwhelmed by Your Majesty's kindnesses and those of the queen."

"Today, Léonard," resumed the king, "I expect from that same devotion, a proof of great importance, and I shall tell you without evasion, that for the mission with which I am about to entrust you, requiring both intelligence and zeal, I do not know of a better agent than you."

"Certainly, certainly!" the queen and Madame Élisabeth added, acting as a chorus to the king's flattery.

Then Louis XVI continued, "You must know all, sir; listen to me carefully."

"Sire, all my interest and attention follow Your Majesty's words," Léonard said.

"You know better than anyone else, the amount of courageous resignation I have displayed in these late days; when my wife, my sister, my aunts, all those about me were possessed of the greatest fear. I was calm and tranquil, because I had nothing for which to reproach myself. My friends, well-advised or ill-advised, I do not yet know which, urged me to leave my kingdom, but I always answered that a father must not leave his children when passion carries him away from his duty.

"Today without entirely consenting to this advice," the king continued, "I have decided to follow it in part, by conforming myself to the plan of a very unfortunate man, Mirabeau. In a few days I shall go to a camp, which the General de Bouillé is going to receive the order to form at Montmédy. That order, my dear Léonard, you are going to carry to the general, with the commission and insignia of the Marshal of France.

"You will appreciate the full importance of such a mission. General de Bouillé has on hand sufficient troops, which he has carefully selected among those not yet possessed of the spirit of revolt. But he must be notified with scrupulous exactness, so that he may have time to operate his movement of concentration first, then to come and meet me."

"Why does Your Majesty not say to meet *us*?" asked the queen.

"Madame," continued Louis XVI, "you will later know my will; allow me to finish what I have to say to Léonard."

And the king continued, "A gentleman of my household, had I known one whose capacity equaled yours would have been much less fit for the duty I wish you to perform. I do not want a man of effeminate habits, a dandified servant able to travel only in a carriage with flexible springs. I need a robust fellow like you, sure-footed, able to walk through fields and swim a river, if necessary, to avoid falling into a patriots' ambush. To reach Montmédy almost as the crow flies, in less than three days, that is the aim of your mission. Do you accept it, Léonard?"

"With joy, sire; I leave in an hour, provided with baggage as light as that which I carried with me on entering Paris twenty-two years ago, and I will reach Montmédy before the expiration of the limit set by Your Majesty."

"I do not doubt it," said His Majesty with a kindly smile. "And do not forget, Léonard, that a King of France can make a *noble* of a messenger who serves him to his satisfaction."

These last words had been said with a laugh, but Léonard saw that the king's promise was a serious one. *Would his journey from the humble roots of Gascony culminate in a title? Would this be the crowning last step of his climb in society?* He suddenly felt as if a "life-giving elixir" flowed through his veins; indeed, this promise of ennoblement would consume Léonard for years to come.

The king then drew a small dispatch from his pocket and handed it to Léonard, saying, "You know for whom it is intended, that's enough." It contained no address.

The queen, who had risen to take something from her desk, returned holding in her hand an object measuring fifteen or sixteen inches, which she gave to the king.

"Here is the marshal's baton for the general," said the king handing it to Léonard. His Majesty likely noted Léonard's embarrassment. He continued, "You think this object somewhat voluminous, perhaps?"

"I confess to Your Majesty that in view of the mystery with which I am to surround my trip," said Léonard, "I fear my purpose may be revealed by this insignia of the highest military rank."

"I had thought of that," said Madame Élisabeth.

"Sister," replied the king, "Léonard is clever enough to conceal this marshal's baton from all eyes. Besides, as last measure, he could hide it under some bush or throw it far from him if danger pressed. But only as a last resort, do you understand, Léonard?

"It has always been the custom during the reign of the kings our ancestors," continued the king, "that the distinctive mark of the highest military rank be handed to the incumbent by the sovereign. To act contrary to this established custom would be to make an attempt against the prerogatives of the throne. We are essentially anxious that General de Bouillé receive the marshal's baton which we hereby bestow on him."

Madame Élisabeth began to smile, surely wondering why His Majesty allowed the marshal's baton to be handed to the general by a mere hairdresser of all people. The princess could not know the reason. The king was unable to find about him a nobleman sufficiently intelligent and devoted to deserve it.

"And now, Léonard, good luck," said Louis XVI holding out his hand, which Léonard respectfully pressed to his heart. "Think that on you rest today not only our hopes but perhaps the sole chance of salvation of the monarchy. I no longer detain you. Go."

The queen and Madame Élisabeth gave the royal hairdresser their hands to kiss, and he took his leave. Léonard was aware that he would be one of the most active agents of court in the execution of this mission, and he zealously accepted it. But he also regretted that the family was determined to follow such an ill-conceived, dangerous plan, a plan that could be the ruin of the monarchy. The escape from the Tuileries would be dangerous in itself, but the people might never forgive the royal family, if caught, for retreating toward the Austrian border, the home of Marie Antoinette and the longtime enemy of France.

By this point, the royal hairdresser turned emissary had a mistress, the pretty daughter of the porter of his house, Lucette. Having a mistress was a mark of respect at the time; in fact, not having one in eighteenth-century France might have cast doubts about Léonard's virility.

The young lady was hardly seventeen years old when she first "desired to be pleasing" in the eyes of her father's employer. She would hide Léonard's letters and newspapers, so that when he asked for them, she would thus have an excuse to bring them to him personally. When she gave an inkling of her desire to live with Léonard, he told her, "My dear child, I don't know how to *live*." He added that all he could do for her was to find her a spot in the French company at the Théâtre de Monsieur, where, in his capacity of proprietor, he could exercise his influence in her favor.

A young girl who wanted to *live* with someone, noted Léonard, was always obeying the dictates of her heart. It was Lucette whom Léonard had employed to discover the secret of the interviews between the Duke of Orléans and Mirabeau for the queen. The young actress had plenty of experience; Léonard noted, "She knew how to make the most of that feminine prattle which is readily taken for wit, when accompanied by a well-timed wink or a pursing of the lips that appears to denote a thought."

Rue Saint-Honoré, area of Léonard's residence, circa 1789
(BIBLIOTHÈQUE NATIONALE DE FRANCE)

When Léonard approached her about spying for him—and by extension, the queen—he asked her if she was interested in making some money.

She replied as only a young lover could. "No, I want to prove to you, Léonard, that the fires of a first love can never be extinguished."

When Lucette later gave him the detailed report concerning the relations between the Duke of Orléans and Mirabeau, Léonard exclaimed, "Really, my dear Lucette, you are a woman beyond price. But withal you are so pretty a woman, so seductive, and above all so delicate in your conduct towards me, that my first homage must be paid to your charms; your talent shall only receive the second." After employing her as a spy, Léonard recognized that he had fallen in love with the young actress.

The report itself was chaotic and frivolous, but all the facts were annotated in great detail, and the important facts of the Orléans conspiracy were gathered and related to the queen. Lucette had managed to befriend an associate of Philippe d'Orléans, and she discovered that if Louis XVI would ever manage to escape, the throne at the Tuileries would be considered vacant. Mirabeau would then propose a constitutional monarchy with Philippe d'Orléans, a supporter of the Revolution, taking his cousin's throne.

Mirabeau would die of a heart attack in April of 1791—though his followers swore that he had been poisoned. The minister's lifetime work was later discredited when it was reported that he had been an intermediary between the Revolution and the court, and that he had taken bribes from the queen.[5]

After hearing of Léonard's new mission for the monarchy, Lucette mockingly asked, "Has the king made you a general?"

"Do not ask any questions; I cannot answer them. You are a good girl, Lucette, and I believe you love me sincerely; so look after my house for I must set out at once."

"Are they going to bring the carriage here then?" she asked.

"No, I am going on foot," said Léonard.

"On foot, like a wandering rogue!" said Lucette.

"In essence, but for my financial resources," he replied, going to his desk and putting two rolls of a hundred louis each in his pocket. "Adieu, adieu, one last kiss."

Léonard left his house at half past midnight; the tower of La Chapelle struck one o'clock as he stepped on to the plain of Saint Denis—up to his ankles in mud. It was the 13th of June 1791, and Léonard left behind his amber, musk, powder-puffs, and ribbons. He had become a royal emissary, almost an ambassador, traveling by night and by the most natural means along the road to Germany. He was under way with an important dispatch, a marshal's baton, and dreams of establishing the "illustrious race of the Barons de Léonard."

His Majesty had commanded him to travel "as the crow flies," which accounted for this route. He was aware of the possibility of being compromised in a part of the country swarming with citizens taking the law into their own hands—especially since he carried a baton covered with those *fleurs-de-lys*, the insignia of the House of Bourbon. It might as well have been a target on his back. Though at first glance it resembled a sugar stick, the inquisitive patriots would surely unwrap it and throw him in some village jail.

Léonard arrived at the gates of Meaux at the break of day, having paid generously for a ride on horseback—of which, he later wrote, "certain notable portions of my epidermis, removed from a part which I will not name."

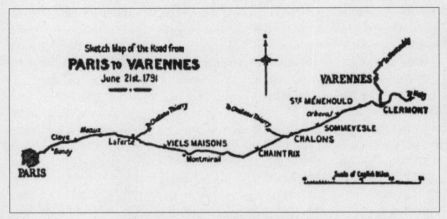

Map of the route to Montmédy

Léonard had succeeded in covering almost forty miles in three hours, and he was resolved to ride horseback as often as possible, despite the suffering of flesh. He couldn't complain, knowing that many illustrious families had formerly paid for their noble titles with blood shed in battle. His posterior was a small price to pay.

Asking for passports in the interior of France was not yet customary in June 1791; nevertheless, a guard was mounted in every village, and travelers were liable to be arrested if their costume or general appearance was in any way out of the ordinary, which Léonard's surely was. His hair, dressed in the fashion of the aristocracy, and his clothing reminiscent of the court, drew the attention of the inhabitants of Meaux. Upon seeing a number of carter's smocks flapping in the breeze, he purchased one to disguise himself. He acted as though he were a neighboring landlord, taking care to explain that the rustic garment was needed for his valet. A little farther down the road, he bought a striped cotton night cap, a large, round, flat hat, and a pair of strong boots.

His royal message was hidden beneath his striped cap covered with the wide six-franc hat, his smock concealed his coat, and the coarse boots helped to complete his disguise. He had sacrificed his handsome beaver and buckled shoes, which he had discarded beneath a heap of dried leaves.

Thus transfigured into a clumsy wagoner with a hazel stick in his hand, Léonard boldly crossed town. Nobody took notice of him, and he casually ate breakfast in a wagoner's tavern just to the north of Meaux. Fortunately, there was no shortage of relay horses along the road to Château-Thierry and Épernay, nor did Léonard fail to use them. He thought of hiring, from post to post, a series of uncomfortable chaises, which were easy to find, but he didn't want to awaken suspicions. Instead, Léonard resigned himself to endure the cruelty of a coiffeur's full-speed journey on horseback. A charitable horseman taught him the remedial properties of a candle inserted in his breeches, which helped.

On the evening of the 14th of June, he reached the little town of Dun-sur-Meuse, and discovered that General de Bouillé was now at Montmédy, some twelve miles farther. Léonard thought it would be imprudent to make his way into a well-fortified camp. He decided to send a local express to the marshal-elect Bouillé, trying to attract his attention without compromising himself.

Léonard met a young shepherd on the road who impressed Léonard as looking humble enough to pass into the camp without arousing any distrust, yet nimble enough to reach Montmédy before the gates were closed. The shepherd could then bring Léonard a reply early the next morning.

"Hark ye, my lad," he said, addressing him with the rough manner of a carter. "Are you the boy to go to Montmédy tonight and do an errand for which you will be paid beforehand, and well paid afterwards?"

"Ay, good man," replied the young shepherd, "I'll go to Montmédy tonight for ye and come back too."

"Tonight?" asked Léonard.

"Ay, indeed I will," said the boy. "I'll just tell the officer at the gate that I want to come home to sleep, and the toll-keeper knows me, you see, good man."

"In that case, my lad, you can start at once," said Léonard.

"Ah, but I must first take my sheep back to the farm," said the boy.

"That's true," replied Léonard. "Well, when will you be ready?"

"In less than half an hour," he said.

"Good, I will wait for you at the door of the *Lion d'Argent*, where I am stopping," said Léonard. "Don't be long."

"No danger of that, good man," he said.

Léonard had prepared a letter for General de Bouillé beforehand. He found a copy of it among his papers with a carter's spelling:

Monsieur the general, one of my wagons holds some furniture and trunks which are for you. I have gone before my mate, who is driving it, because I feared I might meet with some trouble from the customs officers as I got nearer the frontier. And so I pray you, monsieur the marquis, to jump on your horse and come yourself to Dun, where I will wait for you and see that nothing happens to the load I have for you. I am, monsieur, with respect, Jean Robin, carter.

Bouillé, one of the heroes of the American War of Independence, was well regarded in the National Assembly. A load of trunks and furniture forwarded to the general was not likely to raise any suspicions. Léonard hoped that the general, who doubtless expected neither trunks nor furniture from Paris, would readily suspect that some mystery lurked behind this letter. He bet on the fact that the general would ride the short distance to make sure.

Seated on the stone bench before the door of the inn, Léonard saw the young shepherd run up, carrying his clogs in his hand, quite ready to cover the distance from Dun to Montmédy in less than two hours.

He gave the shepherd a big crown of six livres, and promised him another if he finished the errand successfully. He then handed the boy the letter, and off he went. Léonard had chosen a room sufficiently removed from the traffic of the inn to interview with the general privately and waited, too anxious to sleep.

About midnight, a carriage drew up at the door of the inn, and Léonard heard a voice asking for the carter who had arrived that morning. A few seconds later General de Bouillé entered his room with the little messenger, whom he had brought back behind his carriage.

"Is it you, master, who wrote to me?" asked the general, casting his eyes upon Léonard's features as though he recognized him.

"Yes, monsieur," he replied, with a wink that clearly meant, "Say nothing until we are alone."

General de Bouillé bolted the door behind the young boy and stepped toward Léonard. "You are no carter," he said.

"No, monsieur the marshal," Léonard said proudly.

"Why do you give me that title?" asked the general.

"Only because I have come to bring you the patent and insignia," he said.

"You are a messenger from the court?" asked the general, lowering his voice.

"Yes," said Léonard, "and this is the gift which I bring you from the king." Léonard pulled the marshal's baton from under his smock, and handed it to the marquis, together with the royal dispatch. The marquis opened it eagerly.

"You are Monsieur Léonard," cried the general, overcome with joy. "I thought I recognized you. Truly, I might have thought it. I am sure that you are the only really devoted person left at the court of our unhappy king. Well, my dear Monsieur Léonard, embrace me. You are my godfather, since you represent Louis XVI!

"And now what have you to tell me?" he continued. "His Majesty has prepared secrets for me that he was not willing to trust to paper?"

"That is so, monsieur," said Léonard. "Pray be seated, and I will tell you all."

Léonard narrated the changes to the proposed flight of the king, complete with all the arrangements for the plan's execution.

"When does the king propose to start?" asked the general.

"If there has been no change in His Majesty's plans, he will now leave the Tuileries on the night of the 19th," said Léonard.

"And the first intimation I receive of it is on the 15th!" cried the marquis in a stifled voice, turning pale.

"General," Léonard said, "I left Paris at one o'clock at night on the 13th to fulfill the mission which the king had entrusted to me an hour before, and I was here, fifty leagues from the capital, on the 14th at six o'clock in the evening."

"It is not with you, my dear Léonard, that I find fault," said General de Bouillé. "Egad! I can see that, with all the difficulties you have had to encounter, your diligence has not been in vain. But why did the king not let me know earlier?

"How can I now guarantee the safety of this journey?" continued the general. "I ought to have had time to secretly deploy cavalry along the roads from here to the gates of Paris, so that in case any obstacles are placed along the way of His Majesty's journey, my detachments might have been able to cut down that scum of a National Guard and carry away the king. By the way, I hope the king comes alone."

"I think not, monsieur," said Léonard. "I believe that it was arranged by the royal family that Madame Élisabeth and the Children of France should be taken to Brussels, but that the queen was to accompany the king."

"This is the height of folly and absurdity!" said the general. "By God, the queen has chosen a bad moment for this display of conjugal heroism! How could the king have listened to such an unfortunate fancy? And here am I left to execute a military movement, the consequences of which it is impossible to foresee, with a woman!"

He continued, "My dear Léonard, I'm in despair. I have the saddest foreboding about the king's journey, and the sorrow I am feeling spoils the honor the king has bestowed on me by promoting me. Do you return to Paris now?"

"It was my intention to wait for the king to arrive," said Léonard, "in order to acquaint him with the result of my errand."

"It would be better for you to go and meet His Majesty," said General de Bouillé. "Go as far as you can, short of returning to Paris before the king's journey has succeeded—if it is to succeed.

"When you meet the king," continued the general, "be sure to tell His Majesty that I am devoted to his service, and ready to shed the last drop of my blood in aid of his endeavors. Say nothing of the obstacles which I foresee. It is too late now to take any precautions; we must combat them by force, without letting Louis XVI fear that they will beat us. Adieu, I shall return to Montmédy, and will give my orders to the troops at the break of day."

The general took his leave. Léonard would never see him again.*

Léonard briskly retraced his steps in order to meet His Majesty just outside the capital city. This journey was more painful than the first; he had to remain on the road night and day in order not to miss the king when his carriage came into sight. In this way, watching and waiting, Léonard arrived within ten miles of Paris where the bustle of a huge traveling carriage suggested the arrival of the fugitives. Léonard was alarmed when he spotted the enormous coach, heavily loaded, and accompanied by three persons on the box easily recognized as soldiers in disguise. This ponderous carriage, rolling slowly along, was followed by a second coach, also loaded like a stagecoach.

To his dismay, Léonard saw that not only did the queen accompany the king, but that the Children of France were also traveling with His Majesty, and that three or four ladies were seated in the second carriage. Louis XVI would not be able to travel as far as Varennes without being recognized and stopped. Moreover, the king took no precaution to keep his flight a secret; His Majesty, whose portrait was to be found in everybody's pocket, sat by the window, and sometimes stepped out for a walk. Queen Marie Antoinette was no more careful to hide her easily recognizable face.

Although it was the middle of the night and quite dark, he immediately recognized the carriage and called out, "I am Léonard!"

"Léonard, Léonard," came from the back seat of the berline in a woman's voice, which he recognized as that of the queen. The carriage stopped.

The king made Léonard stand on the step of the carriage and tell him about his mission in full detail and the general's words of consolation. Léonard later admitted

---

* General de Bouillé never mentioned the unexpected visit from the famed hairdresser in his own memoirs. However, it was evident that the general did indeed receive a messenger carrying a letter from the king on the 15th of June and this messenger was more than likely Léonard. The royal hairdresser's visit to the general several days before the flight of the royal family was later confirmed in the political publication, *La Revue Bleue*, and as well as being mentioned in archived correspondence written some fifteen years later. The general indeed wrote in his own journal that the letter he received from the king on the 15th of June did announce the family's departure from Paris being delayed for a day, and would not take place until between midnight and one o'clock on the night of June 20th.

This delay, in fact, was needed to conceal the preparations for the flight from one of the queen's chambermaids, an ardent republican whose service in the royal household would not end until the 19th. The family could not depart until the maid was off duty. General de Bouillé was understandably annoyed; he had already issued the orders for the departure of two squadrons to be in Clermont when the king arrived, and now he was obliged to double the time of their stay in that town, a delay that would likely arouse suspicion among the townspeople.

Coins minted in 1789 with the king's likeness

that he might have filled the monarch and his family with unrealistic hopes, but he nevertheless accepted the thanks and gratitude. He also accepted the promises of nobility, but those, of course, would vanish along with the monarchy.

As he took leave of the king, Louis XVI said, "Monsieur Léonard, whatever happens, I hope that we shall soon meet again. Should anything unexpected take place, do not forget that we are to meet again."

Day broke as Léonard entered Paris, and he hastened to get rid of his carter's frock. Eager to know how Their Majesties had managed to escape from the Tuileries, he hurried to Mademoiselle Bertin, whom he knew would be well informed.

Léonard confirmed his role in the flight to Varennes in a letter that he wrote at a much later date to the new ruler of France. However, he was unaware at the time that his younger brother, Jean-François, was also involved with the flight of the royal family—and perhaps even responsible for its miscarriage.

CHAPTER 11

The Other Léonard

". . . but how shall I get back to Paris? I'm in my pumps and my white silk stockings, and I have neither a change of clothing nor any money with me."
—JEAN-FRANÇOIS AUTIÉ TO THE DUKE OF CHOISEUL
PARIS, 20TH OF JUNE 1791

Paris, France
June 1791

Mademoiselle Bertin was eager to relate her story of what had happened at the Tuileries while Léonard was traveling.

"I fear our kind master and mistress will not succeed in their attempt," said the queen's milliner. "I may be mistaken, but it seems to me that their flight is known to the patriots." Léonard was distraught to hear such news.

Mademoiselle Bertin had never left the château during the four days preceding the departure of the royal family. She told him her story:

On the morning of the 18th, as Mademoiselle Bertin was crossing the Carrousel Gardens of the Tuileries to go to the queen, she crossed paths with the Marquis de Lafayette. After exchanging niceties, Lafayette drew a little green Moroccan letter-case from his pocket, opened it, and took a piece of paper from it which he unfolded, showing it to the milliner. It contained two patterns that had been selected for traveling cloaks by one of his acquaintances.

Rose thought for a moment that the blood would freeze in her veins; the material that the general had shown her was the pattern for the clothes that the king and queen were having made for their departure. Although Lafayette looked at her with a fixed gaze, she hid her anxiety; she was certain that Lafayette had been informed of the planned escape of the king and his family. It was also evident that he had no intention of preventing it, because he knew well that Rose was close to Marie Antoinette. The Marquis de Lafayette must have had a motive in speaking to her. *Was he trying to warn the queen?*

The Marquis de Lafayette

The queen had not told Rose of the king's plans—she had overheard them—so she couldn't warn Their Majesties of the risk they were running and Léonard had already left.

The following day, Rose decided to indirectly tell the queen about Lafayette's disclosure. She bizarrely asked the queen if she had forgotten to order her summer toiletries. When the queen demanded to know about what Rose was hinting, the milliner revealed that she knew about the plans to escape. She then confessed that some unfaithful person had sent the Marquis de Lafayette the patterns of the cloaks that Their Majesties were to wear on the day of the departure.

"All is lost," the queen cried out and went to speak immediately with the king. She was puzzled, thinking that there must be some secret treachery lurking beneath Lafayette's conduct. Perhaps he meant to let the family leave, with the intention of accusing them of treason afterward in the Assembly.

When Her Majesty returned, she told Rose that nothing had been changed in the arrangements. For the remainder of the day, the queen allowed her to take part in the preparations for the journey, and Rose promised not to leave the Palace until Their Majesties' departure.

The next day, Queen Marie Antoinette secretly left the Palace later than planned. Count Fersen was there, disguised as a coachman, and as he was preparing to mount the box, the king sharply reminded him that he was only to accompany them as far as the city gates. Louis XVI was grateful, but it was too dangerous for him to help any further. Fersen sadly acknowledged the king's command; the queen was silent, perhaps hinting at another reason they had for rejecting Fersen's offer.

At last, all the royal family had taken their places in the big coach, while the queen's ladies stepped into the second chariot. The carriages pulled away, and Rose Bertin did not go away until the dull rumbling sound of the two carriages had died away in the distance. She returned home at about one o'clock in the morning.

"You can readily believe, my dear Léonard, that my repose that night was neither calm nor prolonged," said Rose after she finished her story. "And what you have just told me of General de Bouillé's apprehensions does not reassure me at all."

It is possible that neither Léonard nor Rose were aware that Léonard's youngest brother, Jean-François Autié, had played any part in the scheme, for they didn't discuss him. They surely had no idea that the younger brother may have been responsible for the king's arrest during his flight to Montmédy, one of the most important events in the history of the French Revolution—indeed, in French history.

The roles of the brothers Autié have often been blurred in the memoirs and the historical accounts of the unsuccessful flight; Léonard and Jean-François were both called "Léonard" and, moreover, they were both employed as hairdressers in the royal household, as was their cousin Villanou. This is something of a nightmare for historians, especially in piecing together the royals' flight.

The Duke of Choiseul, commander of the Royal Dragoons, had been sent by General de Bouillé to Paris from Metz; the duke was to give the king the latest information about the preparations for the flight. Although Choiseul was devoted to the king's cause, he was known to be a frivolous and hasty statesman. However, he was wealthy, the colonel of a distinguished regiment, and able to furnish the relays from his own stables (which the royal party at Varennes needed to continue their voyage to Montmédy.) Choiseul planned to leave Paris ten hours before the king.

On the same day, the 20th of June, Queen Marie Antoinette sent for Jean-François, the Autié brother who dressed her hair on a daily basis. Having an apartment in the palace, Jean-François arrived within minutes. When he approached the queen, she asked in a low voice, "Monsieur Léonard, can I rely upon you?"[1]

"I am your entirely devoted servant," replied Jean-François.

"I am indeed certain of your affection," said the queen. "Take these diamonds, and bury them in your pocket.

"Do you see this letter?" she continued. "It must be taken to the Duke of Choiseul in the rue d'Artois, and it must only be delivered to him in person; should he not be at home you will find him with [his sister] the Duchess de Grammont. Put on a large cloak and broad-brimmed hat so as to avoid being recognized; obey the duke as you would obey me, without question and without the slightest hesitation!"

"Go quickly!" she said, and the court hairdresser scurried away to fetch a hat and a coat from his brother's house.

He arrived at Choiseul's residence at two o'clock that afternoon—with the hat pulled down over his eyes and the cloak covering his court dress. Jean-François handed the queen's letter to Choiseul, which contained instructions that it was to be burned immediately after reading. The letter ended with the following words: "I have ordered my servant to obey you as he would obey me in person, and I hereby confirm this order."

Upon reading the letter, Choiseul said, "And you are satisfied that her intention is that you should do exactly as I order?"

"Yes, Monsieur," replied the hairdresser.

Choiseul's servant arrived to say that the duke's carriage was ready. "Come, my dear Léonard," said the duke.

"What! Am I to come? And the diamonds?" asked Jean-François.

"You'll take them with you," said the duke.

"And where?" he asked

"Where I take you," said the duke.

The Dauphin Louis, Queen Marie Antoinette, Madame Élisabeth, and Marie-Thérèse strolling in the Tuileries gardens
(BIBLIOTHÈQUE NATIONALE DE FRANCE)

"And where do you take me?" cried out Jean-François.

"Some leagues away," he said. "You have a special commission to fulfill."

"Impossible, monsieur!" replied Jean-François.

"Why impossible!" asked the duke. "Didn't the queen bid you to obey me as herself?"

"That's true, but how can I do it? I left the key in the door of my lodging. When my brother goes home, he won't find his riding coat or his hat. Not seeing me return, he won't know where I am. And then there is Madame de l'Aage, whose hair I've promised to dress, and who waits for me. As proof of this, monsieur, my cabriolet and my servant are in the courtyard of the Tuileries."

"Come, come, my dear Léonard, what would you have?" said Choiseul laughingly. "Your brother must buy another hat and another riding coat. You must cut Madame de l'Aage's hair some other day. Not seeing you return, your lackey will surely unharness your horse, and take him back to the stable. Meantime, our team is harnessed, and we must be off."

The duke made the dejected hairdresser get into the cabriolet, which then set off at a fast trot. Jean-François had the duke's assurance that he was only being taken five or six miles from home to receive a special commission from the queen, after which he would be free to go about his business.

At the village of Bondy, Jean-François felt relieved to see that the vehicle was about to stop. He was preparing to get out of the carriage when the duke stopped him, telling him that this was not the final destination. Horses had been ordered in advance, and in a few seconds they were harnessed to the carriage. The vehicle was then off again like a flash.

"But where are we going, monsieur?" inquired the queen's hairdresser.

"What does it matter where we are going, provided you are able to start on your way back by tomorrow morning?" asked the Duke of Choiseul.

"Not much, if I can get back to the Tuileries by ten o'clock, in time to dress the queen's hair!" said Jean-François.

"That will satisfy you then?" asked the duke.

"Of course, but if I could get home a little earlier so that I could pacify my brother and explain everything to Madame de l'Aage, that wouldn't be a bad idea."

"Then you needn't worry, my dear Léonard," responded the duke. "You'll find that everything will turn out for the best."

Jean-François obviously had no idea that the Duke of Choiseul had intended to kidnap him. He quieted for a while, but seeing fresh horses harnessed to the carriage at the village of Claye, and hearing nothing said about stopping, the poor fellow exclaimed, "Ah, monsieur, are we going to the ends of the earth?"

"Listen, Léonard," the duke said, much more seriously. "I am not taking you to some country house near Paris, but to the border."

Jean-François groaned and, placing his hands on his knees, gazed at the duke with a terrified look. He stammered, "To . . . to the frontier?"

"Yes, my dear Léonard, for I expect to find there, with my regiment, a letter of the greatest importance from the queen. Not being able to deliver it myself, it was necessary for me to have someone upon whom I could depend to do it for me. I begged the queen to name someone, and she mentioned you as one whose devotion made him well worthy of such a trust."

"Oh, of course, monsieur, I am very proud that the queen considers me worthy of her confidence," said the hairdresser, "but how shall I get back to Paris? I'm in my pumps and my white silk stockings, and I have neither a change of clothing nor any money with me." The poor hairdresser had forgotten that he had two million francs' worth of diamonds in his pockets.

"Don't worry about that, my friend," said the duke. "I have everything you need here in the carriage—shoes, clothing, and money; so you will want for nothing."

Their coach flew along like the wind. Choiseul had ordered his courier to have two beds and a substantial supper awaiting them at the next stop, Montmirail, where they were to spend the night. Jean-François was partially consoled by the fact that he had been selected for such an important mission.

After supper, the travelers went to bed, the duke having ordered the carriage to be ready at four in the morning. Fifteen minutes before that time, the innkeepers were to knock at his door and wake him, just in case he was still asleep.

Count Fersen was present at the Tuileries palace on the evening of the planned escape, though few were aware that he was perhaps the most active participant in the preparations for the flight. As commander of the Royal Swedish Regiment in the king's service, he was an intimate friend of the king and queen, and on the afternoon of the 20th of June, he had paid a last visit to the royal family. He found them resolved to proceed with the departure, despite Bertin's intimations that their plans had been discovered.

The royal couple was deeply affected by Fersen's visit. The king said, in taking leave of him, that he could never forget all that he had done for them, and the queen wept bitterly. To avoid any more suspicion, she then took her children for a promenade in the Tivoli gardens. While there, she told her daughter that she would need to practice the utmost discretion, and not to be surprised at anything she might see or hear in the hours to come.

Fersen returned to his own house to make final preparations. He visited Monsieur Quentin Craufurd in the rue de Clichy to see whether the new coach that was built for the king's journey had arrived. At a quarter to nine the three bodyguards, who were to act as outriders for the royal party, came to Fersen for instructions.

	Miles.	Arrive at.
Paris to Bondy	6 .	3 a.m.
Bondy to Claye . . .	10 .	4.30 a.m.
Claye to Meaux . . .	10 .	6 a.m.
Meaux to La Ferté sous Jouarre .	12 .	7.30 a.m.
La Ferté to Montmirail . .	20 .	10 a.m.
Montmirail to Etoges . .	17 .	noon.
Etoges to Chantrix . . .	13 .	2 p.m.
Chantrix to Châlons. . .	13 .	5 p.m. {allowing for the break-down.
Châlons to Pont-Sommevesle .	14 .	6.30 p.m.
Pont-Sommevesle to Ste. Ménehould	15 .	8 p.m.
Ste. Ménehould to Clermont .	10 .	9.30 p.m.
Clermont to Varennes . .	10 .	11 p.m.
Total .	150 miles	21 hours.

Paris to Varennes: approximate distances and times

Fersen then mounted the box of the hackney-coach in which he was to drive the royal family to the border.

The queen had returned to her drawing room to find the Count of Provence, who had just taken an affecting leave of his sister Élisabeth. The count and his wife were to leave Paris for their safety that night by a different route than the royal family, not knowing if they would ever see each other again. Indeed the brothers met for the last time that day, before the count left the Tuileries. He would not return until 1814. And then, as King Louis XVIII.

Around eleven o'clock in the evening Queen Marie Antoinette knocked at the door of her son's chamber. He was barely awake, but when she told him that he was about to go to a fortress where he would command his own regiment, he jumped out of bed and cried, "Quick! Quick! Give me a sword and my boots, and let me be off!" However, he was in disguise, dressed like a little girl, in a costume which Madame de Tourzel had provided. His sister, who had been awakened earlier, wore a cheap dress of muslin, which had been purchased a few days beforehand.

The two children, accompanied by their governess and two waiting-maids, gathered in one of the queen's apartments. The queen looked out into the courtyard and saw that everything was quiet. The hackney-coach was just outside the door. Fersen,

Tuileries Palace

who had skillfully made every preparation, was dressed like a coachman and posted on the box of the coach.

The queen solemnly entrusted her children to Madame de Tourzel, who rushed them through the dark passages to the unlocked door and into the courtyard. Fersen lifted the children into the coach, assisted Madame de Tourzel, and drove off. A short time afterward the two waiting-maids were sent down another staircase, where a cabriolet was waiting for them on the other side of the Pont Royal, and they drove off to the first stop in Claye.[2]

Fersen, knowing that the king, queen, and Madame Élisabeth could not arrive immediately, took a turn around the Quais, and then came back by the rue Saint-Honoré to the Petit Carrousel. He waited three quarters of an hour, but no one came. At that moment, General Lafayette's carriage, guarded by dragoons, drove by with flashing lights. Lafayette was on his way to the *coucher* of the king. The guards had been doubled, and everyone was on the alert at the palace.

When Lafayette finally drove away, the king was helped to bed by the servant who had charge of the rooms. The doors of the great gallery were locked by the porter in attendance, and the keys were placed in his mattress, where they were found the next morning. As soon as the king was left alone, he got up and dressed himself for the flight.

After the hackney-coach had been waiting in the Carrousel for almost an hour, Madame Élisabeth approached it. Soon thereafter, the king arrived. They were still waiting for the queen when Lafayette's carriage passed a second time.

The king had to hold his tongue from cursing the general, whom he looked upon as his jailer. The queen had found a sentinel posted at the top of the palace staircase she had to descend, and she had to wait until she could safely pass him. When she finally got into the carriage the king embraced her and cried, "How glad I am to see you here!"

Fersen took a roundabout route to drive to the gate of Clichy. The guard house at the barrier was well lit up, but a marriage was being celebrated with drinking and dancing, so the royal party passed unrecognized. A short distance beyond the gate they found the custom-made coach, a large traveling carriage made to hold six persons. It was drawn by four strong Norman horses. Fersen's coachman was riding postilion on one of them, and Monsieur de Moustier, a tall bodyguard, was on the box. Another bodyguard, who had driven the fugitives through the Carrousel, was on the dickey of the hackney-coach. The third bodyguard sped ahead on one of Fersen's horses to Bondy to ensure a relay of horses would be ready when the travelers arrived.

The hackney-coach was driven up close to the berline. The doors of both were opened, and the royal party stepped from one to the other, unobserved. Then the hackney-coach, having served its purpose, was driven into a ditch. Fersen mounted

Royal family's departure for Varennes
(BIBLIOTHÈQUE NATIONALE DE FRANCE)

the box, with Moustier by his side. When they arrived at Bondy, the fresh horses were waiting for them.

Fersen then took an affectionate farewell. He mounted the horse from which Valory, one of the king's guards in charge of the berline's horses, had dismounted, and headed off—eventually reaching Belgium in safety.

At Claye the maids-in-waiting joined the royal family, and the whole party proceeded in full daylight to Meaux. The king was in high spirits. "At last," he said, "I have escaped from that town of Paris where I have drunk so much bitterness; be assured that, once in the saddle, I shall be very different from how you have seen me up to the present moment." At about eight in the morning the king looked at his watch and remarked, "Lafayette must be in a terrible state of mind now!"

The travelers were amply supplied with provisions that had been placed in the carriage. Before reaching Châlons the horses fell twice, breaking the harness on one occasion, which took an hour to repair. Due to the delay in leaving Paris,* the party was two hours late when it arrived in Châlons.

When the king reached Châlons at five o'clock in the afternoon, he believed himself safe. At the next post, Pont Sommevesle, he was to find a detachment of soldiers from Bouillé's army; similar detachments would be posted all along his route until he finally reached Montmédy. But when they reached the lone post-house of Pont Sommevesle an hour and a half later, not a soldier was to be seen. *Where was Choiseul? Where were the hussars that should have been waiting there?*

The horses were quickly changed, and the coach moved on, but a heavy weight now settled on the travelers' shoulders.

It was not Bouillé's fault that his arrangements miscarried; they had been skillfully and carefully made. His subordinates, however, were inexperienced. Most of them had not been informed of the importance of the mission, believing that they were escorting a valuable shipment of bullion, not the royal family. Troops were to be posted at Pont Sommevesle, Clermont, Sainte Menehould, Varennes, Stenay, and Sedan. But all went awry, owing to a break of the link in the first chain of communication.

M. de Goguelat had been sent by the king and queen to assist Bouillé in making the final arrangements. The choice was an unfortunate one because he disobeyed the most important orders that were given him, and everything left to his discretion was badly executed.

Consequently, when the king arrived at the post-house at Pont Sommevesle to meet his escort, there was not a soul there to meet him. He felt "as if an abyss had opened beneath his feet."

---

* It had been falsely reported that the delay was caused by the king, who behaved imprudently by walking ahead of the coach to enjoy the sunshine; it also is untrue that the children caused delay by repeatedly going for long walks in the hills.

Madame la Dauphine Marie-Antoinette, ca. 1775

Marie Antoinette, Queen of France, ca. 1785

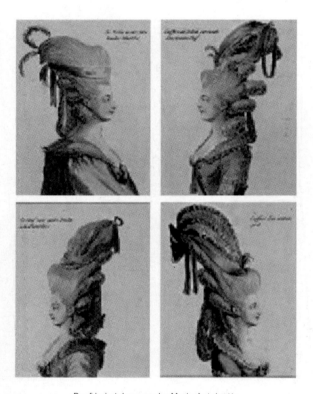

Pouf hairstyles worn by Marie Antoinette
(BIBLIOTHÈQUE NATIONALE DE FRANCE)

Marie Antoinette's hedgehog pouf, ca. 1777

Cœffure
à l'Independance ou le
Triomphe de la liberté.

The coiffure *à Belle-Poule*

Marie Antoinette, ca. 1775

Marie Antoinette *à la rose*

Marie Antoinette's pouf, the *bandeau de l'amour*

Léonard Alexis Autié

(BIBLIOTHÈQUE NATIONALE DE FRANCE)

Marie Antoinette of Austria, Queen of France

Portrait of Marie Antoinette, 1777

Pouf hairstyles worn by Marie Antoinette
(BIBLIOTHÈQUE NATIONALE DE FRANCE)

L'Art de la Coiffure des Dames Françaises, 1767

Marie Antoinette in ermine
(BIBLIOTHÈQUE NATIONALE DE FRANCE)

Marie Antoinette at the Tuileries Palace, 1791

Pouf *à la Victoire*

Pouf *Jolie Femme*

CHAPTER 12

The Fatal Message

"Yes, I know everything. The king has left Paris, but by all appearances he has been prevented from proceeding with his journey."
— Jean-François Autié to the Chevalier of Bouillé
Varennes, France

Pont Sommevesle, France
June 1791

When the queen sent Jean-François to Choiseul on the day of the family's departure, little did the queen's private hairdresser know where the mission would take him. The Duke of Choiseul had taken him in his carriage without telling him where he was going. They slept at Montmirail, left at four the next morning, and arrived at the post-house of Pont Sommevesle soon after eleven. Choiseul found his orderly there with two horses. The hussars appeared an hour later.

Monsieur de Goguelat, who was in command of the party, found Choiseul still dressing, and delivered to him a large packet of orders, which he had received two days before from Bouillé. The orders were very precise. Choiseul was placed in command of all the troops posted along the road, with full liberty to employ force if needed. If he should hear that the king had been arrested at Châlons, he was to attack the town and attempt a rescue. In such a case, he was to dispatch orders all along the line so that support could be sent.

It was from His Majesty that Choiseul would receive his orders once the king arrived at Pont Sommevesle. If the king desired to be recognized, the hussars were to escort him with drawn swords to St. Menehould. If the king wished to remain incognito, he was to allow him to pass quietly. Half an hour later, Choiseul was to follow him along the road, post a body of hussars between St. Menehould and Clermont, who would intercept everyone who came by, either on horseback or in a carriage, from the direction of Paris. In effect, this would prevent the king from being pursued. Further, as soon as he was aware of the king's presence, he was to send M. de Goguelat to inform the several detachments. If this was impossible, he was to carry the news himself.

Choiseul did none of these things.

By some strange miscalculation, the coach was to be expected to arrive at Pont Sommevesle at half-past two in the afternoon at the latest. Choiseul wrote that he became very anxious when three o'clock and four o'clock came, and the courier who was to precede the royal carriage had not arrived. The neighboring villagers, who believed that the soldiers had come to make them pay their rents or seize their property, only intensified Choiseul's precarious situation; the hungry peasants were assuming a threatening attitude and menacing the troops.[1]

At four o'clock Choiseul sent Jean-François off in his own carriage to inform the detachments posted along the road about the delay and that he was still camped in Pont Sommevesle. Choiseul wrote in his memoirs that he waited with his hussars until half past five and then he retreated, not by the highway, but by crossroads to Orbeval. When the king reached Pont Sommevesle at half past six, he found no one there to give him news of the party of hussars, and no sign of any disturbance among the neighboring peasantry.

Choiseul's neglect to wait for Valory, whether preceding the king or not, was inexcusable. He knew Valory to have had orders, if the king failed to reach Bondy, to ride on and inform the detachments that the enterprise had failed.

When Valory reached Pont Sommevesle and found no soldiers, he asked no questions; instead, he ordered fresh horses to be ready for the carriage and he rode on to the next post town, St. Menehould.

St. Menehould was a mix of confusion and uncertainty. When Jean-François passed through with news that the treasury shipment would probably not arrive that day, Captain d'Andoins, the officer in command, ordered his troopers' horses to be unsaddled and his men then dispersed. Half an hour later, Valory arrived at a gallop, and twenty minutes later came the royal fugitives' coach.

The town, by this time, was greatly excited and people were gathering in the streets. Something was happening, but they had no idea what it was.

As the carriage stopped at the post-house it excited much attention. Captain d'Andoins stayed in the background, but whispered to those in the carriage, "Your plans have miscarried. To avoid suspicion I will go away." He also made a sign to Valory to harness quickly, but Valory interpreted this as a wish to speak to him, and their conversation only aroused the attention of the crowd.

Just as the fresh horses were being harnessed, Jean-Baptiste Drouet, the post-master, arrived. A young man of twenty-eight, he had served in the Condé dragoons

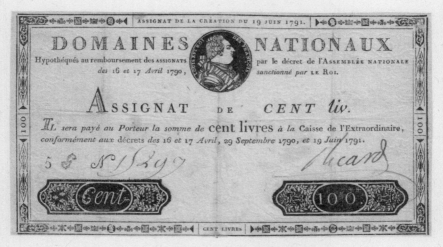

King Louis XVI's likeness on revolutionary currency
(AUTHOR'S COLLECTION)

and had once seen the queen at Versailles; he now thought he recognized her. At this moment the king put his head out the window, and Drouet suddenly remembered the king's portrait on the revolutionary currency, called an *assignat*. He noticed the long aquiline nose, the short-sighted look, and the spotted complexion. He was certain that this was the royal family inside the coach.

Many of the onlookers also claimed to recognize the king. Word spread and the crowd began to hound the travelers; the coach swiftly departed for the next post at Clermont.

Drouet, accompanied by three other citizens, set off at once to spread the news of the royal entourage. As they galloped through the Châlons gate, the newly armed National Guard mistook them for royal soldiers—and fired on them. One was killed and another dangerously wounded. Then a cry arose, "To arms!" The tocsin, the town's warning bell, was sounded and the villagers were all put on alert.

Meanwhile, the king and his family were passing through the beautiful countryside along the banks of the Aire River.* After passing through the upper town of Varennes, they crossed the river by way of a narrow bridge. Just beyond the bridge

---

* The episode at Châlons has been related in various forms, but Princess Marie-Thérèse later noted that the family had certainly been recognized before departing the village.

was the Hôtel du Grand Monarque in the lower town, where, unbeknownst to them, fresh horses were waiting for them. Horses were originally supposed to be there on the road from Clermont, but Goguelat, at the last moment, had mysteriously changed the plans and neglected to give any notice to the travelers.*

Varennes was not used to change horses and postilions; travelers usually took other roads for traveling on to places like Verdun. Varennes was a peaceful little town divided into two parts by the river, and the only means of crossing the river was the ancient stone bridge. Its inhabitants were preparing for a special *fête* when the queen's hairdresser, Jean-François, arrived about eight o'clock with his message for the troops, a message of failure and despair.[2]

"Are you the Chevalier of Bouillé?" asked Jean-François.

Not knowing who was addressing him, Bouillé, the son of General de Bouillé, answered coldly in the affirmative.

"How glad I am to find you here, there are so many things which I must tell you," remarked the hairdresser. But inquisitive and suspicious villagers quickly began to surround them, and Bouillé asked Jean-François to join him in the inn.

"You are to give me the horses that you have here," continued Jean-François.

"Horses, what horses?" asked the chevalier.

"There is no need to be mysterious with me," said Jean-François. "I know everything."

The oblivious Jean-François continued, "Yes, I know everything. The king has left Paris, but by all appearances he has been prevented from proceeding with his journey. I have already warned Monsieur de Damas, who has withdrawn his detachment; the Royal Dragoons regiment has mutinied; there has been a disturbance at Clermont and I had great difficulty getting through."[3]

The Chevalier of Bouillé and another officer, Monsieur de Raigecourt, who were in charge of keeping horses in readiness at the inn, were taken aback by the unexpected arrival of this self-important servant.

Jean-François explained, "I am Léonard, Her Royal Majesty's servant and hairdresser. I know everything. I have with me in this carriage the king's court dress and the queen's jewels. I am going on to Luxembourg where I am to await orders. I shall come to Montmédy if the king arrives there. I am afraid of being arrested, so it is

---

* Choiseul's horses had been stabled in an inn called the *Bras d'Or*, on the outskirts of Varennes, where a change of horses would not likely raise any suspicion. For some unknown reason, however, Goguelat had ordered them to be taken to the *Hôtel du Grand Monarque*, on the other side of the village. General Bouillé ordered that the horses be immediately returned, but the soldier in charge, Bouillé's son, was afraid to order their removal for fear of creating a "fresh commotion" in the village.

essential that I should resume my journey. Therefore, give me therefore the horses you have here and, if you will take my advice, you yourself should leave, because if you remain here you will be exposed to grave danger."[4]

The chevalier assisted Jean-François in finding two fresh horses with the aid of the innkeeper, hoping to get rid of him as soon as possible.[5] The hairdresser had thus accomplished his mission, but he had left behind him a trail of frustration, confusion, and mistrust.

Jean-François, perhaps saddened by the unfortunate news of the aborted flight of the royal family, decided to take the road to Verdun instead of the road to Montmédy, where the General de Bouillé with his staff was awaiting the king's arrival at Stenay. Having been the bearer of bad tidings all along the king's route, he now discontinued his mission—ironically, at the very moment when he might have been of use. Had Jean-François continued on the road to Montmédy, he would have met General de Bouillé en route. And the tales of the bizarre and least-likely messenger could certainly have prompted the general to take his troops along the Châlons road to escort the coach to its final destination.*

The royal family stopped at the entrance of the town of Varennes, where they expected to find horses waiting for them. Yet, there was nothing to be seen and no lights in the villagers' windows. In vain, the king knocked at one of their doors, only to be angrily scolded and told to go away. The three bodyguards set off to look for the missing horses.

Then the two riders, Drouet and a friend, galloped past the carriage, crying out to the postilions, "Don't go on. Unharness your horses. Your passenger is the king!"

"We are betrayed!" Valory responded after a fruitless search for the horses. Their only course was to press forward, but the postilions refused to continue, saying that their mistress had charged them to go no farther than the entrance to Varennes—they were needed the very next day for the hay harvest. It was said that this mistress never forgave herself for having thus caused the misfortunes of the king and queen. The bodyguards at last threatened the postilions to remount and drive the carriage into Varennes. But it was too late.

Drouet pulled up to the Auberge du Bras d'Or, where a few young men still lingered. He entered in haste, drew the landlord aside, and told him the news. They immediately left at once to rouse all the villagers; the king had to be arrested. The landlord woke his neighbor, Mayor Sauce, while Drouet set out to barricade the

---

* Had it not been for their encounter with Léonard, the two soldiers would probably have decided to transfer the horses at nightfall to the appointed position at the entrance to Varennes. The people were now safely in their houses, and many had gone to bed. The only place that remained open was the Bras d'Or, and only a few men still remained in the inn. Transferring the horses would surely have gone unnoticed, and would have possibly been the salvation of the royal family.

The royal family in flight
(BIBLIOTHÈQUE NATIONALE DE FRANCE)

bridge that united the two parts of the town. Two captains, Bouillé and Raigecourt, were sitting at the window of their hotel and heard a little movement in the town, but paid it no attention.

The mayor sent his children to rouse people from their beds. Seven young men armed themselves and prepared to stop the carriage. The post chaise with the two chambermaids came first. They were asked for their passports; replying that they were in the second carriage, the maids were allowed to pass.

The occupants of the royal coach were detained and questioned, claiming that they were on their way to Frankfurt. Mayor Sauce held up a lantern, and scrutinized the faces of the travelers. When the passports were handed to him, he remarked that they were signed by the king, but not by the President of the National Assembly. Due to the irregularity, he felt compelled to detain the travelers until the matter could be settled.

When the postilions attempted to proceed, they were stopped by the armed men, who cried, "If you go a step further, we will fire!"

The royals had no choice but to get out of their carriage. The mayor offered them the hospitality of his house. On the ground floor was a grocer's shop, emitting a strong smell of mutton fat that was particularly disagreeable to the queen. The upper story, reached by a narrow corkscrew staircase, contained two rooms: one looking onto the street, the other onto the courtyard. The royal family gathered in the back one.

The king seated himself in the middle of the room in an armchair. The queen asked for some hot water, wine, and clean sheets. The dauphin and his sister were placed upon a bed and were soon asleep, with Madame de Tourzel seated at their side. The bodyguards sat on a bench beneath the window.

The king could have quite easily been rescued at this moment. Sixty hussars were in their barracks just a short distance from the bridge with their horses saddled and ready. That they were useless in this crisis was due to Goguelat's errors. For some reason he had sent their commander off to General de Bouillé's camp, where he could be of no use. The Chevalier de Bouillé and Raigecourt did the same.

By this time the whole town of Varennes was in chaos. Barricades were being built across all the streets leading out of the town. Choiseul arrived with his forty dragoons at about one o'clock in the morning. They were halted by a barricade and two old pieces of cannon, but they pushed easily through and entered the town. Choiseul marched straight down the street, continued past the house where the royal party was held prisoner and on to the hussar barracks, which he found empty. The hussars and their young commander had already galloped off toward General de Bouillé.

Choiseul drew up his German soldiers and told them that the king and queen were prisoners in the town, and that it was up to them to rescue them. He rushed his troops back to Major Sauce's house. The soldiers might have saved the king, but the customary hesitation and delay prevailed.

In the mayor's house the king had acknowledged himself. Some of those around him were moved to tears, and Sauce was almost ready to give way. Outside, however, was a surging crowd, being stoked by Drouet. The king assured the crowd that he had no intention of leaving France, and he was not going beyond the French border, but a voice cried out, "Sire, we don't believe you!"

Inside the house, the queen wisely tried to draw sympathy from Madame Sauce and Sauce's mother. Old Madame Sauce, a woman of eighty, fell down upon her knees bursting into tears, and kissed the hands of the children. The poor old dame, born in the era of the great King Louis XIV, had venerated royalty all her days, and she still clung to the ways of the past. But the mayor wavered on whether or not to let the royals go.[6]

When Goguelat entered the room, Louis XVI said to him, "Well, when shall we set off?"

"Sire, we await your orders," he answered, and suggested placing the whole party on seven horses belonging to the hussars and carrying them off under guarded protection. But King Louis feared a stray ball might kill one of them. It would have been far easier to have cleared the road with a charge, and then to have driven off in the royal coach. But it was finally decided to wait for General de Bouillé. This decision would be disastrous.

The royal family in Mayor Sauce's house
(BIBLIOTHÈQUE NATIONALE DE FRANCE)

By four o'clock in the morning, word had traveled quite quickly and thousands of peasants had reached Varennes from the neighboring towns and villages. Goguelat had just been wounded by a pistol shot in an altercation with a National Guard; this might have triggered a massacre, but the hussars, instead of attacking the crowd, began to fraternize with them. Jars of wine were passed from guard to guard, and soon the soldiers were half drunk, calling out, "Vive la nation!"

As the sun rose over the lovely valley of the Aire, Sauce asked the king to show himself to the crowd from the window that overlooked the street. Louis saw a dense throng of peasants armed with muskets, scythes, and pitchforks; some women were staggering, half tipsy, among the crowd. When he appeared at the window, there was a deep silence, and when he told those who could hear him that he was going to Montmédy, but that he would afterward return to Varennes, there was a thunder of applause, and reiterated cries of "Vive le roi!" and "Vive la nation!"

At five in the morning an officer of hussars, holding a bare sword, burst into the room where the royal family was assembled. It was Captain d'Eslon, who had been sent off to Bouillé by the blundering Goguelat. At three o'clock in the morning he had heard that two carriages had been stopped at Varennes, containing a man, some women, and children. The captain took seventy of his men and galloped back to Varennes. He was stopped at the bridge, and having little ammunition with him, he dared not charge. After some negotiations, he was permitted to enter the town on foot, and, presenting himself to the king, asked for orders. The king replied he was a now a prisoner and had no orders to give him.[7]

The town officials were deliberating what they should do about the king's departure, when two messengers from the National Assembly arrived. One of them handed the queen the assembly's decree, ordering the return of the royal family to Paris. Louis read it over the queen's shoulder. "There is no longer a king in France," he said.

The queen was less accepting, to say the least. "What insolence!" she cried. Seeing that the paper had fallen on the dauphin's bed, she seized it and threw it on the ground, saying that it soiled her son's bed.

The only chance for the king was to stall until Bouillé arrived. The deputies and the people were eager that he set out for Paris immediately, but Louis entreated that they be allowed to wait until eleven o'clock. In turn, a hasty breakfast was served for them.

As a last resort, Madame de Neuville, one of the waiting-maids, pretended to be seized with a violent illness. The king refused to desert her, and a doctor was sent for to care for the servant. But all these distractions produced only an hour and a half's delay, and General de Bouillé and his soldiers never appeared.

The shouts of the impatient mob surged upward from the street. The carriages had been harnessed and brought up to Sauce's front door; the royal family slowly and sadly descended the winding staircase. The king walked first, followed by Madame de Tourzel and the two children; Choiseul gave his arm to the queen. The bodyguards were placed on the box, guarded by two grenadiers with bayonets fixed in their muskets. Once the royal family had entered the carriage, Choiseul closed the door and bid his king adieu.

The heat and the dust during the royal family's return journey were intolerable. They reached St. Menehould in the afternoon and were held at the gate while the mayor delivered a municipal address. The royal family lunched in the town hall. The queen showed herself to the crowd with the dauphin in her arms. As the king and queen passed through the chapel where the prisoners attended mass, they distributed money to the poor; in the queen's opinion, their circumstances were much like their own. The royals would soon be forced to grovel, just like the masses that they had helped to impoverish had been doing all their lives.

On Saturday, the 25th of June, the royal family returned to Paris. At the perimeter of the city, they were met by a dense crowd of citizens. No one raised their hat or spoke a word. They entered the garden of the Tuileries by way of the swing bridge, and were protected by the care of Lafayette as they dismounted.

Proceedings were set in motion by the revolutionaries against Bouillé and all the agents involved in the king's abduction. The assembly had devised this euphemism to implicate the royalist party as a whole. All those who had taken part in the flight—whether they had emigrated or not—were issued arrest warrants. Curiously, Jean-François was not indicted, and still more curious, he seemed to be in no hurry to return to France, though he could have quite safely. Léonard's youngest brother, who was so anxious about dressing his noble client's hair and so destitute for money when he left Paris, somehow found the means to live in a foreign country for three months without anything being heard of him.

Jean-François did not return to Paris until the end of September, taking up residence in the Tuileries again as hairdresser to the queen until the 10th of August. Despite the ineptitude he showed on the mission, he was able to regain his position in the queen's household and continue his services honorably. After the fall of the monarchy on the 10th, Jean-François lost his means of income, but soon found an administrative position in the army, thinking it prudent to let himself be forgotten.

Royal family escorted back to Paris
(BIBLIOTHÈQUE NATIONALE DE FRANCE)

CHAPTER 13

Léonard in Exile

"Do you scorn hair powder now, and are you longing for the smell of gunpowder?"
—THE COUNT OF ARTOIS TO LÉONARD AUTIÉ
COBLENZ, 1792

June 1791
Paris, France

As soon as Léonard heard of the melancholy return of the royal family, he hastened to the Tuileries Palace. He found Mademoiselle Bertin in the queen's apartment with Marie Antoinette.

"Well, Léonard," said Her Majesty, "I have come back. In spite of all your zeal, Monsieur de Bouillé could not find the means to have us escorted in time; and what is so difficult to believe, he was not able to deliver us when we were arrested, although there was only a handful of peasants around us."

"I would only venture to share some observations with Your Majesty," said Léonard. "The departure was delayed by twenty-four hours; the officer in command of the troops which were to advance into France may have thought that the king had changed his intentions; and the corps, marching without instructions from the Minister of War, could not penetrate into the heart of the kingdom without compromising Your Majesties. In this circumstance it would have been too dangerous to support an order received directly from the king."

"True," said Marie Antoinette, "an order from the sovereign is not sufficient, now that France has twelve hundred kings. Besides, our destinies are written on high, and I truly believe that God sometimes sends us mysterious warnings in our sleep."

The queen then turned toward Mademoiselle Bertin. "I dreamt of you last night, my dear Rose, you were bringing me ribbons of all colors, and I chose several, but as soon as I had taken them in my hands, they turned black, and I threw them back into your boxes in horror. I took up others: green, white, lilac, and no sooner did I hold them, than they too became covered with the color of death. I began to weep, and you wept also, for you loved me in my dream as well as you love me in reality."

"That dream is not surprising after the disagreeable events that have come to pass of late," replied Mademoiselle Bertin, "but please God, it contained nothing that is real except my respectful attachment to Your Majesty."

"You are wrong, Rose," said the queen, turning her head away slightly, "the cannibals of the 5th and 6th of October will force their way into my apartments again; they will murder me."

"Good God, madame, suppress that horrible thought!" exclaimed Mademoiselle Bertin.

"I cannot, my friends," said Her Majesty. "I try to banish those melancholy forebodings, but they return incessantly. I feel almost certain that I shall be murdered. Oh, Heaven grant at least that the hideous tragedy may not take place at the feet of the king! If I was their only victim, and if my death could fix the crown firmly upon my son's head, I would gladly shed my blood for him.

"I am wrong to trouble you thus," said the queen. "Let us change the subject. I must tell you that the only result of our voyage, apart from the complete imprisonment which it has gained for us, is a very bad cold which has fallen to my lot. That good bodyguard, whose devotion, alas, will perhaps cost him dearly, made me walk in the gutter of the rue du Bac, and my feet were wet all through the night. It has been a long time, I should think, since such a thing happened to a queen of France."

When autumn approached in the early part of October 1791, Léonard noted a very remarkable change in Marie Antoinette's habits. Her Majesty seemed to have laid aside that air of grandeur and pride of which the Parisians always complained. The queen moved about in her apartments among the militia; they had been posted in the palace as a guard of safety rather than a guard of honor. She often talked with the officers and even the private soldiers in a familiar manner, asking them about their families, their position, and their happiness.

The queen had many devoted and loyal supporters, but few were very smart. In a revolution, where all the strength is in the hands of the masses, cleverness was the only quality that stood a chance of succeeding against the rebels. On the other hand, it was those devoted subjects who lacked cleverness entirely who were often the most heroic. It seems the two qualities work in opposition to each other, especially in crisis.

Shortly after the removal of the court to the Tuileries, Madame the Princesse de Lamballe, superintendent of the queen's household and longtime confidante, had gone abroad to seek alliances against the revolutionary movement. Unfortunately, Louis and Marie Antoinette could not have employed anyone less likely to succeed in such a mission. The princess was quite beautiful, but seriously lacking in any

The Princesse de Lamballe

diplomatic gifts. She followed the monarchy's fall from power in the French newspapers in England. She resolved to return to France and help—whatever the risk.

One cold, wet evening in October, Léonard went to the Tuileries to report to the queen regarding an errand. He found Her Majesty doing needlework in a small drawing room on the ground floor with Madame de Campan by her side. The king was sitting before a scanty fire with the young dauphin on his knees, giving him a lesson in geography. The rain was beating violently against the window panes, and the wet wind whistled through the branches of the bare chestnut trees.

The queen had begun to permit Léonard to enter after gently scratching at the door—he didn't need to be announced anymore. Assuredly no sovereign was ever so accessible in the final years of her life. Though she was still the Queen of France by title, she was no longer surrounded by the solemn pomp of Versailles. She no longer stood on the purple-carpeted step to the throne with an audience of brilliant courtiers. Instead, the veil was lifted; she now welcomed sympathizing deputies from the government, royal guardsmen, and groups of ladies from the *faubourgs*, the Parisian suburbs, who were still devoted to Her Majesty.

Whenever Léonard had traveled far on foot for Her Majesty, she always made him sit down and tell her about his excursion. Before sitting down on this occasion, Léonard told the queen that a traveling carriage had drawn up as he entered the palace.

"A traveling carriage!" cried Marie Antoinette in surprise. "I can't think who it can be."

At that moment, the door opened and the Princesse de Lamballe entered the room. Léonard would never forget that "sweet, noble face, pale with the fatigue of the journey, but lit up with an expression of the tenderest attachment." She was wearing a bewitching English beaver hat, turned up at the side with black silk cording and three black feathers nodding above it. The princess also wore a little wadded coat, fastened in front with bows of ribbon that failed to spoil the elegant outline of the princess's figure.

The princess must have been shocked when she first saw the queen's condition and the miserable state in which the royal family was living at the Tuileries.[1] The queen's hair had become quite gray, her eyes sunken, and her face haggard. The king, sad inarticulate Louis, crushed with humiliation, scarcely spoke; he warmly took her hand. She too had to submit to the constant watching, now the lot of every member of the royal household. Her old apartments in the Pavillon de Flore of the Tuileries palace were quickly made available. Léonard would soon leave for England, and he would never set eyes on Madame de Lamballe in person again; however, he would later see a likeness of her in the British press—an incredible image that he would never be able to forget.

Toward the close of 1791, when the Tuileries palace had become nothing more than a prison to the royal family, the queen sent for Léonard one evening. After explaining the terrible financial situation in which she and the king found themselves, she ended by informing him, in tears, that they had been reduced to a condition of perilous need. "You will be convinced of the truth of what I say, my dear Léonard, when I tell you that I am obliged to sell some of my own diamonds in order to meet our expenses."

"My heart bleeds for Your Majesty," Léonard said in a broken voice.

"My poor Léonard, your zeal and devotion have never failed us," said the queen. "I expect a new and striking proof of this from you today; for I have something to ask you which will perhaps vex you."

"Nothing could vex me, madame, which Your Majesty thinks right to command me," he said.

The queen took a casket of green leather from her secretary, and handed it to him to open. "These diamonds," said Her Majesty, "have never cost France a penny. They are the stones I brought with me from Vienna in 1770, and nobody has the right to prevent me from using them as I please. Take them to England, Léonard. In London you will easily find a jeweler who will purchase this casket from you. I rely entirely upon your discretion for the management of this business, and upon your integrity for the service that you will render me.

"When you have sold them," she continued, "pay the proceeds to the London representative of Vandenyver, who will see that they are remitted to their proper destination. When this is done, await my instructions in London; they shall be sent to you without delay. It is essential that you depart as soon as possible. The assembly has withdrawn its decree as to passports, but this formality may soon be re-established, and then your voyage could not take place ... and this would distress me greatly, for I am entirely dependent upon its result."

"Madame," he replied, "I shall soon have made my arrangements for departure, if Your Majesty will only give me four and twenty hours."

"That is well, Léonard, I expected no less from your devotion," said the queen. "Such zeal, such perseverance displayed in our service shall not go unrewarded."

"Ah! Madame," said Léonard, "the best reward Your Majesty can extend to me is to believe that I am sufficiently rewarded by the confidence which you place in me."

"Go, then," she said. "The day will come, I hope, when we shall be sovereigns once more, to the advantage of our friends and the confusion of our enemies."

Léonard left the palace that evening and immediately started making preparations for his departure.

Upon the royal family's ignoble return to Paris on the 24th of June 1791, Léonard's Théâtre de Monsieur had been officially renamed Théâtre Français. He had strongly argued against changing the name of the theater, but Monsieur was the king's brother and it was becoming too dangerous to be associated with anything royal. The name change was the least of his worries. Put simply, the name *Léonard* had become so unpopular that the theater asked Léonard to give up his post. He steadfastly refused but after an altercation at the theater one evening, he soon changed his mind. One of the spectators had approached him and chastised him, "What are you doing here, you evil wigmaker? Go take care of your business with the queen at the Tuileries. You will be in welcome territory there."

Léonard, having consented to the removal of his name from the front of the theater and its billboards, now occupied himself solely with the queen's new mission. He had given up his profession as hairdresser some time ago now, but he was still known as the "Coiffeur de la Reine." Although his brother, Jean-François, tried his best to stay out of the public eye, there were too many rumors spreading about Paris; the most scathing one accused him of stealing the queen's diamonds, the jewels that had disappeared mysteriously on the ill-fated flight to Varennes.[2] Jean-François—also known as Léonard—had unwillingly sullied both his brother's first and last name.

Léonard set about shutting up his house. He regretted leaving Paris, but he regretted leaving his little Lucette even more. He considered taking the actress with him, but there was too much uncertainty attached to his current trip. Unable to confide to her about the secret affairs, he consoled himself by writing, "A woman in the midst of armies is always a much compromised article of luggage." He left Lucette behind, reserving the right to send for her at a later date.

As for Léonard's wife, she refused to leave the country with him. In fact, he later learned abroad that she had obtained a divorce. Tellingly, he would never mention her again.

After collecting all the capital he could find, Léonard purchased letters of credit for ten thousand louis, or eight hundred thousand dollars, on London and Amsterdam banks. The queen's diamonds, which he estimated at some 350,000 livres, or about 1.5 million dollars,[3] were divided and carefully concealed among his luggage. Before setting out on the 27th of December 1791, he left his brother Pierre in charge of administering what fortune he still possessed in goods and real estate, but not for long. The revolutionary government began confiscating all the property of those who emigrated.

Very little was written about Pierre Autié; he had held a post in the household of Madame Élisabeth, the king's sister, as coiffeur and valet. When it became too dangerous to be associated with the royal family, he gave up hairdressing, not wanting to dress the "ordinary" heads of Paris.[4] After years of serving the royals, he may have felt himself above it; but the "ordinary" heads of Paris more than likely could not afford his services during these troubling times. At the time of his wife's death, Pierre was a tobacco shopkeeper, living in Versailles. Discouraged, and perhaps financially ruined, he abandoned his children and emigrated to England. He briefly resurfaced on a visit to Paris many years later, but otherwise he too was never heard from again.[5]

Arriving in London on the 30th of December, Léonard took up residence at the Golden Cannon in Piccadilly, an inn which was at that time considered the best in London, at least among French visitors. He was told that the establishment specialized in Parisian cuisine, but Léonard was not at all convinced. When he asked for some thick soup, he was served a "decoction of an alarming paleness, in which swam three great slices of half-cooked beef," which he left untouched. When he received the fricassee of chicken à la française, they brought him a would-be fricassee, consisting of a few bits of fowl stewed in water and served dry. When Léonard asked for the sauce, they pointed to a glass bottle, which the waiter had just placed on the table. He poured a few drops of the bottled seasoning on his plate, and after tasting it claimed, "No highway robber of the Forest of Bondy ever took an unoffending traveler by the throat more violently than did this fatal sauce." He swallowed the remaining fragments of chicken with plain salt, and pretended to have finished his supper, after washing down his meal with three glasses of so-called port—which "burnt the gullet."

"Oh, industrious and learned British nation! How badly you feed and lodge your neighbors!" he exclaimed, as he stretched himself upon a bed which did no more credit to the art of upholstery than the chicken did to the art of cuisine. Nevertheless, he slept as he had dined—out of necessity. But the next morning, he accepted that he had to find a French lodging house.

Léonard must surely have felt alienated in the foreign country. His old partner, Frémont, had died in London some time before and he was without friend or family. Compounding Léonard's travails was the fact that he did not know one word of English, and the French language was far from being widely spoken in London at that time. Although he was certain that a number of people he knew must have emigrated here, how would he ever find them?

Suddenly he remembered that the former court purveyor of feathers and flowers, Madame Martin (au Temple) had started a new business in London, having recently

Piccadilly in the eighteenth century

closed her Paris shop in order to follow a large number of her illustrious debtors abroad.[6]

He discovered that she was situated just yards from the Golden Cannon. Her showrooms were on the first two floors; the workrooms of the flower and feather makers were on the second; and on the third, the "garret," slept the colony of pretty assistants whom Madame Martin had brought with her from France.

She heartily welcomed Léonard, whose profitable business relations with the artificial flower maker in Paris had covered a span of nearly nineteen years. Whenever a lady of the court's new whim promised Léonard a handsome reward in gold coins, he would excite the client with promise of the most fantastic hairstyle. Then he would hurry to Madame Martin and tell her of the "impossible" order they had for that day. The two would split the handsome profit. Madame Martin was known to call the two of them "the fairies of the toilet."

"You in London!" cried Madame Martin when he found her in one of her showrooms, surrounded by a circle of French priests. She penetrated through her black entourage, came toward him, and whispered:

"This must seem very strange to you; and yet these good ecclesiastics are clients who come to me every day from France. Sometimes I also receive visits from titled people, as destitute of money—and even shirts—as they are rich in coats of arms."

"What, my dear lady?" Léonard exclaimed. "Do you harbor at your own expense all those pious veterans of the priesthood?"

"What am I to do, my dear Léonard?" she asked. "A fair wind from Normandy brings them to England with no hope save an unpledged allegiance, no resource save my address, no capacity for work. How can I close my door to them, when I know that no other will be opened for them? But let us speak of yourself: what good errand brings you to London?"

"I am here, dear Madame Martin, in as awkward and helpless, but not as poverty-stricken a position as your worthy Norman priests. Nevertheless, I am commissioned by the queen with the conduct of an important business." Léonard proceeded to tell his old friend about the royal family's financial crisis.

"Poor queen!" she said. "To be reduced to such a strait! I can think of none but the jeweler William who can do your business. My eldest son will take you to him whenever you please, and act as interpreter while you conclude your bargain."

Léonard accepted Madame Martin's kind offer. She insisted that he remain for dinner, and arranged a tour of the workshop for her old friend by one of her cutters. Léonard followed him to the second floor, remarking that he had never seen so active a flower factory before.

"They think," said the young cutter, "that we only make bouquets and garlands here. If the English ladies knew that we made all the different sorts of flowers ourselves, they would cease to buy them. To listen to them, one would think that the climate of the British Isles was as unfavorable to the production of artificial pinks and roses as to the growth of these flowers in their natural state."

Léonard watched the cutter attentively, noting that he seemed to have "suffered the shipwreck of his fortunes through some gust of the wind of adversity."

The guide then led Léonard to a small and almost elegantly furnished room, in which the forewoman was seated at work. Her head was bent over her table as he approached, and she did not seem to notice his presence.

"Mademoiselle Julie," said the cutter, "look up! Here is Monsieur Léonard, who has done us the honor to visit our workrooms."

"Léonard!" exclaimed the worker.

"Julie!" cried Léonard.

The work table was thrown over, and Madame Martin's forewoman was in Léonard's arms, pressing him to her heart, while the guide watched in bewilderment. Léonard found himself face to face with his first mistress in Paris, the fairy of Nicolet's Theatre—the head upon which he had laid the foundation for his fortune.

"Yes, Monsieur Léonard, it is me!" she said, overcome and keeping Léonard's hands captive in hers. "It is the pretty little Julie of Nicolet's, only with twenty-two years added to her age."

"Which do not prevent me," Léonard said, "from still seeing before me the beautiful Julie."

"My work for the day is done," continued Julie, laying down her scissors on the work table. "There are still three hours before dinner time. Sit down in that rickety chair, Monsieur Léonard, and I will tell you the story of my life."

Julie had become the Countess of Norkitten, and when her husband died, she became a very wealthy widow. Her next great love, however, turned out to be a Polish swindler, who stole everything and left her financially destitute in Paris, which is what led to the job with Madame Martin. Léonard and Julie reminisced of their days in Paris, and how Léonard had been most unfaithful with a certain countess—a crime, she said laughingly, that she had repaid him with interest.

Madame Martin kept her promise, and the next day, her son accompanied Léonard to William's jewelry shop on the Strand. Through the intermediary of his young interpreter, he openly told the jeweler about the commission with which he had been charged by the Queen of France; he even displayed the diamonds which Her Majesty had entrusted to him.

"Oh!" said William. "Those stones have been set in Germany, and not recently either. Here is one which I recognize as having belonged to the Empress Maria Theresa."

"Yes, it was from her," Léonard replied, "that her august daughter received them."

"I presume, sir," continued the English merchant, "that before bringing these diamonds you had them valued in Paris, and that you informed the queen approximately of the price which you expected to obtain for them."

"I did, sir, take that precaution," said Léonard, "not that I thought that a purchaser in your nation would not give me a fair price, but in order that Her Majesty might know pretty nearly the value of the jewels she was placing in my hands."

The jeweler weighed the stones one after the other in his hands. "And do you think," he asked, "that you have received a fairly correct estimate of their value?"

"The jeweler to whom I went is looked upon as one of the foremost experts in his trade," said Léonard.

"Well, then, at how much did he value them together?" asked William.

"My countryman thinks that these diamonds are worth to the trade purchaser 350,000 livres," Léonard said, determined to protect the queen's interests as much as possible.

"Your countryman," William replied, "has either a very light hand or a very light conscience; it is easy to see that all these brilliants, which have been set with the want of experience common to the workmen of the last century, are half hidden in their settings. I need not take them out and weigh them to be able to tell you that they are worth one hundred thousand livres above the valuation of the Paris jeweler; and I will at once prove to you that I am able to form an idea of what they weigh without the setting.

"See," the jeweler continued, "here is a single stone which I value at nine thousand livres of your money, without its setting; I will have it taken out, and we will then weigh it, and by comparing it with the tariff, you will see that I am not two louis off."

The experiment was made, and the brilliant diamond, taken from its setting and weighed with the greatest care, proved to be worth 8,974 livres and ten sous.

"You see," continued the English jeweler, laughing, "that my estimate is pretty correct. And so I offer you 450,000 livres, payable at sight on any place in Europe you may be pleased to mention. This is only a trifling transaction, and it is no use to waste time in examining the jewels. Does my proposal suit you?"

"The more so, sir," Léonard said, shaking the merchant by the hand, "since it is the proposal of a man of honor and of conscience."

"And so it is a bargain?" asked William.

"Certainly," Léonard replied, "and I will ask you, sir, to pay over the amount to the correspondent of M. Vandenyver, the banker of the French Court."

"Since you wish to receive the money in London, you must dine with me," said William. "I will serve up your 450,000 livres in banknotes at dessert. Good day, till two o'clock."

When Léonard arrived at two o'clock, he found William in a sumptuous living room; Léonard had since discovered that William had served as Lord Mayor of London in 1788. In the morning Léonard had met a brusque merchant; in the afternoon he was received by a sort of *grand seigneur,* with easy and polished manners, who welcomed Léonard and introduced his family.

The dinner was sumptuous, but long; Léonard discovered that the English love the pleasures of the table, and that they employed their time well. Except when one was eating, however, an English evening passed very sadly. Léonard noted that one elbowed another; the atmosphere was saturated with a *pot-pourri* of perfumes; people yawned at such gatherings without measure and almost without restraint.

The jeweler had taken advantage of a pause between a fantasia on the piano and an Italian song to count out to Léonard the price of the queen's diamonds, and Léonard and his guide took their leave of the merchant and his family at nine o'clock.

Léonard wasted no time in remitting the proceeds of the sale of the queen's diamonds to one of M. Vandenyver's agents, recommending that he transmit the amount to Paris with the least possible delay. William had promised Léonard to keep this transaction secret; but Léonard still worried about Marie Antoinette's enemies, who could easily find some wrongdoing on the queen's part. Despite his precautions, the transaction would cause him much anguish months later.

The sale of her diamonds was not the only task that Queen Marie Antoinette had entrusted to Léonard. He was charged with a number of errands for Her Majesty both in England and on the banks of the Rhine, where he was instructed to travel after completing his business in London. One of his first commissions was to find the infamous Countess La Motte, knowing that in times of revolution it is best to purchase silence than to hope that contempt merely fades away.

By March 1792 Léonard had completed his missions in London and prepared for his departure to the banks of the Rhine, where he was to continue to do the queen's bidding. He had to report back to Her Majesty on the characters, habits, and even the occupations of the emigrants collected in England. This was indispensable—she needed to know how much she could trust those nobles, and if their assistance could really be reckoned on for the restoration of the monarchy in France.

The information Léonard collected and transmitted to the queen from London was not reassuring. The noble fugitives were not in the least interested in the French monarchy. They focused solely on the comfort of their present circumstance, sparing no intrigue and pretense. London had suddenly become a sort of universal academy, in which the more or less titled Frenchmen appointed themselves professors or *virtuosi,* driven by the struggle for existence. Here a marquis opened a philharmonic; there was a fencing academy, under the management of a brigadier general; and on

St. James Street a drawing school prospered under the direction of a captain of the navy.

More than once Léonard came across a certain countess, around whom three years before had fluttered all the butterflies of Versailles. Now she could be seen hurrying along to give a private piano lesson in London, her pretty feet almost touching the pavement through her worn shoes, and her solitary black velvet gown splashed with mud. But sadder still, it was said this countess was now reduced to abandoning herself to the caresses of the "milords" deprived of their favorite French dancers.

Léonard finally embarked for Ostend (part of modern-day Belgium), where he landed after a ten hours' crossing. He commenced a series of communications to the queen upon the habits of the emigration, and even more information awaited him at Coblenz, Cologne, and the surrounding districts. He even gathered some information of such an immoral nature regarding the sexual habits of the emigrants that he refrained from sending it to Her Majesty.

Léonard had for some months been waiting for the Count of Artois, who had made a journey to St. Petersburg. He returned at last, bringing with him a sword with which the Empress Catherine had presented him. His Royal Highness, upon whom Léonard waited in a castle in the neighborhood of Longwy, received him with that charming airiness of manner that he retained throughout his life, in misfortune and in prosperity, so long as love and money remained at his beck and call.

"Well, Léonard," said the prince, "so here you are with the army. Do you scorn hair powder now, and are you longing for the smell of gunpowder? It would not surprise me, my lad. The king my brother, when he substituted the baton of a marshal of France for the stick of cosmetic in your satchel, already initiated you into the calls to arms and the excursions of war."

"*Excursions* is the word, monsieur, and mine, although entrusted to a hairdresser, would have succeeded, if the king had had friends more active to support the movements of the General de Bouillé."

His Royal Highness, passed his tongue over his lips, bit them for a second, and changed the conversation.

"Has the queen given you any message for me?" he asked, pulling on one of his boots, for Léonard had caught him as he was getting out of bed.

"Yes, my prince," Léonard replied, "and if Your Royal Highness would grant me a moment's interview in private, I will communicate various matters to you which Her Majesty did not think fit to entrust to paper."

The prince dismissed the Marquis de Digoine and some officers who were present. Then, Léonard detailed the queen's messages for the count.

"My poor Léonard," said the prince, "I am really sorry the queen did not send you to Monsieur rather than to me; he is so very observant. In order to tell Her Majesty all that she wishes to know, it would be necessary to go very laboriously through a vast mass of papers, and none of my suite has the time to busy himself with it."

The prince showed Léonard two tables placed together and covered with enormous heaps of letters, the greater part of which were still unopened.

"You see, there is enough there to frighten away the most inveterate rummager, except Monsieur, my brother of Provence. Oh, he's different; I remember, in the time of those damned Notables who drove us here, with what delight he used to wade among the petitions, remonstrances, supplications, and all the litter of papers with which we were inundated.

"But I have an idea," continued the prince with a smile. "Why should not you, Léonard, undertake to gather from all this correspondence the information which the court desires? You can follow my staff for a fortnight, with a wagon loaded with all that baggage, and when your work is done, you will be able to report on it directly to Their Majesties."

"Monsieur, I will obey Your Royal Highness's commands."

"Well done, Léonard. You are now promoted to be my secretary *pro tempore*. Tell me, is not my hair a little out of curl?" asked the prince.

"A touch of the comb will put it right," said Léonard.

And the prince's new secretary *pro tempore* rearranged his curls and covered them with a sprinkling of powder. The Count of Artois next donned, with Léonard's assistance, his uniform as Colonel General of the Swiss Guards, and asked for his sword.

Once the prince left, Léonard began to occupy himself with his new task. For three days he went through the papers that had accumulated on the prince's desk. However, he never found more than a few lines showing devotion to the imprisoned royal family in Paris; rather, he found requests for money or advancements, empty words, and threats.

On the fourth and last day in the prince's archives, Léonard found the most alarming letter. The Counts were planning on placing sovereign authority in the hands of Monsieur, the Count of Provence, who would thus become the regent of France while his older brother, Louis, was jailed in the Temple.

The princes' army in exile did not favor regency in the Monsieur's name; it hardly ever saw him. When Madame Balbi, his so-called favorite in exile, heard that he had not been to the French camp, she advised the prince to "go and see them more frequently."[7] The support of the troops was imperative for any mission to save the imprisoned king, but the Monsieur did not follow her advice. This inactivity speaks to the Monsieur's "come what may" attitude; in any case, he was still next in line for the throne, as Léonard knew. The discovery was something Léonard could not share with Her Majesty, who was still holding out hopes that her monarchy would be saved by the foreign powers. The news would simply flatten her.

PART FOUR

The Struggles to Survive

(BIBLIOTHÈQUE NATIONALE DE FRANCE)

CHAPTER 14

Sorrowful Events

*"Ah, my sweet Versailles! My charming Paris! Where are you? Come, Léonard,
tell me a story of our good days to enliven me a little. Rummage once more in your
powder bag and bring out an anecdote. Tell me of your career as a hero, when you
were a duke, a count, a marquis, a president . . . by proxy."*
—THE COUNT OF ARTOIS TO LÉONARD
SEPTEMBER 1792

Coblenz, Germany
August 1792

Léonard left Verdun to rejoin the two princes near Coblenz, where their uncle generously provided for them at his summer residence of Schonbornlust. Léonard was carrying with him the papers that the princes had forgotten when they departed. After
handing them to the king's brothers, he informed them of his intention to return to
England—to continue carrying out the queen's instructions.

The Count of Provence was confused, wondering how Léonard could possibly
receive the queen's instructions considering that she was "confined in the Temple."[1]

"My prince," said Léonard, "since the occurrences of the 10th of August I have
never ceased receiving the queen's instructions."

Léonard was referring to that morning in August when the palace of the Tuileries was savagely invaded by Parisian mobs. A great number of the palace's inhabitants were slaughtered, all its luxurious furniture and art destroyed, and its royal family
escorted to the National Assembly nearby for safety. There it was decided that the
family should be removed to the Temple, a medieval dungeon built by the Knights
Templar; two days later they were imprisoned there to await their fate. In a flash, the
French monarchy was no more.

Attack on the Tuileries, 10th of August 1792
(BIBLIOTHÈQUE NATIONALE DE FRANCE)

The count was surprised that Léonard was able to maintain contact with the royal prisoners. "That seems very extraordinary," the king's brother said, "but I think, Léonard, you ought to communicate to me the nature of the intelligence which you have kept up with the crown."

"I meddle, monsieur, neither with war nor politics," said Léonard. "True, what the queen deigns to ask of me has nothing to do with the ordinary attributes of a humble hairdresser; but as those who second me risk their lives at every moment, I could not, without sacrificing them, extend my relations. Your Royal Highness will understand that so dangerous a secret must not leave my breast."

"Very well, Léonard, very well," replied the count. "I will not ask you for a confidence which you cannot give. And when do you return to London?"

"As soon as I have received Your Royal Highness's orders and those of the Count of Artois," said Léonard.

"I shall devote tomorrow to preparing mine," said the count. "I shall be glad when you are over there. Our agents in London are worthless: they go about drinking tea, making love to the English ladies, and listening to strains of the famous Viotti."

The royal family escorted to the Temple Prison
(BIBLIOTHÈQUE NATIONALE DE FRANCE)

"You shall be our emissary to these gentry, you must rouse them for us," he added. "Do you understand me, Léonard?"

"Perfectly, monsieur," he said.

"Go and see Monsieur the Count of Artois, who will give you his instructions also. Have you a good memory?" asked the count.

"Certainly, my prince," said Léonard.

"That is fortunate, for my young brother never writes a line. It takes up too much time, he says, and yet God knows that he generally does not know what to do with his, unless it is the time between night and morning."

There was a touch of sarcasm in the prince's remark, as there was always a tug of war between the princely brothers. The Count of Artois was perhaps unwilling to accept his brother's unofficial, self-proclaimed regency while King Louis XVI was imprisoned. The Count of Provence no doubt was displeased with his brother's refusal. Léonard knew better than to respond and get in the middle of the brothers' dispute; he immediately took leave to ask the Count of Artois for his orders.

When Léonard arrived, the Count of Artois was with an officer who had just brought news of the death of Vicomte de Mirabeau, the great minister's brother. The officer was about to give the details of the funeral honors to be rendered to the general when His Royal Highness interrupted him, saying, "That honest vicomte, his belly is bound to have caused his death. On the battlefield, it was too big to escape the enemy's bullets for long; and outside the lists of war, it was too greedy to escape indigestion.

"Since you tell me that the vicomte died in his bed," he continued. "I am sure he must have succumbed to the consequences of a great dinner, as he would otherwise have succumbed to the consequences of a great battle. Go on."

The soldier did not respond to the levity. The prince turned to Léonard and said, "Oh, laugh, Léonard. There is no harm in laughing; it foils our most formidable enemy, weariness. As for me, I am eaten up with weariness, and if it lasts long, I believe on my honor I shall end by joining that poor Vicomte de Mirabeau.

"What the devil is there for me to do here?" continued the prince. "The emigrants are all ruined. There is no play possible, the lady emigrants are growing old, and I am tired of my studies in ancient history. The German women are sentimental and cold; and as to the German princes, you can't go hunting with them for an hour without fearing to step out of their estates.

"Ah, my sweet Versailles! My charming Paris! Where are you? Come, Léonard, tell me a story of our good days to enliven me a little. Rummage once more in your powder bag and bring out an anecdote. Tell me of your career as a hero, when you were a duke, a count, a marquis, a president . . . by proxy."

After listening to Léonard reminisce about his days at Versailles, the Count of Artois then gave him his orders for England in the usual fashion; as the count's brother warned, it was all done verbally, not a word was written down. The prince then drew a note from his pocket which he had received that morning and asked Léonard to read it.

Léonard read aloud: "Three of the count's carriages and nine others belonging to French noblemen, although deposited in a place of safety, have just been discovered and seized by one Michael Horn for the sum of 1,104 livres owed to him by the princes."

"We did invent a means," said the prince, "which, with the aid of the engraver's art, was of some use to us. But it did not last long; the people of Coblenz saw through our secret.

"We were never so unfortunate as at present," he continued. "Assignats [revolutionary currency notes] given in payment or discounted by messieurs the emigrants are continually being sent back from Paris, with reports declaring them counterfeit. They say there are four million of them in circulation."

"Your Royal Highness knows how selfish the people of Coblenz are," said Léonard, "and you may imagine their outcry, but it is we who are the victims."

"You can understand, my dear Léonard," said the prince, "that to be called pickpockets is not pleasant for the Princes of the Blood; the position ceases to be tolerable. Should there really be any means of helping us, it is high time to do so now."

"The means are there, monsieur, and I have an appointment in Dover with someone well known to Your Royal Highness, who is assisting us greatly."

"Oh, oh, and the name?" asked the prince.

"I may not tell yet but it is quite certain and the assistance will be one of two or three millions."

"It must be a woman of the court. Go, and be brave, for we are reduced to selling our breeches. Don't think I am joking. See here, Léonard, read this letter written to one of my staff officers, by his friend, Madame Le Bouhour."

Léonard was shocked by what he read:

I have sold the clothes of which you spoke, and also your breeches. I have made every effort to sell them for as much as possible; I assure you I have had a deal of trouble, for I had them taken to every house. At last I sold them to Monsieur Cul for one louis. As to your waistcoat and your breeches, I could get nothing for them. What wretchedness, my heart![2]

On an evening in October 1792, Léonard stood on the jetty at Dover, watching the arrival of another ferry from Calais. It was low tide and the passengers had to be carried ashore on the backs of sailors. With his spyglass Léonard attempted to get a

Docks of Dover

better look at the travelers who were disembarking. Among them, one lady seemed to be a rather heavy burden for her sailor. She was careless in her position on the Englishman's shoulder, exhibiting an entire leg.

Léonard knew that leg quite well. Moments later he received Madame the Countess du Barry in his arms as she leaped from the back of her carrier. She was over forty, but still as fresh and pretty as ever. She greeted Léonard graciously, and when she squeezed his hand he vividly remembered his times at Luciennes.

"We are old friends, Léonard," said the countess. She leaned on his arm as he led her to a "French"-run inn.

"You speak of old friends, madame; in truth, it is difficult to believe, when one looks at you, that you can have any of that sort," said Léonard, turning up the flattery.

"True, I have some young ones too," she said.

Chatting along the way, they reached the inn where the countess quickly found her rooms. Eager to speak with Léonard, she sent her maid and her manservant away, telling them to see to her trunks and her carriage.

When they were alone, Madame du Barry made Léonard sit by her side and told him that she had received all the letters he wrote her from the Rhine, as well as the response to her offer of financial assistance made in 1789. She explained that it was not possible to send anything from France either into the Temple or to the emigrants in Germany, because her house at Luciennes was being watched day and night by the patriots. "To remove a toothpick from it would ensure a search," she said, "and I dare not even expose the treasures it contains to the light of the sun."

Madame du Barry had no choice but to leave France in order to come to the assistance of the royals. She led the municipals of Luciennes and other government officials to believe that she came to London in pursuit of her diamonds, which were stolen. But this was only the pretext of her journey. The story of Madame du Barry's diamonds, filled with historical, illustrious personages, was as thrilling a tale as that of the famous Affair of the Necklace.

When Louis XV's favorite was politely banished from court, Louis XVI gave her a pension—although she had been one of his and the queen's bitterest enemies. She retired from the court, spending the next fifteen years in a convent and then at her château in Luciennes.

On the evening of the 10th of January 1791, Madame du Barry had paid a visit to a friend in Paris, and remained in the city overnight, leaving her valet in charge of the château. He made the tour of the house on the following morning, and when he came to the bedchamber of Madame du Barry, he was startled to find that it had been ransacked during the night.

He immediately reported the case to the authorities, and a sergeant and two mounted police returned with him to make a careful examination of the château.

Papers and letters scattered over the floor of the chamber implied that the thieves had been searching only for jewelry or money, not for documents. When the countess returned, she submitted a list of the vast number of diamonds, rubies, and sapphires that were missing.

The announcement of the daring crime produced ambivalence among the French people. They could not forget that the countess had profited from the oppression of Louis XV, and had amassed her fortune from the money "extorted by violent means from the toil-worn people." Yet there were those who discredited the whole story as a fabrication, maintaining that it had been invented so Madame du Barry could have an excuse for leaving France.[3]

Madame Countess du Barry

Madame du Barry could find little repose until the mystery could be cleared up. Having already made three trips to London, thinking that the diamonds and the thieves were holing up there, she decided to make a fourth.

"I have really come to discuss with Monsieur and Madame de Crussol, with Madame de Calonne, with the President Deville, and with you, my dear Léonard," continued Madame du Barry, "the best means of selling two diamonds valued at two millions which I had buried in a safe spot in the woods near Saint-Germain. The proceeds shall be at the disposal of the illustrious captives, or of the princes, according to the more or less pressing needs of either."

"If you will believe me, madame," said Léonard, "go to none of those whom you have mentioned. They are all in want of money, and the sum which may be of use in fighting for the cause of the Throne would be greatly diminished to the advantage of private necessities.

"It is on the banks of the Rhine that the source of the blood shed for the king should be nourished," he continued, "even then, the division of the supplies will be a difficult matter enough. Listen, madame, I know an English jeweler who will buy your two diamonds and pay for them on the spot."

"What? Two million?" the countess inquired.

"He may even offer more than you ask for them; that is his way," said Léonard.

"Well, I will put myself in your hands," she said.

"But madame, watched as you are, have you not felt any alarm lest your diamonds should be stolen?" asked Léonard.

"That would be impossible. I carried them on my person," she said.

"All the more reason," said Léonard with a smile.

Madame du Barry and Léonard set out the same night for London, where they arrived early the next morning. The countess was expected, already having had lodging arranged by Monsieur de Bouillé. The son of the Duke of Orléans, the Princess of Henin, the Duchess of Mortemart, Monsieur Bertrand de Moleville, and the Baron de Breteuil were living in the same house, forming a colony of supporters for the royal cause. Their mission was to persuade the Cabinet of St. James to declare war on the Republican government of France. The British government and aristocracy were aligned with the French Court, though the British people were not. In 1792, notions such as liberty, equality, national sovereignty, and Republican principles were as freely invoked in London as in Paris, putting the government in a very precarious position. It was fearful that the revolutionary spirit would travel across the Channel.

Léonard took up quarters again in his little lodging on Air Street, where Madame du Barry visited two days later. It was barely seven o'clock that October morning and he was still in bed. The countess entered without hesitation and plumped herself down at the foot of his bed.

"I could not wait before coming to see you, my dear Léonard," said Madame du Barry. She was anxious to tell him that his thoughts on the French nobility had proved absolutely true. They had all asked her for money and more than twelve thousand francs had already passed from her pockets into theirs. She was now determined to assist those "poor devils" on the banks of the Rhine who had sold their breeches, and before the emigrants swallow up her two diamonds, she wanted to place them in safekeeping.

"Nothing easier," said Léonard. "Since you have determined to sell your diamonds in order to assist the princes and hasten the release of the illustrious captives of the Temple, let us go this very morning to my jeweler William, and let us finish this piece of business at once."

"That is a good idea," she said. "Well then, I am ready to start, Léonard."

"But, madame, how can I proceed to make a so very elementary toilette in your presence?" he asked.

"Chaste and shy Léonard," Madame du Barry said with a hearty burst of laughter. "I have always heard that when anything alarms one, one should proceed as far as possible in its direction, so as to know what one has to deal with . . ."

"Alarms? Ah, what a word, madame!" he said, remembering his earlier visits to her château in Luciennes.

Just before they were about to enter William's shop together, Madame du Barry decided that it would be better if Léonard conducted the business alone, and she asked him not to reveal that the diamonds belonged to her. Madame du Barry did not wish all of Europe to know how lucrative Louis XV's affection proved to be.

Madame du Barry waited for Léonard in her carriage outside William's door. He went in alone, and while he was concluding his business with William, a gentleman passed by Madame du Barry's carriage. Recognizing Madame du Barry in the carriage window, he reproached her for not telling him earlier about her arrival in London.

The countess replied somewhat coldly, but he continued to speak with her, not noticing her tone. He wondered what she was doing outside "the richest jeweler in the world."

When she replied that she was waiting for Léonard, who was helping her with a "little diamond" to pay off her debt, the man seemed surprised, both at the countess's precarious situation and the fact that "Léonard, the confidant of the French court, and the vainest man in the world, should consent to sell a *little* diamond."

He then bowed to Madame du Barry, who was delighted to see him go away—though he did not remain so for long.

Pure joy is always indiscreet. In his delight at having sold Madame du Barry's two brilliants for 2,200,000 livres, that is to say for two hundred thousand livres more than she had hoped to obtain, Léonard called out this enormous figure to her from the jeweler William's door. He did not notice at that moment that a shoeshine, whose box stood near the carriage, suddenly ran off.

During one of the three journeys that the countess had made to England, she had made the acquaintance of a very polite young man, who came to her aid when she suffered an attack of seasickness. This gentleman had asked and obtained permission to wait upon Madame du Barry in London; she was unaware that the amiable countryman was Republican Blache, a sworn enemy of the court.

Within an hour after leaving Madame du Barry, the shoeshine Blache told one of his fellow Republican spies that he was certain that the missing diamonds were actually stolen by the agents of the dethroned king. Having heard that she was selling diamonds (and hearing Léonard's profit from William's door), he was convinced that they were part of the stolen diamonds from Luciennes. If so, they could be used to fund the king's return to the throne.

It was ten o'clock in the evening, and Léonard had just returned from spending the day with Madame du Barry and her noble colleagues at the hotel. The nobles had become so friendly that they allowed Léonard to dine with them—as though Louis XVI's promise of nobility had finally been realized. The exhausted Léonard was preparing to go to bed when suddenly a woman rushed into his room, panting with terror. It was Julie.

She cried out for Léonard to follow her. There wasn't a moment to lose; he was about to be arrested! There was already a constable at the door.

Léonard resisted, saying he had nothing to fear. Julie then seized his hand and dragged him toward the staircase, but it was too late. The constable and his men were already in the house, at the foot of the staircase.

Julie then pushed Léonard into a little passage with a window at the end of it. She opened the window and told him to jump; it was hardly eight feet to the grass below and she would follow him.

Léonard landed on the ground below. Grasping his hand once more, she hurried him across the little garden, opened a gate, and they soon found themselves at a house on a little street near Piccadilly. Having climbed to the second floor, they entered Julie's room and she said, "Here, friend Léonard, is all that is left of my wealth. I pay four guineas a quarter to my landlord, and I do not share it with anyone at present."

"What? And where is your cutter?" asked Léonard, referring to Julie's protégé and lover.

"Yesterday you did not give me time to tell you, so eager were you to go and play Louis XV the Second!" she said, referring to his rendezvous with Madame du Barry. "The count has been in Poland for the last two months."

"Mischief, this Count Delvinski! And after all you have done for him?" said Léonard.

"He is struggling to do much more for me," she said, "and endeavoring to recover in Poland some last remnants of fortune, but especially honors, which he will invite me to share."

Léonard found a place by the fire blazing in the hearth as Julie continued her story. She had been delivering flowers to a noble client when she encountered three gentlemen speaking English. She overheard them discussing the immediate arrest of the famous Léonard, who was accused of having sold some of the diamonds stolen in France. The English minister had consented to his arrest; it was a clear case for extradition. Madame du Barry would have been questioned, but the minister said there was no case against her.

Léonard was taken aback when he heard he was proclaimed the thief of the crown diamonds. Worried that the news would compromise Madame du Barry, he decided to immediately go to the countess, but Julie persuaded him to remain in her room; he would be arrested the minute he set foot in the street. Julie offered to take a letter to Madame du Barry for him the next day. He agreed, and thanked her.

Léonard brought up the more immediate matter of where he would sleep that night. Julie pointed to a likeness of Count Delvinski, painted in the uniform of a Polish officer, and told Léonard that she had promised to marry the count. And she wished to remain faithful to him.

"I am abject," said Léonard.

"That should be quite easy," Julie said with a smile, "after a whole day devoted to the Countess du Barry."

Léonard made no reply aloud, but said to himself, "She shall pay for that impertinence."

Julie laughed and threw a pillow and a mattress on the floor, making two beds out of one, and said, "There, dangerous Léonard, there is your bed. Envelop yourself, as the wise man says, in your virtue. You shall be quite comfortable."

Léonard said nothing. She put out the lamp, and they climbed into their own beds. But half an hour later she exclaimed, "Léonard, Léonard, they are right—you are a thief! But I am good-natured, and I shall not ask for your extradition!"

According to an old French proverb, "Night brings counsel."[4] Léonard had time to reflect upon his situation, which was much more critical than it had first appeared. He could either leave London immediately and cross the Channel to France, or stay and be forced to explain the origin of the diamonds he had sold to William. If he left London, he would not be able to fulfill his mission for the exiled princes, but if he remained and revealed that the diamonds he sold belonged to Madame du Barry, he would arouse royalist suspicions, compromising the countess herself and thus making her return to France impossible. He saw no middle ground.

Julie went to the flower factory, but quickly returned. She had found a letter for Léonard at Madame Martin's and she brought it to him, knowing that it had been delivered by Madame du Barry's own servant. Léonard promptly opened it:

> Set your mind at rest, my dear Léonard, you shall not be taken back to France bound hand and foot; your interests have been secured. I learned yesterday what had taken place; it was a little late in the evening to wait upon the Chancellor of the Exchequer; but the danger was imminent, and Mr. Pitt never sleeps. I went to his house, and on giving my name to the footman was immediately shown in.[5]

The letter explained that Mr. Pitt had authorized the arrest of Léonard for taking part in the alleged robbery of the diamonds. She showed Mr. Pitt the invoice from the jeweler who sold them to her in 1773; however, he already knew the diamonds were actually her own personal property.

Louis XVI bids farewell to his family
(BIBLIOTHÈQUE NATIONALE DE FRANCE)

Mr. Pitt told the countess that William was under orders to inform him of any purchases from the French emigrants; he knew everything that had transpired at the shop of the jeweler. He also knew that the countess wanted him to stop Léonard's arrest, because it was only through him that the princes could receive financial assistance. And, thanks to Lucette, Léonard was the only conduit of information to the royal family in the Temple prison.

Léonard was to be arrested only for appearance's sake. In fact, he had fled the scene too quickly; the policemen were only instructed to take him to supper and then let him go. The minister then told the countess that Léonard was free to travel throughout London. She ended her letter on a lighter note:

> So that is our case, my dear Léonard. Little snail hiding in your shell, come out again without fear; the Patriots' big feet shall not crush you. I would not go to bed before writing you all this. I am racked with sleep, but I shall not get into bed before I have sent this letter to Madame Martin, who will doubtless find a means of conveying it to you. Come and see me in the evening. Au revoir.[6]

209

Léonard saw the countess that evening in bed, surrounded by almost as numerous a court as that in her days at Versailles. Once the distributor of great offices, titles, and orders, now Madame du Barry was only courted for the sake of obtaining money. Many of the courtiers were broken-down priests, ancient lady emigrants, and faithful servants who had gone into exile for love of masters who were unable to support them.

"Young men of fashion and pretty women on the right side of forty," said the ex-Favorite, "are never in want, wherever they may be."

When the crowd of courtiers had all departed, Madame du Barry and Léonard arranged for a considerable sum to be sent to the princes. This would enable them to reacquire their carriages and to pay an installment on the money due to the Royalist troops without being driven to counterfeit more assignats. By this time, however, Louis XVI had perished on the scaffold in Paris. Day after day, torrents of blood deluged the square that had come to be known as the Place de la Révolution.

CHAPTER 15

The Queen Is No More

"Ah, how I regret the smiles which I have lavished on those monsters! How I hate myself for granting them my favors! Léonard, I have become a Royalist I think . . . and yet I am not sure; for I know that among your party there are many deplorable passions, too.

Had this been otherwise, they would at least have saved that unhappy queen, whom the cannibals dragged to execution in a cart after a slow agony of misery, privation and outrage. The wretches!"

—LETTER FROM LUCETTE TO LÉONARD
DECEMBER 1793

London, England
January 1793

After several days of mourning for his brother Louis XVI, the Count of Provence declared himself the regent of the Dauphin Louis Charles, the young child still imprisoned at the Temple with his mother Marie Antoinette, his aunt Madame Élisabeth, and his sister Marie-Thérèse. According to the fundamental laws of royal inheritance, the count would serve as regent while the dauphin—now known as Louis XVII by the royal supporters—was still a minor.

To restore the Bourbon monarchy, the Count of Provence had been leading the emigrants against the Revolution and the forces of the Republic. These forces were made up of hordes of rebels who defended the French border and invaded its neighbors to attack the count's armies; they were the very same rebels that had attacked the Tuileries, murdered the king's guards, and guillotined their sovereign.

The death of Louis XVI was known in London on the 23rd of January 1793; the entourage of French emigrants in London put on their morning dress for their martyred king.[1] Léonard saw Madame du Barry that evening, surrounded by courtiers once again. After the crowd departed, Léonard and the countess made arrangements to send a considerable sum to the princes on the Rhine.

To Léonard's dismay, and despite the advice of her friends and the accounts of the danger to which she would expose herself, Madame du Barry revealed that she was determined to return to France.

"Wait," said Léonard, "the storms of the Revolution, like those of nature, can be but passing ones. You are certain to win your lawsuit, and the diamonds stolen from you will be returned. Their proceeds and the capital which you brought to England with you should suffice to assure you an honorable existence throughout a long life; and I once more repeat, the troubles in France cannot continue."[2]

"My dear Léonard," she said, "but what can those people do to me, when full of confidence I return to live among them?"

"They will accuse you of plotting," he said.

"Impossible!" she said. "An impenetrable mystery surrounds the remittances which I have made to the banks of the Rhine; and now that the British cabinet is about to declare its position against the Republic, I have no reason to fear that Mr. Pitt will break his word."

"The services which you have rendered to our exiled countrymen will be made into crimes," said Léonard. "And then, madame, realize that your wealth will be looked upon as a proof of your guilt, though you should dress your head with a red cap. Have you forgotten how they cried, 'War to the châteaus, peace to the cottages!'"

"I shall tell them to take all I possess!" she said.

"Madame Countess, I am in despair at seeing you so obstinately determined upon your unfortunate project," said Léonard. "They will kill you."

"I do not think so," she replied. "And besides, I must absolutely return to France. Léonard, I am forty-two years old, and love has become to me as soup or beef. But there is one passion which seems to spring from the ashes of the myrtles consumed; a passion which no longer fires the breast, but dominates the mind—I mean the love of riches."

And rising, the ex-Favorite went to her desk, took a large sheet of paper from it, and handed it to Léonard. She said: "I have no secrets from you; read this."

Léonard took the paper and started to read. It was the accounts of Madame du Barry's hidden treasures at Luciennes. Silver and gold place settings, diamond necklaces, thousands of gold coins, pearls, and emeralds were hidden throughout the château, its cellars, and its gardens.

"Yes, madame," he said, returning the paper to Madame du Barry, "I can imagine that one does not willingly abandon such riches as these."

"And note this," she said, "to anyone who said that all this cost me no great trouble to acquire, I should reply, 'Possibly. But since I am no longer able to procure any more by the same means, I must preserve what I have, even at the risk of my life.'"

"Ah, madame, that is a very high price," said Léonard.

"You are always thinking of the cost, Léonard," she said, "but I only look at the absolute value. I shall go in a week."

About this time it became impossible for French people, undecided between emigration and business, to remain in England—Great Britain was at war with the stormy French Republic. It was necessary either to declare oneself an emigrant, become a naturalized English citizen for reasons of business, or leave England immediately to keep from losing one's French citizenship. Madame Martin, for one, had been forced to leave England because she owned land in the Touraine and it would have been confiscated if she applied for naturalization. No foreigner was ever permitted to own property in France.

Léonard had again subsumed his own life for that of the court. Up to that moment, Léonard had been so preoccupied with his mission for the royals that he had not given much thought to his own exile in England. His splendid household goods in the Chaussée-d'Antin and his stake in the Théâtre Feydeau were about to be confiscated and sold for the profit of the nation. His brother's letters detailed the situation in France, which prevented him from returning. Léonard was regarded as an agent of the princes and of Minister Pitt. Lucette also wrote to Léonard; the little actress had succeeded in preventing the confiscation of his property up to this time.

Lucette, although a Royalist, found herself admired for her Republican virtues, allowing her to flit between the Temple and the Committee of Public Safety, between the red cap of the Republic and the fleur-de-lys of the Monarchy. She was so confident of her position that she strongly recommended that Léonard return behind the shield of her own popularity. But Léonard found that too risky. "Wait, wait," he wrote, "and see what happens."

Léonard escorted Madame du Barry to Dover, deeply saddened by her departure. As he stood on the shore, after bidding farewell, she appeared in his view, standing on the bridge of the ferry—for a moment it appeared as though she was already mounting that terrible instrument of the Revolution—the guillotine.

On his return to London, Léonard received a morning visit from Julie. As a French woman and not naturalized, she was forced to leave England. She was too old to go and join the patriots in Paris; instead, she would travel to Poland, marry her Count Delvinski, and grow old as a Polish princess.

When Léonard asked her if she had any means, she replied that her furniture and her cutting tools were more than sufficient for the journey. But Léonard was not convinced; she required more than that to rejoin her count and he reminded her that she had a good friend of some twenty-two years' standing in London.

"I should have thought that I proved to you the other night that I remembered it very well," said Julie.

"Then remember it altogether," he said, "and permit me to be your banker to the extent of two or three hundred louis."

But Julie refused Léonard's offer; their friendship was not based on such an unnatural souvenir. When she told Léonard that she was leaving at the earliest opportunity, he decided to accompany her and they would part in Holland, where she had some business.

In vain Léonard urged Julie to take his money. Perhaps the famous fairy of Nicolet's Theater had forgotten that she had helped Léonard move from the decrepit rue des Noyers to the boulevard du Temple—bringing only his magical comb with him. When he decided to leave London, he was already leaving behind four or five hundred louis. Hoping not to lose any more, he thought it was high time that he should depart.

After a crossing of thirty-six hours, Léonard and Julie reached Ostend on the Flemish coast. Early the next morning, they then embarked on a barge on the canals to Holland; a means of transport he only consented to after Julie begged him.[3] After a month in Amsterdam, Léonard had finished the queen's business that had brought him to the capital, but the couple remained another six weeks during which they enjoyed a renaissance of their love. "What I also learnt for the first time," he noted, "was that when old bonds are refastened, they can never again be broken off."*

Duty soon called for Léonard to rejoin the princes. There also had to be many letters awaiting him at the different addresses he had given in Germany. Julie reproached herself for having delayed so long before going to Poland. When Julie finally made up her mind to go, she said, "I will take ship for Danzig. One should always hasten voyages in which one has regret and sadness for sole traveling companions."

"And I will leave at the same time," said Léonard, kissing her, "so as not to find sadness and regret lurking in every corner of this lodging which we have occupied together."

"You are right," she said. "After any separation, the person who suffers most is the one who remains behind."

Léonard took Julie on board the ship that was to separate them, while the horses he purchased were being harnessed to a carriage. The postilion was in his seat, and the track of the ship was still visible on the surface of the sea as his carriage was rolling along the road to Germany.

---

* When Léonard wrote this line in 1812, Julie, who must have been more than sixty years of age, occupied all his thoughts: "I truly believe that if I were to meet her again, I should still be in love with her."

By the time Léonard reached the Royal Army, it had been forced to retreat. The line of the Rhine had been threatened in more locations than one, and the headquarters of the princes were moved to Paderborn, a city in northern Germany. Despite the setbacks to the royal cause, Léonard found the Count of Provence in great spirits.

"Our affairs are taking a good turn, Master Léonard," said His Royal Highness. "Toulon has proclaimed my nephew King Louis XVII. The name of that child would be useful to us, if only the queen would understand the interests of the Monarchy better, and would once and for all convince herself that it is not possible to conspire in prison.

"Egad, my dear Léonard, if I was quite free to act as I pleased, I would let things take their course until the Republic perished through its own excesses or its own follies, and the latter would probably be the most expeditious means."

The Count of Artois rarely set up his headquarters in the same town or village in which his brother, the Count of Provence, established his camp. Léonard visited the Count of Provence in a small château near Paderborn, which the prince occupied with his principal officers.

It had been four months since his return to the princes' headquarters, and Léonard was beginning to question why he was there. He was still considered a banker, and already more than half the capital he had brought with him from France had passed into other hands. Noble borrowers were everywhere, and all of them had known Léonard in France. His supply of gold coins continued to disappear rapidly.

He also received some disturbing news from Lucette. Things back home had been upended. All of his possessions had been confiscated by the revolutionaries, and his theater had become national property and put up for sale. Stuck in London, and without any recourse, he had no choice but to focus on what he could do for the queen—and for himself. The letter also revealed that his "brother Villanou" had been guillotined by the revolutionaries.[4] Léonard did not discuss this tragic event in his memoirs, writing only that it was "the most distressing news."

The report that Léonard's brother Villanou had been executed was perplexing; Léonard had only two brothers, whose names were Jean-François and Pierre. He did have a cousin, Jean-Pierre Villanou, but according to the Revolutionary Tribunal's list of those guillotined on the 25th of July 1794, the person convicted and executed was Léonard's brother, Jean-François.

The matter became even more complicated when reports surfaced that Jean-François had never mounted the scaffold. One report stated that on the 25th of July 1794, a condemned man, handed over to the executioner and subsequently certified to be dead, was nevertheless still alive. The ruse was accomplished by substituting some unfortunate person for him during the hours between his condemnation and his removal from prison, then placing the unfortunate in his place upon the scaffold.[5]

---

7 thermidor an II. — 25 juillet 1794.

2527. AUTIÉ dit Léonard (JEAN-FRANÇOIS), 36 ans, né à Pamiers.
2528. BESSUÉJOULS ROQUELAURE (FRANÇOIS-ROSE-BARTHÉ-
LEMY), 46 ans, né à Toulouse.
2529. BOURDEIL (HENRY-JOSEPH), 36 ans, né à Paris.
2530. BUQUET (FRANÇOIS), 46 ans, né à Conge.
2531. CHARLOT-DARTIGUES (MARIE-MARTHE), veuve Maron,
46 ans, née à Coulommiers.

List of victims of the Revolutionary Tribunal of Paris on the 25th of July 1794

There was also evidence that foreigners, labeled spies and not knowing how to speak French, were often taken to prison in the place of others. Moreover, the revolutionary prisons of France had such abominable conditions that many of these prisoners would beg to be next in line to be executed.

There was nothing improbable about a ploy to save Jean-François. If he did survive, he remained silent for the rest of his life, undoubtedly to protect his brother and Lucette if they were accomplices, and to protect himself if he made a new life for himself in America, as was rumored. Replacing a prisoner condemned to the guillotine's blade would have been a very costly undertaking. The jailer, the porter, and the registrar, among others, all would have had to be bought. Léonard certainly had the wherewithal during his travels abroad, Lucette had valuable connections in the various government offices, and, conjecturally, Jean-François may also have had access to the queen's jewels that were once in his hands—jewels which disappeared so mysteriously the day after he had given them up during the royal family's flight to Varennes.

Did Jean-François manage to escape as one eyewitness reported, and was he replaced with another prisoner with the help of his wealthy brother? Or did another prisoner, sick of living any longer in his fetid cell, possibly exclaim, "It doesn't make any difference, take me!"

Lucette had herself been very nearly arrested for her loyalty to Léonard, assisting him with his mission abroad, and facilitating communications with the court in exile. Fortunately, she had friends in high places, which enabled her to escape imprisonment and death. They did warn her that, as pretty and witty as she might be, she must abstain in the future from defending the royalists and their cause.

This latest letter from Lucette—which reached Léonard by means that the revolutionaries never were able to discover—contained a horrifying picture of the Revolution. Léonard showed it to the Count of Artois, who wiped his forehead several times as he read it, returned it to him, and said, "This is horrible!" He next showed it to the Count of Provence, who read it with great attention, but to Léonard's surprise, *smiled*.

"My lad," said the count, "this looks well. Yes, yes, this looks well, but do not look so surprised. A few more months of this reign of blood, and our cause is gained. Those scoundrels are following in every detail the plan which I would have laid down for the Revolution in order to be quickest rid of it."

The Count of Provence expected the revolutionaries to turn on their own ranks once they had eliminated all the royalists. After cutting each other's throats, the count would then ascend to the throne of France. Léonard must have shuddered when the count talked of his nephew and sister-in-law in the Temple; they would fall beneath the terrorists' blows. If all were demolished, the Count of Provence would be in a position to build everything up again, this time as King of France.

The count's premonition would come true. Toward the middle of October, Léonard received the gloomiest of news—this time regarding the queen herself.

After the execution of the king earlier in the year, Marie Antoinette was taken from the Temple prison to the Conciergerie to await trial. At a quarter past one in the morning on the 1st of August, she was awakened—if indeed she slept—by the commissioners of police with their orders for arrest; twenty gendarmes waited in the prison yard to escort her.[6] The police allowed her to retain a small handkerchief and a small bottle of smelling salts, fearing that she might faint on the way. She embraced and kissed her daughter, knowing well that it was for the last time. The little princess was petrified, unable to return her mother's embrace.

The young Louis XVII had already been taken from his mother's arms months earlier; she only saw him, through a little crack in a wooden partition, when he was taken for a breath of fresh air on the roof of the Temple by the guards. She would stand in that particular spot hour after hour every day, just to catch a glimpse of her little boy.[7] The queen then turned to the Princess Élisabeth and recommended her children to her care; after a few whispered words, Marie Antoinette turned and went to the door without turning back.

The queen had nothing with her but the dress she originally wore from the Temple that first night. Day after day she earnestly entreated that she might have a supply of linen, but so strict were the orders that the concierge's wife dared not supply her. The queen was not allowed the use of a mirror until after repeated requests, the concierge permitted the prison maid Rosalie to lend the queen her own little, cheap looking-glass.

Marie Antoinette's prison cell in the Conciergerie

Her hair was only permitted to be dressed by the wife of the new concierge Bault, but only in his presence. Rosalie noted that the queen had patches of white hair on both her temples, but there were hardly any over her forehead, or in the rest of her hair. Her Majesty told her that the graying was caused by the troubles of the 5th and 6th of October, the days when the mob of Paris marched to Versailles and attacked the palace.

Marie Antoinette, seating herself on a wicker chair in her cell, asked Rosalie to do her hair. The concierge Bault, started forward, thrust Rosalie aside, and cried out that it was his business to do it. Marie thanked him, and immediately arising, arranged her hair herself, and put on her cap.

On the 16th of October 1793, the former queen of France, now the widow Capet (she was given the surname of her husband's ancestor, Hugh Capet, the first "King of the Franks"), was collected in a tumbril, a two-wheeled cart commonly pulled by oxen. Dreadful indeed would be the contrast between this procession and another that wound its way through the streets of Vienna twenty-three years earlier. Then she was the adored and beautiful dauphine whom France was about to welcome. Now she was simply a ragged widow, her hair whitened by sorrow, about to be seated on the cart of death.

The years of violence, executions, and the horrific separation from her children had finally taken its toll on the dethroned queen. After spending seventy-six days in the Conciergerie, she was led to the cart that would convey her to the Place de la Révolution. Marie Antoinette had a moment of weakness before she stepped into the wagon, losing control of her bowels in the Conciergerie courtyard. Beside her were the executioner, Samson, and a Constitutional priest, whose services she refused to receive.

On the route to the scaffold that morning, the artist Jacques-Louis David, who had earlier voted for her execution, sketched a quick portrait of the former queen on her way to the guillotine. The drawing depicts her last moments: She was passive, plainly attired in white muslin, and motionless—while some spectators grieved, others cursed and spat on her. She is almost unrecognizable.

Her hair had been cut, with only a few strands poking out of her cap, a far cry from the magnificent coiffures Léonard once adorned on her head, the envy of all of Paris. If her past hairstyles were the highlights of French fashion, helping her to become embraced by her subjects, the linen cap that replaced her crown is just as telling. She was now simply known as *l'autrichienne*, the Austrian or the *ostrich bitch*.

And then she was no more.

The widow Capet

The Count of Artois felt the keenest sorrow at the news of the queen's death and that of his sister, Madame Élisabeth, who was also guillotined. His brother, the Count of Provence, displayed a more stoical, more resigned grief. "I expected it," said His Royal Highness. "Events are now taking the course which I foresaw."[8]

The arrest of Madame du Barry

At the end of December 1793, Léonard received more gloomy news in a letter from Lucette, about the execution of poor Madame du Barry, who did not go quietly.

"Would I could find a desert in which to spend the rest of my life," Lucette wrote. "Ah, how I regret the smiles which I have lavished on those monsters! How I hate myself for granting them my favors! Léonard, I have become a Royalist I think . . .

and yet I am not sure; for I know that among your party there are many deplorable passions, too.

"Had this been otherwise, they would at least have saved that unhappy queen," she continued, "whom the cannibals dragged to execution in a cart after a slow agony of misery, privation and outrage. The wretches!

"Madame du Barry is less worthy of interest, no doubt, and is yet interesting because of her benevolence and the good qualities which incline one to forget the errors of her life. She followed the queen closely to the revolutionary tribunal: the blood of Marie Antoinette had barely dried upon the scaffold, when it was covered by that of the ex-Favorite. Just before her execution, the poor creature's mind left her entirely. She was heard to cry, 'Help! Help!'"

Lucette's account of Madame du Barry's execution is not far from the truth. An eyewitness reported that, when she arrived at the foot of the scaffold, two of the executioner's assistants had to lift her upon it. When they were on the point of fastening her to the plank, she managed to escape and run to the other side of the scaffold, but she was soon brought back and tied to the plank. She offered to give up all her worldly possessions and wealth if her life would be spared, but her last minute pleas were ignored. When the plank was tipped to bring her head under the blade, she uttered a final, terrifying shriek.

According to other reports, Madame du Barry did not display the calm courage with which other victims met their fate; her cowardice was openly contrasted with the calm reserve of Marie Antoinette. History was perhaps unfair in this comparison, considering the pride of the condemned queen and the months of illness she suffered in the dungeons of the Conciergerie. Madame du Barry, on the other hand, was a strong, healthy woman. It was as natural for her to struggle as it is for "the bird to peck at the hand that comes to take it out of the trap."[9]

In her defense, Madame the Countess du Barry had known nothing of the politics of the day. She was not an aristocrat, but rather a peasant by birth and a prostitute by profession before she became the king's mistress. The most damaging charges against her were not that she led an immoral life, had wasted the public money, and had hidden the royal jewels—which were later found buried in her château's gardens. Rather, her crime was that she had worn mourning clothes for the death of the late king.

Lucette ended her letter in a stirring tone: "When Jeanne Vaubernier [Madame du Barry's original name], the ex-Favorite, had been dragged onto the scaffold, she recovered enough presence of mind to say to the executioner, in pitiful tones, 'One moment more, I beg you, monsieur.' But this last word was drowned in the flood of blood that suddenly inundated the beautiful neck—in which once had nestled the kisses of a king."

CHAPTER 16

Léonard Resumes the Comb

"Our affairs are going well, and you shall not remain long in St. Petersburg. There will soon be crowned heads for you to dress in France ..."
—King Louis XVIII to Léonard
August 1798

Verona, Italy
July 1795

Upon the death of Louis XVI, the Dauphin Louis Charles was too young to head the House of Bourbon, and his uncle, the Count of Provence, was regent-in-exile. Because the French monarchy had been abolished for several months, the young Louis XVII never actually ruled, and any claim to regency by his uncle would have been in name only. The child died of tuberculosis in the Temple Prison on the 8th of June 1795 after a long period of cruel treatment by his jailers; he had also been isolated for long periods of time in a dark, damp cell infested with rats and accumulated human waste.

Léonard and the royals in exile were not aware of the horrific story of the young king's death. Six years earlier Léonard had witnessed Marie Antoinette and Louis XVI's grief over the death of their son Louis-Joseph. Having dressed the queen's hair in bed while she was carrying Louis Charles as a baby, Léonard would surely have been distraught had he heard of the young prince's ignoble fate.

The only surviving descendant of King Louis XVI was his daughter, Marie-Thérèse Charlotte. She was also kept in the Temple prison, but under much better conditions. The princess could not be considered a candidate for the throne, however, because of France's Salic law—allowing only male heirs to rule. Therefore, on the 16th of June, the princes-in-exile declared the king's brother, the Count of Provence, "King Louis XVIII" of France.

Louis XVIII successfully negotiated his niece Marie-Thérèse's release from the Temple prison in 1795 in exchange for Austrian prisoners. The new king desperately

Uncrowned Louis XVII in the Temple

wanted the princess to marry his nephew, Louis-Antoine, Duke of Angoulême, son of the Count of Artois. Marie-Thérèse was an important prize because her hand in marriage could quite possibly lead her husband to the throne of France. On her mother's Austrian side of the family, her cousin, Archduke Franz Karl, also sought her hand. But Louis XVIII deceived his niece by telling her that Marie Antoinette and Louis XVI's last wishes were for her to marry his nephew; Marie-Thérèse, loyal to the late royals, agreed.

223

Marie-Thérèse,
sole survivor of the Temple

Like her mother, the princess would be married for political reasons to a shy and indecisive foreign prince, and she would one day be Queen of France, albeit for only twenty minutes in 1830. (Though not acknowledged by most historians, the couple reigned between the time her father-in-law signed an instrument of abdication and the time her husband reluctantly signed the same document.) Unlike her mother, Marie-Thérèse would spend most of her days in exile and would die without any children.

When Léonard arrived in Verona, Italy, he found the exiled King Louis XVIII organizing his court and appointing his new ambassadors. Kings had their favorite hobbies like any other men; Louis XVI enjoyed tinkering with locks, but Louis XVIII's only pastime was to sit upon his symbolic throne, no matter where, and no matter the circumstance. While waiting for an audience with the king, Léonard was struck by the contrast of the new sovereign's grandeur with the extreme modesty of his household. He occupied only part of an ancient building furnished with worm-eaten tables and worn out armchairs in faded red velvet—horsehair stuffing was escaping at the corners. Léonard noticed a few footmen clad in patched and threadbare royal uniforms, and a few hungry-looking officers in shiny uniforms, walking up and down a dismantled anteroom. The whole scene was almost ghostly.

The king's kitchen remained calm and cold even at midday. This rather pathetic situation at the court of Verona was due to the habitual negligence of His Majesty's allies in discharging the pension that they allowed him.[1] Austria took no part in the aid, refusing to acknowledge the Count of Provence as King of France for fear that Napoleon's armies would retaliate. The royals were, in essence, entirely on their own.

The first time Léonard had an audience with the king, Louis XVIII was personally drafting one of the first acts emanating from his newly acquired royalty; he granted his favorite the Count of Avaray the right to bear the fleur-de-lys in his arms, thus becoming the Duke of Avaray. The king explained that the Duke of Avaray had shown him devotion on the occasion of his departure from France, which His Majesty described as his terrifying escape from the "prison of Luxembourg Palace."

However, Léonard clearly remembered that King Louis XVIII's flight from Paris, coinciding with the royal family's flight to Varennes, proceeded without the slightest obstacle. The only calamity that this Louis had encountered on the road was the need to dine on roast veal instead of wild game.

The king said he would show his gratitude to any servants who might lend him a little money, enabling him to warm his kitchen upon occasion and to have the guards' boots soled and heeled. Léonard had already squandered so many gold louis in this direction, so he decided to at least wait until he was *asked* for the loans which he had formerly volunteered of his own accord. Léonard may have grown disillusioned with the court of the gluttonous, gout-ridden protector of the exiled monarchy. Many of the nobles of Verona took no heed of Louis XVIII; even the French emigrants in the area abstained from attending his court, keeping themselves prudently in the background.[2] The journalists of France referred to Louis as the King of Verona, never the King of France. Back home, in fact, the exiled royals and the emigrants were found guilty of treason and their property confiscated by the French government.

In many ways, Léonard was tied down—the same thing that once gave him such mobility and influence was now shackling him. He had so intimately been identified with the royalist cause that he did not see how he could—without disgrace—separate himself from it. Things were taking such a turn at the close of 1795 that it seemed to him very unlikely that Louis XVIII would be able to move his court to Versailles anytime soon, and his own ruin appeared to be near, and inevitable. Perhaps too proud to admit it, Léonard claimed in his diary that this did not greatly alarm him, resolutely declaring to himself, "Well, when I have exhausted my last resources, I will stoically turn my steps back to their origin; I will go to St. Petersburg, where the fine manners and the curls of the reign of Louis XV have taken refuge, and there resume my comb."

Although in exile, the king still held court with all the regal rituals and trappings that he could muster. One evening, the king became charmingly familiar with Léonard, pleased that he alone would assist him with his *coucher*, the king's going-to-bed ceremony. Léonard was surprised when the king began to reminisce about Marie Antoinette.

"The late queen, my sister-in-law," said Louis XVIII, "sometimes opened her mind to you, Léonard, on the subject of her likes and dislikes. I will wager that she told you more than once that she disliked me."

"Never, sire," replied Léonard.

"And yet it is true that Queen Marie Antoinette had an aversion for me, and I will tell you the reason," said the king. "I clearly saw that she had been instructed by her mother, the Empress Maria Theresa, to annul our credit, the credit of us Princes of the Blood, as far as she was able; and you will agree, Léonard, that Her Majesty acquitted herself with tolerable thoroughness of the instructions which she had received.

"Dignity," continued the king, "is perhaps the quality with which a sovereign is least able to dispense; it atones for many failings, and nothing is better fitted to bring out his other qualities. If God permits me one day to return to my realm, I hope to prove to the French people that I possess all the conditions for the want of which the Revolution broke out. Shall I tell you my whole thought, Léonard? I believe that in me there is more of the stuff which kings are made of than in all the rest of my family put together.[3]

"I have found among my nobility a sordid egoism," the king said, "where I expected to find unlimited devotion. Is it not a disgrace to all those nobles, whose resources are well known to me, that they should allow themselves to be pre-empted by you, Léonard, in advances to the Crown, which they could themselves have made without the least difficulty?"

"Sire," Léonard interrupted, "I have always made these advances with equal pride and satisfaction."

"Egad, I know it, my lad," said His Majesty, "and at this same moment, when my returns have been a little delayed, I am sure that you will gladly hand the Duke of Avaray five hundred louis which it is absolutely necessary that I should have."

"Your Majesty does me honor by relying upon my eagerness to meet your wishes," said Léonard.

"That is fine of you, Léonard," said Louis XVIII, giving Léonard his hand. "I expected as much from you."

Léonard would have been more pleased if His Majesty had expected less, but the new King of France was indeed clever in leading up to such a delicate request. Once again Léonard was cajoled to play the loyal supporter of the royal cause; he had no choice but to acquiesce to his sovereign's wishes, despite its quite obvious threat of financial ruin.

Louis XVIII had hoped that he would be permitted to establish his nomadic court, at least for some time, in Verona. However, no one could have predicted the arrival of Napoleon Bonaparte, who would make so triumphant a military entry into Italy in 1795.[4] Understanding that he could no longer hope to "reign" peacefully in Verona, and that his court would be subjected to constant wanderings and negotiations, the king decided to leave for Blankenburg, in Germany. Far from the front lines of combat, the king could find protection there from the Duke of Brunswick. Léonard, ever the dutiful servant, followed His Majesty—practically to the end of the earth as far as Europe was concerned.

Blankenburg was a very insignificant German town in the Duchy of Brunswick. Its inhabitants were known as great smokers and fearless beer-drinkers. Léonard found their women to be a feeble sort, "vegetated in their household like a mushroom in its bed, and faded almost as quickly." It was not a particularly inspirational respite for Léonard, who said, "One who remembers the delicious turmoil of Paris yawns regularly once a second in this Brunswick town."

His Majesty did not take Léonard into his political confidence except insofar as the financial department was concerned, so Léonard left the king's court for Brunswick, the capital of the Duchy, where he hoped to find less monotony and a better investment for the few remnants of his fortune. Léonard was left with two thousand louis, putting him dangerously close to having to resume his magical comb in order to live.[5]

Brunswick was closer to Léonard's style, a lively, bright city in whose midst arose an elegant palace, the charming residence of the reigning duke. The town might well have been called a miniature Paris; it had its own rue Saint-Honoré, its handsome cafés, its little milliners with their provoking glances, a number of tastefully arranged shops, and comfortable coaches.

The hotels were furnished in good style, and Léonard found one complete with a French table d'hôte and baths. He had no sooner removed his traveling boots than he was asked to be shown to the part of the house containing the baths; they were not luxurious, but at least they were not disgusting. According to the custom of the country, the bath attendants were all women. Léonard paid no notice to the woman who came to turn on the taps. When she later returned and brought the towels, she looked at Léonard from the corner of her eye, and cried out, "You are Monsieur Léonard!"

The bath attendant, a large, buxom woman in her mid-forties, continued, "I am Laura, the sweetheart of poor Frémont and the friend of Julie, the fairy of Nicolet's Theater!"

"Ah! I remember you perfectly now!" said Léonard. "But what strange series of events has turned you into a bath attendant in Brunswick?"

A violent ringing summoned her away, but Laura promised to visit Léonard in his room that evening to tell him a story that he would find most amusing.

That evening, at exactly ten o'clock, she came to his door and told her story.

"You will expect to hear, Monsieur Léonard," Laura said, "that a long series of follies have formed the links in my chain of adventures. If so, you are mistaken. Since the year 1775 my life has been mainly ecclesiastical."

Léonard looked surprised, but she added, "Yes, Monsieur Léonard, ecclesiastical, but not orthodox!"

Laura then told Léonard the long story, beginning when she and Julie had joined the opera. One evening at the theater she was approached by Dom Joseph, a very wealthy monk visiting Paris from the city of Tours. They instantly fell in love and Laura gave him two daughters, who fifteen years later both became dancers in the opera ballet. When Laura's husband was appointed captain of a Parisian battalion and sent to the front, Laura later joined him there; but he was seriously wounded in a battle in 1796 and taken to a hotel in Brunswick. After languishing for two months, Joseph died in Laura's arms, leaving her in debt and owing the hotel for their lodging. Needing a bath attendant, the hotel gave the starving general's widow the humble position, in order to pay off the debt.

"My dear lady," Léonard said, "when, twenty-eight years ago, I arrived in Paris carrying all my luggage in my pockets, I found two charming women who gave me a helping hand to move from a wretchedly furnished room in the rue des Noyers into a nice apartment on the boulevard—such things are never forgotten by honest minds. Julie became the wife of a Prussian general, you the wife of a French general; and I have met both of you, after a period of prosperity, struck by unpredictable fortune.

"You can leave for France as soon as you please," continued Léonard. "Tomorrow we will settle accounts with the hostess of this house, and I will give you the where-withal to go to the French authorities to ask them for the pension which is due you, the widow of a Republican soldier who died of his wounds."

Laura was very grateful for Léonard's generosity. In fact, her invoking of providence proved that Laura had surely become religious in the intervening years. Léonard thought of the risqué conversations of the young dancer at Nicolet's, the nonchalance of fastening her garter above the knee in the presence of bystanders, her inclination for tipsiness, and a thousand other little foibles of her youth that had pointed everywhere but to spiritualism. "What oddities time carries in its bosom!" he noted, invoking the French saying.

The next morning Léonard settled with the hostess for Laura's account, and he offered Laura one hundred louis, but she refused to accept more than fifty for her journey home; she even pretended that fifty louis was too much. When she arrived, the bath attendant received news that she would receive a regular and punctual pension of one thousand francs—as befit the wife of a fallen hero.

In Brunswick, Léonard was relieved to not have run into any of those noble borrowers whom he had found in London, on the Rhine, on the Danube, and everywhere else in his travels. It had become time for him to think of himself, and he became more and more determined to go to Russia, there to resume the comb, which alone among the elements of his fortune, had never failed him.

He proceeded to Blankenburg to receive the king's orders for his audience with Emperor Paul I of Russia and for any noble Frenchmen who might have taken exile in St. Petersburg. When Léonard reached the little town where he had last left the

Jelgava Palace in Mittau

court of Louis XVIII, His Majesty had already departed for the Kingdom of Prussia. Léonard immediately set out for Berlin, but when he arrived he discovered that the new king had, for political reasons, already left for Mittau in Courland.

Léonard made his way to Mittau, where he found a letter waiting for him from Julie, now the Countess Delvinski, in which she had enclosed a draft for the sum he had lent his old friend. Of all the money Léonard had scattered about since his departure from Paris, this was the first that was returned to him.

"I must confess, my dear Léonard," wrote Julie, "that whenever I pass along the boulevard du Temple, before the very modest lodging which I occupied in 1770, my heart beats very hard. Ah, how often I think of that time! How happy those years seem, though they were rich in nothing but folly, voluptuousness, and thoughtlessness! And when a woman who is completing her ninth lustrum [forty-fifth year] has such lively memories, it is not without a certain emotion that she writes to a friend of that time. You know, Léonard, that after forty a woman may talk of friends, but not of lovers.

"Heaven, how Paris has changed from what it was! Do you remember, Léonard, the monstrous hoops of our former great ladies of the Court, the full skirts which, the petticoats aiding, were such a protection to their chastity, as everyone knows? Well, the Frenchwomen of 1798 have reached the antithesis of that voluminous attire. If you walk in the Tuileries on a fine sunny day, you can have the pleasure of examining at your ease the figures of our *merveilleuses,* fashionable ladies, and the soft shades of their skin. There is no longer any need for painters and sculptors to pay heavy fees to models for their Venuses—the ladies pose everywhere and at all times in true academic nudity."

In sharp contrast to Julie's description of Paris, Louis XVIII's court in Mittau offered very few attractions or even simple comfort; in fact, His Majesty discovered the hard lesson that safety and contentment do not always go together. No longer was the exiled king's ear caressed by the warm and balmy zephyr of the Adriatic, but by the chilly blasts of the Baltic. Living amid a population composed almost entirely of wool or leather merchants, all fanatically devoted to the practice of freemasonry, the king did not find himself among a citizenry with common predilections. "Where can I go," the king would say, "not to hear people speak of liberty or equality?"

It had been a long time since Léonard had first entertained going to St. Petersburg, but he hesitated leaving the king. The reason was not that His Majesty Louis XVIII might have granted the title of nobility that had been promised him, but rather, the more he hesitated to part from the king, the more it became a matter of self-esteem. Léonard's resources in the year 1798 had diminished to such an extent that the simplest calculation sufficed to show him that there was too little remaining on which to live.

He saw clearly that he must resume his comb, and in Russia, where the ladies' hairstyles had more or less attained the point where he had left them in 1769 in Paris. Too old and out of date for France, his talent might still appear young in inspiration and fresh in imagination in St. Petersburg; he could revive all the fashions that had formerly sprung up beneath his comb at Versailles.

Yet one thing troubled Léonard once he first considered retreating to Russia: telling the king. Léonard knew he was one of the last remaining figures of the court and he worried that his absence would be too painful to the monarch. He recognized the absurdity of this vanity and finally summoned up courage to announce to the king that he was compelled to return to his profession. He had been so obedient for so long that he might have feared striking out on his own, but he was determined to proceed to the Court of Paul I—with the object of recapturing some scraps of his past fortune.

"What, my poor fellow, has it come to that?" asked Louis XVIII.

"Alas, sire, yes," he replied. "Events, as Your Majesty knows, have deceived the expectations of all of us, and I had sown abundantly in the hope of a speedy harvest."

"Yes," said the king reflectively, "we have all made a blunder. I thought too late of diversions from the inside, from the center. Remember what I say, Léonard, one man alone is to be feared by our cause, and that is Bonaparte, that little general whose body could be blown over by a breath, but whose soul would brave a tempest.

"If he had remained in Europe, we should have had great difficulty in checkmating the Revolution. Fortunately, he embarked on an expedition to Egypt. We shall be able to operate on a large scale, and the English fleet is blockading the French army on the Nile.

Louis XVIII, King of France
(BIBLIOTHÈQUE NATIONALE DE FRANCE)

"Our affairs are going well, Léonard," added the king, rubbing his hands, "our affairs are going well, and you shall not remain long in St. Petersburg. There will soon be crowned heads for you to dress in France."

Léonard could hardly believe these last words. It seemed incredible that, to the royal family, he should still be Léonard the hairdresser, that is, *only* Léonard the hairdresser. "How backward my political education!" he noted.

Had Louis XVIII just promised Léonard he would return to the restored court of France *as a hairdresser*? Was he to resume the thread of his career where he had left off in 1789—as though his commitment and sacrifice in the intervening years *never happened*? The king seemed to think that Léonard could recover his powder box, his powder puff, and his curling irons just as the noble emigrants were to be restored all their possessions, their titles, and their privileges.[6]

Léonard surely found it now easier to leave the king who still regarded him as nothing more than a man who could frizz hair. Disappointed, he also noted that his departure would not have made any more difference "than a poor spaniel who gets up and goes, after amusing his master for a time by playing fetch."

Léonard finally left Mittau for St. Petersburg in 1798. The king had handed him some dispatches for Paul I, insisting that he hand them to the czar in person. The czar famously trusted no one; absolutely everyone was suspected of conspiracy. But the name of the famous coiffeur had long been a household name in St. Petersburg. The Chevalier d'Éon, Paul's fencing master when he was younger, had entertained His Imperial Highness with stories of the hairdresser's expertise; and when the czar had visited Paris before the Revolution, he had viewed Léonard's masterpieces firsthand at the court of Versailles. His Imperial Majesty was actually looking forward to his visit with the same curiosity one attaches to the sight of a rare monkey.

When Léonard was admitted to the czar's presence, he found Paul I in his study, seated before a desk covered with maps of Italy and Switzerland. When the czar saw Léonard enter, he rose, came toward him, and took the king's dispatch from his hands. He cast his eyes over it rapidly, and then tossing it on to his desk, he began to speak.

"Well, Léonard," he said in excellent French, and as though he were addressing an old acquaintance, "so you have decided to transfer the empire of hairdressing to Russia? Like the King, your Sovereign, you want a throne somewhere."

"Sire, in adversity we seek consolation sometimes in fantasy," said Léonard.

"Ah, your sovereignty will prove no fantasy here," said the czar. "You will be able to do a good business. Just think, the Empress will protect you! I know that you have faithfully served the unfortunate Queen of France; all my nobility will follow their sovereign's example and show their appreciation of your conduct."

"I shall be indebted to your Majesty for a prosperity on which I dared not reckon," replied Léonard.

"Oh, you will have to purchase it!" said the czar. "Do you think that our ladies are free from caprices, and that your patience will not be put to every possible test? No, no, Léonard, to grow roses in the North of Europe you must cultivate them, and with ardor. But you come here with a famous name; that is a great thing to begin with!"

Czar Paul I

Maria Feodorovna

Just then the Empress Maria Feodorovna appeared. Léonard, who had only seen the voluminous princess for a moment at Versailles, recalled thinking at their first encounter that she would have been a superb woman in a country where athletic proportions were considered a charm in the fairer sex.

"Madame," said Emperor Paul, "this is Léonard, whose arrival was announced to us some time ago. He brings with him the best traditions of Versailles: I hope you will employ him."

"I will, sire, and from today. My hair is in a hideous state of disorder. I really do not know, monsieur," said the empress, turning to Léonard, "whether you can make anything of it. It is as one might say a long-neglected flowerbed, in which the plants have grown up at random. Our Russian hairdressers don't know how to handle a pair of scissors."

"Madame, I am at Your Majesty's orders," said Léonard.

While he was speaking with the empress, the Czar Paul returned to his maps, and Léonard assumed his audience was finished. He approached the emperor respectfully to take his leave. "Your Majesty has no orders to give me for the king?" he asked.

"No," the czar replied. "Louis XVIII has no very fervent ally here."[7]

Léonard learned to know Paul I very well during the last three years of the czar's life, and the czar would never be able to understand Louis XVIII's qualities. In his eyes, a monarch's chief virtue consisted of military knowledge and, in this respect, the new King of France was still learning his first lessons. It was this value system that caused the czar to proclaim himself an admirer of Napoleon.

Czar Paul was at the same time a man of education. He was witty and intelligent, but was also fickle. Léonard would find him one evening pleasant, chatty, and familiar; the next morning he would appear haughty and authoritarian.

One thing troubled Léonard as he returned to his hotel: Almost ten years had passed since his hand had rested on a woman's head, and he was just about to perform his first experiment on the illustrious head of the empress. When he returned home, he asked a pretty little girl whom he had seen with the hostess to come up to his room and begged her to let him do her hair. She readily consented, in return for an allowance of sweets. He found his hand a little heavy and found himself having to struggle to find the inspiration with which his imagination formerly overflowed. Nevertheless, his hand had not lost all of its magic; the very same evening he unraveled the long and silky hair of Empress Maria.

Her Majesty, tired of the clumsy fashion in which her hair had been previously dressed, was greatly pleased with his creation. Léonard saw that it was going to be easy for him to recapture in St. Petersburg the *vogue* that had withered away in Paris beneath the blast of the revolutionary tempest. Yet, he could not say much of his career as coiffeur to the Russian court; it was but a pale copy of his very first

St. Petersburg, Russia (eighteenth century)

successes—a languid succession of mornings and evenings devoted exclusively to the service of the comb.

Those delicious accessories with which his life had been strewn at the courts of Louis XVI and Marie Antoinette, those sweet prerogatives with which his talent and audacity had formerly rewarded him, could not be reproduced in St. Petersburg. In fact, he was threatened one day with a flogging for hinting that two or three duchesses had honored him with their favors, certain gratuities thrown into the bargain for their coiffures.

Léonard was fifty-two when he arrived in Russia in 1798, and he would have been a fool to try to lay siege to the soul of the local beauties. What he had heard about the ladies from younger and more attractive men only confirmed his opinion of them. He had come to the conclusion that voluptuousness, as it was understood in France, Italy, and Spain, had never crossed the Rhine.

Léonard had no lack of clients in St. Petersburg, and his business would have been lucrative—had he been able to collect the gold imperials that were due him. But hard times had come upon the splendid capital. The fortune of the Russian nobles depended upon the number of peasants (*moujiks*) that they possessed, but the Napoleonic Wars were annihilating them. For more than ten years, misery stalked through the superb palaces that adorned the banks of the Neva.

The Empress Maria took a great interest in Léonard, afterward shared by the noble and beautiful Czarina Elisabeth, consort to the next emperor, Alexander. The autocrat Paul had shown Léonard many kindnesses that he would never forget, despite having to frequently bear the brunt of those foul moods.

Paul I had died suddenly on the 23rd of March 1801, murdered by some of his nobles.[8] The czar, a vindictive and spineless ruler, had been asked to step down from the throne for the good of his people. When he refused, a conspiracy was organized and a band of dismissed officers broke into his bedroom, finding him hiding behind some curtains. They tried to force him to sign the abdication, but he resisted. A soldier struck him and knocked him to the ground; another strangled him with an officer's sash and the others trampled him to death.[9]

The czar was far from being a handsome monarch; in fact, the artist Madame Vigée-LeBrun wrote that "a flat nose and a very large mouth furnished with very long teeth made him look like a death's head."[10] Nevertheless, it was necessary that, according to custom, he should be exhibited before the eyes of the people; and it was necessary, as much as possible, to diminish the effects of the revolting decomposition of His Majesty's features. The empress sent for Léonard.

Realizing that the alteration in the face was due to the actual color of the skin rather than any change in the facial muscles, Léonard decided that a little white and rouge, cunningly applied, would succeed in giving the czar a more lifelike color to his face. Léonard next brushed and curled the emperor's hair, and in the end he succeeded in restoring this face, in which decomposition had already begun its hideous work. In fact, Léonard did so well, that Paul I was actually less repulsive on his state deathbed than he had been when alive.

In his career as hairdresser, Léonard had distinguished himself in the invention of every style of headdress, and no shade or texture of hair had escaped the exercise of his art, but one thing was precluding him from achieving his glory. This last complementary feat he achieved on the 24th of March 1801; Léonard had just turned fifty-five when he thus crowned his reputation. He had successfully dressed the hair of a corpse.

CHAPTER 17

Sixteen Years Later

"And has it never entered your mind, simple man that you are, that there is some compensation due to you?"

—LUCETTE TO LÉONARD
JUNE 1817

April 1814
Paris, France

Léonard had become an old man at sixty-eight. After a sixteen-year sojourn in St. Petersburg, where he spent his years dressing the hair of the amiable, but lackluster, Russian nobility, Léonard learned in 1814 that he could finally return to France as he wanted. Although his country had been open to him ever since the famous amnesty of 1800, he did not consider himself important enough to "assume any airs" toward the imperial court of Napoleon.[1] If Léonard had returned to France earlier, he would have been obligated to accept the rule of the dictator Napoleon, displeasing the royals in exile and perhaps sacrificing any rewards or titles he had been promised.

Additionally, had he returned earlier, hairdressing would not have been as lucrative in Paris as it was in St. Petersburg. Napoleon's court dressed its hair, male and female, short and curled, "like Titus." Gone were the days of poufs and towering coiffures that made Léonard a rich man. The misfortune of the times in France also meant that hairdressing was simply not as fashionable in Paris. He was still dressing the Russian ladies' hair in an embroidered silk coat with point lace cuffs, while hairdressers in Paris wore meager hunting frocks and spurs. He still drove to his clients in a carriage in St. Petersburg, while in Paris they traveled on horseback. There was now a core of equestrian hairdressers in the capital of the French Empire; Léonard had not been in the saddle since his first horrible experience in horsemanship on the road to Montmédy in 1791.

Due to a fire that destroyed all the hairdresser's papers in Russia, little is known of Léonard's last years in Russia.[2] However, it is clear that the return of the Bourbons to the throne in France in 1814 gave him fresh hope:

> It is no longer Léonard the coiffeur whom His Majesty Louis XVIII will reward; it is the faithful Royalist who has given proof of unlimited devotion in the services which he has rendered not only to the late king and queen, but also to the reigning monarch and his august brother.[3]

Léonard left St. Petersburg eagerly, undoubtedly leaving more than one object of affection behind him. The hairdresser and banker of the Bourbons was certain he would be rewarded for his lifetime service and sacrifice in France and abroad. He no doubt felt it was coming to him:

> Among the many appointments, His Majesty is no doubt reserving some honorable and lucrative place for his old servant Léonard, or rather, for his banker at Verona. Ah, I shall be a happy man in France, and I shall at least find in my dear native land a corner in which to lay my mortal remains.

When Léonard arrived in Paris, the entrance to the Tuileries, where the new royal family had been established, was so obstructed by soliciting courtiers that Léonard was unable to make his way to Monsieur the Count of Artois. He wished to see the count first, hoping that he would be kind enough to present him to Louis XVIII—perhaps with a good word for him and a reminder of Léonard's faithful service. However, it was so crowded that a whole week passed before he could even catch a glimpse of the king across the crowd.

Along with the new regime, Paris had also changed. For one, the nobility had been educated during Napoleon's Empire; the counts now knew Latin and Greek, having taken their bachelor's degrees. Their sisters played the piano, painted landscapes in oils, and knew how to read. In the shops along the rue Saint Denis, all the tradesmen knew arithmetic; they kept their books by double entry and signed their names with a flourish.

These tradesmen were also expanding their businesses. There were no cobblers in Paris now, no bakers, no grocers, nor wine shopkeepers; in their places were booteries, bakeries, grocers, and wine dealers. It would no longer be possible for the corps of wigmakers to ever bring an action against Léonard's colleagues, because there were no longer any wigmakers in Paris. There were only hairdressers, although Léonard had not yet seen a single remarkable headdress since he arrived.

The reception of Louis XVIII

Before the Revolution the typical cafe was a gloomy resort, painted in gray with clumsy tables, uncomfortable benches, and a huge stove with an enormous copper pipe on top of it. At the counter usually sat a woman, generally ugly, in a cap of doubtful cleanliness. Her bosom would be concealed behind a loosely tied kerchief, while a waiter in a filthy apron with a corkscrew hanging from his belt slowly served the customers beneath the light of a smoky lamp. But by 1814, every cafe had become a little temple glittering with gilding, brilliant with mirrors and paint, and flooded with light.[4]

Paris boasted three thousand cafes, and all were crowded with people chatting and sipping, much like the cosmopolitan cafe culture of today. The counter had become an altar for the woman sitting behind it, an intoxicatingly beautiful hostess, dazzling with jewelry. The waiters had to run from table to table for their gratuities; women were too often "driven to vice" by the effect of such competition for tips from their male customers.[5]

Léonard had ample time to discover the new Paris before he was finally permitted an audience with the Count of Artois. When the prince finally received him, he remarked that Léonard had become "very ugly." Though the insult hurt slightly, Léonard was relieved that the prince at least *remembered* him.

Léonard told the prince that hairdressers could not make their fortune in Russia, especially when they resumed the comb at fifty-two and continued using it until they were sixty-eight. His Royal Highness did not appear to take the hint. Whether he had forgotten Léonard's devotion or not, Léonard didn't know; he took leave of the prince without obtaining anything.

At last the king deigned to grant Léonard a post: doorkeeper to his private apartments. Considering Léonard's opinion of himself, his long wait, and his sacrifice for the court, this must have stung quite a bit. It was a far cry from the patent of nobility promised him by Louis XVI; yet, the king had smiled at him from a distance, and Léonard thought he saw a kind recollection in his smile. So, he waited and he hoped.

When Léonard succeeded in obtaining several consecutive audiences with King Louis XVIII, His Majesty always received him with kindness, but Léonard's position remained unchanged; he simply remained the king's doorkeeper. Whenever His Majesty came across Léonard in his black coat with the key chain around his neck, he always honored him with friendly words and a gracious smile. The princes and

The Restoration of the Bourbons

the Duchess of Angoulême, Queen Marie Antoinette's daughter, also showed great interest in Léonard, but in words only. His return to France was decidedly less auspicious than he had planned.

Léonard also never mentioned whether he regretted leaving Russia, but one can assume he couldn't resist returning to the lively streets of Paris, the theater, and the gala balls. Although there was no lack of noble ladies' heads to dress in St. Petersburg, life in the low and marshy city was languid and lethargic. Winters were severely cold, and summers very short. People were generally very listless, and even the artists were "absolutely void of inspiration."[6]

It struck Léonard that he might give a hint to Count Blacas as to the old debt due him. Blacas was the minister of the royal household, an official of considerable power in matters of the king's court. He had the opportunity of seeing the count, who was always very friendly to him, and he decided to speak to him about his former functions as banker to the royal family in exile. He told Blacas his story, giving the count a little memorandum of the sums he had loaned the princes. *Would he possibly bring the matter up before the king?*

Count Blacas wagged his head several times before replying: "It's a bad business, my dear Léonard. I have no doubt that the king and the princes of his family have every intention of paying, sooner or later, the debts which they contracted during the emigration; but I fear that at present your demand would be decidedly premature. I will go further: I think it would be dangerous."

"What, dangerous?" asked Léonard.

"Well, yes!" he said. "At court as elsewhere, the best way of conveying that a request is considered inopportune is to get angry at it. Listen, you are a discreet man; I will give you an insight into the matter in question. Monsieur the Count of Artois had a creditor in England who for a long time displayed the greatest patience and had even perhaps resigned himself to a loss, but who has become very pressing since His Royal Highness has taken his place on the Throne.

"In fact," he continued, "that is just what I have now come to discuss with the count. I have had further conversations with him on this subject, and up to the present I have never been able to get a word out of him which I could convey to the anxious Englishman."

"That I can imagine, monsieur," said Léonard. "The Count of Artois has many calls upon him; he is perhaps pressed, and I should refrain from reminding him of a little claim which I also have upon him personally. But the king . . ."

"The king, my dear Léonard, is much worse," said the count.

"Really?" asked Léonard.

"Listen, I will tell you of someone you know. I have on my desk a properly authenticated claim from your old friend, Mademoiselle Bertin, to whom Madame of Provence owed about sixty thousand francs.* What should you think the king replied when I mentioned it to him? He said, smiling, 'The King of France does not pay the debts of the Count of Provence.' The king finds this jest so merry that he repeats it whenever the question crops up of his other debts of the old days when he was Monsieur the Count."[7]

"But mine dates back to a time when His Majesty was already reigning as king," said Léonard.

"You are mistaken, Léonard," he said. "Where his debts are concerned, the king only commences his reign in 1814, when he arrived in Paris. Believe me, do not mention that topic for the present; it would make a most unwelcome sound in the king's ear. Have patience, better times may come, and then we can bring the matter up again. I will tell you when the proper moment arrives."

The official then asked him to open the Count of Artois's door for him, gently reminding Léonard of his new role. Léonard did as asked, and thanked Count Blacas for his advice. Thus was shattered the beautiful castle in Spain which Léonard had imagined for years.

He regretted the news, but what could he do? In the Paris of 1814, he was a doorkeeper—it's as though his past were wiped clean.

Léonard had found many of his old acquaintances in Paris, and many tried to be of assistance to him. Others, whose credit had fallen with Napoleon's Empire, could offer nothing but a cordial welcome. Julie, now Countess Delvinski, and her husband were among those who opened their purses as well as their hearts. Count Delvinski, the brave Polish general, had received promotion, crosses, titles, gifts, and wounds on every battlefield where he followed Napoleon, but nothing now remained save his pension. Julie, now sixty-eight, appeared younger than the general who was not yet fifty-five. After having danced at the Opéra, created artificial flowers in London, and fought in Poland, Léonard's one-time fairy now pruned her fruit trees and grew her cabbages in the valley of Montmorency. Never had Léonard seen a woman more resigned to adjust to the fickleness of fortune.[8]

"There is only one thing I cannot get used to," said Julie as they were walking in her garden, while the general, reclining in a chaise, smoked cigar upon cigar in a sad reverie.

---

* Rose Bertin was in fact owed over 1,500,000 francs (six million dollars) by the court and the entire royal family at the time of the Revolution. She and her heirs could not make any claims when the monarchy was restored; Rose, out of loyalty to Marie Antoinette, had destroyed all her account books and any trace of the sums owed to her, fearing any additional charges against the queen.

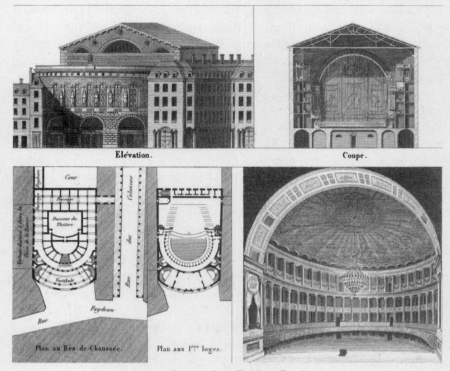

Leonard's creation, Théâtre Feydeau

"What is that, countess?" Léonard asked, still mindful of their former intimacy.

"I cannot get used to growing old, Léonard. And Laura, what has become of her?" she asked.

"What I expected . . . she has turned to religion," said Léonard.

"What are we coming to!" she asked.

"Yes, the wife of a general, or if you prefer, of Father Joseph, has just entered one of the convents which Louis XVIII has authorized to serve as an asylum for hundreds of old women who have not your privilege, Julie, of remaining young while aging, and who having nothing more agreeable left to do on earth but to start at a gallop on the road to Heaven, to make up for the time devoted to ambling in the opposite direction."

"I assure you, Léonard, that Laura has no time to lose."

Léonard also reunited in Paris with another woman of his past, one who had no intention of taking the veil, like Laura, nor of planting cabbages, like Julie. It was Lucette, who was reaching the age when the older one grows, the younger one pretends to be. Lucette only confessed to be thirty-seven, although Léonard knew the truth behind this lie that she shared with her many adorers. She had enjoyed the spoils of the Republic, the Consulate, the Empire, and the commencement of the Bourbon Restoration. One could say it was a harlequin destiny, but richly spangled.

Lucette was the same good-hearted soul; she had loved the brilliant Léonard as his mistress, and now she liked the old Léonard as a friend. One morning when he called upon her, her servant had hardly announced his name before she cried, "Come here, Papa Léonard," and she tapped with her hand upon the sofa on which she was sitting beside a middle-aged man, sparkling with jewelry like a rich widow of the rue Saint Dominique.

She continued, as soon as he was seated, "Do you ever pass the Théâtre Feydeau, which used to belong to you, without experiencing a deep emotion?"

"Truly, no, madame," he replied. "The sight of that theater always gives me a great pain at my heart."

"And has it never entered your mind, simple man that you are, that there is some compensation due to you?" she asked.

"Ah, my child, I have no right to look to Louis XVIII for it," he said.

"And why not, monsieur?" she asked. "I hold, on the contrary, that it is His Majesty who owes it to you. Was it not for his family that you left France? What am I saying? Have you not made personal sacrifices for His Majesty himself, too?"

"No doubt, my dear Lucette, but all that is almost forgotten," said Léonard. "I have noticed, generally, that everyone concerned in the emigration has lost his memory on crossing the Channel, as if this sea had been the Lethe [the river of forgetfulness] of my debtors."

"Very well, but supposing the king could make your fortune without disbursing one louis d'or?" solicited Lucette.

"Ah, nonsense," he said.

"Yes, my dear Léonard," she said. "A big royal signature at the bottom of a little order ten lines long, and we recapture the fortune you have lost. Listen to me, the French are just as they always were. They want sights; they want many sights, even when they have no bread to eat. Now that the great theater of war, in which each was an actor in his turn, is closed for a good number of years, naturally the play within four walls must atone for what we have lost in the open air. The theater, therefore, has become a subject of speculation, and our fondness for emotions is already being quoted on the Bourse.

"Now it is certain that a second Opéra-Comique Theater would do better business now than our Théâtre de Monsieur did twenty-six or twenty-seven years ago," she continued. "But a privilege is necessary before opening a second opéra-comique, and that privilege is due to you, incontestably due to you. It is only a question of asking for it. Monsieur the Count of Provence is now King of France, and he cannot refuse this slight favor to the former proprietor of his favorite theater."[9]

"And the building, where is it?" asked Léonard.

"In the quarries of Arcueil, but do not bother about that. As soon as you have the order in your pocket, this monsieur here," said Lucette, nodding to the man in the diamonds, "will place two million francs at your disposal."

Léonard was so taken with this proposal, that he rose on the spot, grabbed his hat, and made his way to the Tuileries Palace to speak to the Count of Artois about the privilege—it seemed to him that it'd be quite easy to obtain. After all, he had been confidant to the kings and queens of France, his artistic flair had smitten the courts of France and Europe, and he once reigned as proprietor and artistic director of Monsieur's theater. He was *not* a doorkeeper.

Léonard would wait no longer for fortune to shine down upon him. He was simply too old for that. It was time for Léonard to take control of his fate.

CHAPTER 18

Léonard's Final Ruse

"No, Léonard, as to your privilege, you must not think of that anymore."
—Count of Artois to Léonard
April 1818

November 1817
Paris, France

Three years. Three years had passed since Léonard had first returned to Paris, expecting King Louis XVIII to repay him for his loans to the royal family and reward him with a title—as was promised by the king's brother, Louis XVI. But receiving an audience with the new king was nearly impossible. When Léonard reached the Pavillon de Marsan at the Tuileries, he was determined to take matters into his own hands. The moment seemed favorable for speaking to the Count of Artois; he was with Monseigneur the Duke and Madame the Duchess of Angoulême, who had both assured Léonard that they took the greatest interest in him. Léonard would get his privilege approved, and approved thrice.

His Royal Highness had granted Léonard the right to enter his apartments at all times, independent of his function as usher. He entered the drawing room, and respectfully assured the personages that he had come to solicit their kind recommendation to His Majesty the King.[1]

"What is it about, Léonard?" asked the Count of Artois.

"Your Royal Highness will perhaps remember that I was at one time the owner of the Théâtre de Monsieur, which has now become the Théâtre Feydeau."

"And national property," said the prince.

"Alas, yes, my prince, and unfortunately there is no recovering it," said Léonard.

"Oh, oh, oh," said Monsieur, "how quickly you make up your mind, Master Léonard. But to return to what you were going to ask me . . ."

"This is my case, monsieur," said Léonard. "I have just been told that it would be an excellent speculation to establish a second Opéra-Comique Theater, and that if I was so fortunate as to obtain a privilege, the rest would be very easy."

"Easy to build a theater which would cost fifteen to eighteen hundred thousand francs!" cried the Duke of Angoulême. "Who told you that?"

"A person who is holding two million francs at my disposal, against the sight of the royal order," said Léonard.

There was a moment's silence in the room. The three royals exchanged questioning looks. The Duke of Angoulême picked his nose with his customary activity, while the princess crossed her legs alternately one over the other, a sign of impatience. Léonard could see that their decisions were already made. Queen Marie Antoinette's daughter was the first to reply.

"What, Monsieur Léonard, do you wish to embark upon a theatrical enterprise?" said Madame d'Angoulême, using the loud voice she favored when expressing displeasure. "You are wrong; there are quite enough theaters in Paris!"

"There are even too many," added the Count of Artois, "and they are nothing but meeting places of the opposition in which they proclaim every night the acts and deeds of the Revolution."

"That's true, that's true," said the Duke of Angoulême. "There is not a farce performed nowadays that does not provoke either revolutionary or imperialist sympathies."

"But those sympathies are nowhere to be met with," said Léonard. He hoped a little speculative flattery would forward his cause. He had gotten quite far in the past with this tactic.

"Master Léonard," said the duke, "I regret to see one of our faithful servants, a man of a religious tendency, at least I hope so, thinking of becoming a theatrical manager."

"I do not wish to become a manager, my prince," said Léonard. "I have not the knowledge to become so, for that matter. I only propose to profit by the privilege."

"And thus to add to the number of schools of scandal and immorality," said Madame d'Angoulême, in a tone that didn't try to hide her displeasure. The princess's reaction must surely have disappointed Léonard. After all, it was he who had saved her mother from an angry mob on that October night in 1789. This court had short memories, indeed.

"What do you think of it, Berry?" asked the Count of Artois of the prince who had just entered.

"Well, really, sir, I do not think that the king's government can be compromised if there is one more theater in Paris. You know my way of looking at these things: The more we give way to the tastes of the French, and the less we drive them out of their habits and preferences, the more they will love us. Besides, if Léonard is refused the privilege of a second Opéra-Comique, another will obtain it, because ministers will always make kings sign documents so long as commissions and bonuses continue to keep up the persuasive eloquence of statesmen."

"Oh, as for you, monsieur," said Madame d'Angoulême, "your decided taste for the theaters is well known, and you would be quite happy to see them multiplying."

"Why not, madame, since it pleases the people among whom we live?" he replied. "For if God gives us the right to govern them, there is surely nothing to oppose our doing so."

"That will do, my children," said the Count of Artois. Then turning to Léonard with some humor, His Royal Highness continued, "As for you, Léonard, since you are bent upon your Opéra-Comique, draw up a petition for the Minister of the Interior. We shall see that it is supported."

Nothing about his interview with the Count of Artois impressed Léonard as very reassuring; he bowed and withdrew. Leaving the palace, again empty-handed, Léonard's imagined new life was put on hold. He was doubtful that the fortune and prestige he had imagined would ever come to pass.

Later that evening, Léonard saw Lucette and recounted what had happened at the palace.

"You will receive no support from the royal family," she said. "Madame the Duchess of Angoulême has spoken against your request, and that is

Madame d'Angoulême
(BIBLIOTHÈQUE NATIONALE DE FRANCE)

sufficient. It is really a pity that Monsieur the Duke of Berry has not a more influential voice in the council; he understands the era in which we live and knows that the theater is one of its necessities, even apart from the price he pays for throwing his handkerchief to the dancers of the Opéra. But in the Pavillon of Marsan it is his illustrious sister-in-law, the daughter of your late patron Marie Antoinette, who takes the chair, and we shall have some trouble in counteracting the veto which she is sure to pronounce against your privilege. However, I wouldn't throw up the sponge."[2] And parodying the count's phrase, Lucette said with dignity, "Draw up a petition to the Minister of the Interior . . . we shall see that it is supported."[3]

Léonard had renewed acquaintance in Paris with Madame Martin, the kind-hearted dealer in artificial flowers in London. Her youngest son, whom Léonard had last seen in London in 1792, introduced himself to the famed hairdresser, whose adventures he had heard told many times by the maternal fireside.

Monsieur Martin listened to Léonard's plan and was kind enough to draw up his first petition. He even promised to have its progress through the ministry watched by one of his friends, a clerk in the office. Léonard later learned that his petition had mysteriously never made it to the minister's office, having been tossed in a porcelain vase with some twenty others in the audience room.

Fortunately, Léonard's second petition found its intended recipient. On the recommendation of the clerk, and upon the urgent advice of Lucette, Count Blacas, the superintendent of the royal household, put the petition in a new envelope on which he wrote, in his finest hand, "Privilege for a second Opéra-Comique," and he left it on the desk of the minister's chief officer.

There it slept peacefully for some four months, gradually getting buried under more and more petitions. When Lucette, bent on visiting the Pavillon de Marsan, went to speak to the chief in Léonard's favor, he replied by pointing to the immovable bundle of documents and saying, "I am keeping M. Léonard's matter before me." And he spoke the truth; he could not sit down to his desk without seeing his papers, but that was *all* he was doing with them.

Lucette advised Léonard to stimulate the chief's zeal with a dinner at one of the most famous taverns in town. Dinners, then as now, were a well-known medium for seduction, transaction, and conclusion. Léonard invited the official with several of his colleagues, Monsieur Martin, and Lucette to dine at the Café Riche. The chief was both a *gourmet* and a *gourmand*. He found the dishes exquisite, the iced champagne delicious, and the next morning Léonard's report was made.

However, a fortnight passed, and Léonard heard nothing. Finally, when he was visiting the palace one morning, the Count of Artois came to the door of his chambers and beckoned Léonard in, telling him he had some news.

"Your business is settled, my dear Léonard," said His Royal Highness.

"Has the king deigned to sign the order?" asked Léonard.

"It was not necessary, you will receive . . ." said the prince.

"The privilege to establish a second Opéra-Comique!" interrupted Léonard, carried away by an outburst of gratitude.

"No, Léonard, as to your privilege, you must not think of that anymore."

Léonard humbly acquiesced, replying that a man of seventy-three should not have to beg; though, he admitted, "old age has its needs." The count explained that Léonard had a formidable competitor; some dramatic author had persuaded Madame the Duchess of Berry to speak to the king, and the king granted his rival the preference.

"As for your privilege," continued the Count of Artois, "I repeat, you must think of that no longer."

"Ah, I understand, my prince . . ." said Léonard.

"But you shall receive the post of Orderer-General of State Funerals," said the count. "I am not jesting, Léonard, you are officially the Orderer-General of State Funerals. The position carries a salary of twelve thousand francs, with no trouble, without even any functions."

These last words were spoken in a tone that suggested no reply was needed. Léonard was silent for a moment to affect a natural-seeming shift from disappointment to gratitude. Then he answered, "In all this I owe Your Royal Highness the sincerest thanks; for not only were you so good as to support my petition, but when you saw that success was impossible, you deigned to take the trouble to obtain for me a place more in conformity with my age and my incapacity. I lay all my gratitude at Your Royal Highness's feet."

Count of Artois at the Tuileries
(BIBLIOTHÈQUE NATIONALE DE FRANCE)

"Say no more, Léonard, you were always devoted to my family. I even *believe* that I have formerly been under a personal obligation to you. You can always rely upon me. Good day, my friend, good day."

Léonard understood that these last words signaled his dismissal; he was now Orderer-in-Chief of State Funerals. He went to the Hotel de Ville, where he officially received the papers containing his appointment, a promotion from doorman to funeral director—an ironic jump from a greeter in this world to a greeter into the next.

The next day he was installed by the department's somber administrators with all the ceremony accorded to a high dignitary. Like a Marshal of France, who has come to take over the command of an army, Léonard passed in review, in a large courtyard with all the staff that was to be under his orders. Those long files of mourners, the men in black coats, crepe hatbands, and weepers, and those batteries of hearses that paraded before him were certainly not as magnificent as a review of the Royal

"The Preposterous Headdress" (1786)

(COURTESY OF THE LEWIS WALPOLE LIBRARY, YALE UNIVERSITY)

Guards. The scene was melancholic: No medal or title of nobility was awarded; neither King Louis XVIII nor the Count of Artois was present; there was no gilding of the sword. Yet this curious inspection possessed a certain romantic character.

At the conclusion of the ritual, those who took part in it offered Léonard a splendid dinner, at which they were very lively and gay. Later in the evening they took him to the Opéra, proving that though these gentlemen spent their day with the dead, they did indeed know how to live. And certainly in a way that Léonard approved.

But when Léonard returned home, he took time to reflect. When one is seventy-three years of age and has seen much of the world, one is always a philosopher. And undoubtedly there was a very decided grotesqueness about the varied sequence of events that had composed his life. The Revolution had ended his career as entrepreneur in the theater; it forced him into exile as far north as the frozen banks of the Neva River in Russia; and it took the very head that had once showcased his magnificent poufs at the court of Versailles.

Léonard would only once ever serve at the head of a state funeral procession; it was upon the death of the old Prince of Condé, the 13th of May 1818, shortly after his appointment as orderer-general. The prince's mortal remains were transferred to Saint Denis, and Léonard was seen preceding the prince's magnificent hearse on horseback, in a black coat of curious cut and a Henri IV hat with black feathers. Léonard had made no progress at all in the art of horsemanship since his journey to Montmédy; he still held himself in the saddle like the hairdresser that he was.

Only a year later, Léonard was summoned to court by a former associate, Madame Montansier, who had invested in his Théâtre de Monsieur in 1789. The original agreement called for Madame Montansier to receive an annuity of twenty thousand francs for twenty-five years; the court awarded her five hundred thousand francs, or about two million dollars, plus interest. Léonard, employed as orderer-general at the age of seventy-three, didn't know how he would ever be able to pay her off.

As fate would have it, he would never have to. Léonard Alexis Autié died on the 24th of March 1820.

Léonard did not leave a will and testament; his only survivors, his daughters Louise and Fanny, shared his remaining assets of 716 francs and a small collection of jewels. The most important object of the succession was a jeweled brooch, a bird of paradise that had belonged to Queen Marie Antoinette. To this day, it is unknown if Léonard had anything to do with the missing crown jewels from the flight to Varennes, though there isn't evidence to support such a betrayal on Léonard's part.

His liabilities included 375 francs owed his maid, Sylvie Martin, for fifteen months of service, and 250 francs to his landlord for six months' rent. His servant,

(BIBLIOTHÈQUE NATIONALE DE FRANCE)

Léonard Autié

Pierre Menchin, did not ask for any payment. His daughters did not attend his funeral; it was a modest occasion with only his nephew, Joseph Blair Autié, following the funeral hearse. It had thus become the Orderer-in-Chief's turn, and in 1820 his staff rendered him the same honors that he had assisted in rendering to the Prince of Condé.

Léonard Autié, who arrived in Paris on that day in 1769 when Venus glided across the face of the sun, was the first to use this dynastic name. His only son, Auguste-Marie, had died young, and there would be no Léonard II to inherit his legacy. His fortune was comprised of a trusty shell comb, and the art that he possessed in a higher degree than any other; Léonard Autié's art lent an air of elegance to folly. Along with his unfailing audacity and ruses, his story reveals Paris in all its sublime glory and the climactic end of all its illusions.

When Léonard felt death approaching, his last wish was to be conducted to the cemetery in the most magnificent coach of his department. And he left the world in the style to which he had once been accustomed, just like the towering and celestial poufs that once adorned the head of his beloved Queen of France.

AFTERWORD

My interest in Léonard Autié's story began with a simple question: Who in the world was this famous hairdresser to Marie Antoinette who supposedly died twice? In the French monthly review, *l'Intermédiaire des chercheurs*, the historian Alfred Bégis discussed this paradox in 1890; the "legende de Léonard le coiffeur" purported that the royal hairdresser was guillotined in 1794, but died of natural causes in 1820.[1]

In the midst of dusty, archived documents in the Bibliothèque Nationale de France, a clipping dated 1905 reported: "Another legend shot down: that of Léonard, the queen's hairdresser, dead twice."[2] In this article, the French historian, G. Lenotre, proposed a thesis to explain the paradox.

He cited two cases in which a condemned man had escaped the guillotine's blade during the Revolution. Although it was a very costly and risky enterprise to bribe the prison concierge and guards, Lenotre delicately insinuated that Léonard could very easily have concealed some diamonds on his person during his imprisonment. After all, Marie Antoinette's diamonds, which were in his charge, went missing on the royal family's fateful flight to Varennes. As for the tale of him dying twice, the author ended on a humorous tone:

> In 1818 he was Superintendent of Burials, and it must have been an edifying sight to see him—the gay Léonard, once the Queen's hairdresser—marching in short breeches and mourning cloak, with a black cane in his hand, at the head of a funeral procession. And when the chances of his office took him to the cemetery of Picpus, where were buried all those who perished with him on the scaffold, he must have experienced the most unusual sensations.[3]

To add strength to Lenotre's argument, Joseph Autié, Pierre's son, published an article in 1838, claiming his uncle Léonard could not have been guillotined in 1794; he was still alive after the restoration of the Bourbon Monarchy in 1814, and did not die until 1820. In fact, Joseph was the only relative who attended his funeral. But if Lenotre's thesis proved true, Léonard would not only have been a thief; if a prisoner was substituted for him at the scaffold, he would have been a murderer as well. The historian Bégis confirmed Lenotre's thesis, concluding that Léonard's escape was due to fraud at the expense of a very unfortunate prisoner—a very grave accusation against the queen's hairdresser.[4]

To set the record straight, *Marie Antoinette's Head* has established that there were three hairdressers, all known as Léonard: Léonard Alexis, Pierre, and Jean-François. The eldest, Léonard Alexis, our protagonist, created the incredible headdresses for

Marie Antoinette. After he gave up the comb, he opened the Théâtre de Monsieur in the name of the king's brother, only dressing the queen's hair on special occasions. He played a small role in the flight to Varennes, and later emigrated to England and Northern Europe in 1791, where he carried out missions for the queen and aided the royals in exile. He returned to Paris in 1814, where he died in 1820.

Pierre was known as Léonard, hairdresser to Madame Élisabeth, the king's sister. Fearing the guillotine at the onset of the Revolution, he left the princess's household, and was employed in a tobacco shop. Possibly ruined, he abandoned his eight children and left for England. He did not return to Paris until after the Restoration, but he brusquely disappeared after two weeks and was never seen again.

The youngest brother, Jean-François, was also referred to as Léonard; he was employed in Marie Antoinette's household as hairdresser, but he only tended to her daily needs. Like Léonard Alexis, he also played a role in the flight to Varennes, but, as the book recounts, he may have inadvertently been responsible for the royal family's arrest. Documents prove that Jean-François was indeed convicted of treason, and condemned to death in July 1794. Whether he was actually guillotined remains a mystery; a story later surfaced that Jean-François had escaped the executioner's blade.

While abroad, Léonard Alexis briefly mentioned the death of his brother in his memoirs. The question arises, however: Why was Léonard mostly silent about such a tragic event? He was also ambiguous when he reported the execution, calling his brother "Villanot," which was actually the name of his cousin, Jean-Pierre Villanou.*

To make matters more confusing, archived documents reported that it was his brother Jean-François who was guillotined, and not Villanou. Léonard's account of his brother's death is suspicious, especially when it was reported that a prisoner had managed to escape the guillotine's blade on the very same day. Could this have been Jean-François Autié?

It is not only possible, but probable. And Léonard may have played a role in his brother's escape. But why would Léonard use his cousin's name instead of his brother's? Knowing that Léonard had valuable court jewels in his possession in England, he may very well have had the means to financially assist his brother. He may also have invented the story of his cousin Villanou being executed, not wanting to be suspected as an accomplice or accused of skimming profits from the diamonds sold for the crown's causes.

There is reason to believe that Villanou also went into exile. An archived note reports that Jean-Pierre Villanou left Paris in August 1794, leaving behind furniture that his wife Marie-Françoise then acquired. Villanou, also hairdresser to Queen

---

* Léonard alluded to a brother, called Villanot, in his memoirs. At first I thought he was referring to his brother Pierre, but I am convinced that Villanot was not a given name, but the surname of one of the queen's valets, Jean Pierre Villanou, a cousin of the Autié's.

Marie Antoinette, may have feared for his life, and it is quite possible that Léonard may have helped him escape as well. There are no official records of Villanou's execution, but this possibility cannot be overlooked.

A rare document, which may shed light on Léonard's finances, was an indictment found in the National Archives charging Léonard, the hairdresser of the former queen, with sending a large quantity of counterfeit gold coins and money to the counter-revolutionary cause in France while he was in England. The question arises: Could Léonard have kept the receipts for the diamonds he sold, remitting the amount in counterfeit money? While there may not be enough evidence to accuse Léonard of any theft, it should be remembered that he did have one of the queen's diamond brooches in his possession when he died in 1820.

Léonard had no fortune at the end of his long career to bequeath to his two surviving daughters, but his wife, Marie-Louise Jacobie, about whom he hardly ever spoke, led a very gay and sumptuous life in Paris before her death in 1837 at the age of eighty-five. Archived documents have also revealed that she asked for a pension in 1824, given that she was the widow of a renowned civil servant. Her request was denied because Mademoiselle Malacrida had been divorced for some thirty years. As for her marital status, church documents revealed that on special occasions Marie-Louise merely signed *"père absent"*—not wanting to be associated with the name "Léonard."

Léonard's memoirs were those of a Gascon, as he himself admitted. He inflated his role in the scenes he portrayed; yet, he was seen, he acted, and he maneuvered his way in and out of the important historical panorama of the French Revolution. Perhaps his memoirs could have been entitled "Léonard the Opportunist," considering the fascinating times and the affluent circles in which the artistic genius lived. His clients, spirited and pretty with fortunes at their disposal, were all actresses, and Léonard used his art to help them realize their roles.

It will be the task of historians to eventually determine whether Léonard's story is based more on verifiable facts or his vanity, but few documents of his time evoke the *époque* in such a striking and lively fashion. His adornment of Queen Marie Antoinette's towering hair earned him the title of "Léonard, the Great." In spite of his celebrated status, Léonard also endured the unimaginable hardship of privation, ignominy, disappointment, and contempt. To these must be added his loneliness, and the adversities of a wandering and perilous life, which easily could have led him to the guillotine's blade.

Such were Léonard's tribulations—all for the glory of fame, prestige, and title. It will be up to readers to decide if he was an entrepreneuring artist, a shallow scoundrel, or a pitiable victim of one of the most tumultuous times in French history.

In any event, one can only assume that Léonard would be thrilled about one thing: being back in the spotlight again.

Acknowledgments

There are a number of people and institutions that I must thank for their help in guiding this project. I must first of all express my gratitude to the staff at Lyons Press and my editor, Jon Sternfeld, whose patience, editorial criticism, and invaluable advice were exemplary and greatly valued by a sometimes fidgety author. Meredith Dias, the book's project editor; Casey Shain, the layout artist; and Vicky Vaughn Shea, the cover designer, also contributed unconditionally and skillfully to make this book possible.

Secondly, I would like to thank all those who have provided me with personal assistance over the years in my studies and in my European travels, including my professors from Arizona State University, Ohio University, the American Graduate School of Paris, and McGill University. I can also never forget the numerous staffs at the libraries and archives that I utilized while researching and writing this book, including the Archives Nationales de France, the Bibliothèque Nationale de France, the Ohio State University Library, and Yale University's Lewis Walpole Library.

It is with the greatest respect and deepest gratitude that I acknowledge the magnificent work of Marie Antoinette's biographers, Antonia Fraser, Caroline Weber, and Chantal Thomas, who spurred my interest in bringing Léonard's story to life again.

Final recognition must go to my family who has always supported and encouraged me, even though the miles between us were many at times. It saddens me that my grandmother cannot see this book—she would have been so proud. My mother and my brother remain a constant source of inspiration, and this book is lovingly dedicated to them.

Selected Bibliography

Abbott, J. S. C. *The Life of Marie Antoinette.* London: Sampson Low, 1850.

Adhemar, La Comtesse de. *Souvenirs sur Marie-Antoinette.* Paris: L. Mame, 1836.

Agnew, John Holmes. *The Eclectic Magazine: Foreign Literature.* New York: Bidwell, 1858.

Alison, Sir Archibald. *History of Europe from the Commencement of the French Revolution.* London: Blackwood, 1870.

Ambs-Dalès, J. B. *Amours et intrigues des grisettes de Paris.* Paris: Roy-Terry, 1830.

Anonymous. "Bienfaisance." *Journal de Paris* 57 (1789): 257.

———. *Essais historiques sur la vie de Marie-Antoinette, reine de France et de Navarre.* Versailles: Le Montensier, 1790.

———. "Rough Materials." In *Metropolitan Magazine* 11 (1841): 92–94.

———. "Memoirs of the Late Duke de Biron." In *Monthly Magazine and British Register* 55 (1800): 43–46.

Arnault, Antoine Vincent de. *Souvenirs d'un Sexagénaire.* Paris: Librairie Dufey, 1833.

Aulard, François-Alphonse. *The French Revolution under the Monarchy.* New York: Charles Scribner's Sons, 1910.

Autié, Léonard Alexis. *Recollections of Léonard, Hairdresser to Queen Marie-Antoinette.* New York: Surgeon & Williams, 1909.

———. *Souvenirs de Léonard, coiffeur de la reine Marie-Antoinette.* 2 Vols. Paris: A. Levavasseur, 1838.

Babeau, Albert. *Le Théâtre des Tuileries sous Louis XIV, Louis XV et Louis XVI.* Paris: Nogent-le-Rotrou, Daupeley-Gouverneur, 1895.

Barthou, Louis. *Mirabeau.* London: William Heinemann. 1913.

Bearne, Catherine Mary Charlton. *A Royal Quartet.* London: T. Fisher Unwin, 1908.

Beaumarchais, Pierre-Augustin Caron de. *La Folle journée ou le Mariage de Figaro, comédie en cinq actes.* Paris: A. Quantin, 1784.

Bentham, Jeremy. *Rational of Judicial Evidence.* London: C. H. Reynell, 1827.

Bicknell, Anna L. *The Story of Marie Antoinette.* New York: The Century Company, 1898.

———. "The Dauphine Marie Antoinette." *The Century Magazine* 54 (1897): 841–60.

Bidwell, W. H. *The Eclectic Magazine of Foreign Literature, Science, and Art* 47 (1859): 102.

Bingham, Denis. *The Marriages of the Bourbons*. New York: Scribner and Welford, 1890.

Blaze, François-Henri-Joseph. *L'Opéra Italien de 1548 à 1856*. Paris: Castil-Blaze, 1856.

Boigne, Comtesse de. *Memoirs*. New York: Charles Scribner's Sons, 1908.

Bord, Gustave. *La Fin de Deux Légendes*. Paris: Henri Daragon, 1909.

Bouillé, Le Marquis de. *Collection des mémoires relatifs à la révolution française*. Paris: Badouin, 1823.

Bouillé, Louis de. *Mémoires sur l'affaire de Varennes, comprenant le mémoire inédit de M. le Marquis de Bouillé*. Paris: Badouin, 1823.

Browning, Oscar. *The Flight to Varennes*. London: Swan Sonnenschein, 1892.

Cabanès, Augustin. *Le cabinet secret de l'histoire*. Paris: Albin Michel, 1908.

Campan, Jeanne-Louise-Henriette. *Memoirs of the Private Life of Marie Antoinette*. London: Henri Colburn, 1822.

Campan, Madame de. *Mémoires sur la vie privée de Marie-Antoinette*. Paris: Badouin Frères, 1822.

Campardon, Émile. *Marie-Antoinette et le procès du collier*. Paris: Henri Plon, 1863.

Challamel, Augustin. *Histoire de la mode en France: la toilette des femmes depuis l'époque gallo-romaine jusqu'à nos jours*. Paris: Hennuyer, 1881.

———. *The History of Fashion in France*. London: Sampson Low, Marston, Searle & Rivington, 1882.

Chambaud, Louis. *A Grammar of the French Tongue*. London: Cook & McGowan, 1816.

Chambers, Robert. *Popular Antiquities*. London: Chambers, 1832.

Chastenay-Lanty, Victorine de. *Mémoirés de Madame de Chastenay*. 2 Vols. Paris: E. Plon, Nourrit et Cie, 1896.

Chauveau-Lagarde, Claude-François. *Note historique sur les procès de Marie-Antoinette d'Autriche, reine de France, et de Madame Élisabeth de France au Tribunal révolutionnaire*. Paris: Gide, 1816.

Choiseul-Stainville, Claude-Antoine-Gabriel duc de. *Relation du départ de Louis XVI, le 20 juin, 1791*. Paris: Badouin Frères, 1822.

Coches, F. Feuillet de. *Marie-Antoinette et Madame Élisabeth*. Paris: Henri Pon, 1873.

Goncourt, Edmond et Jules de. *Histoire de la société française pendant la révolution*. Paris: G. Charpentier, 1880.

Dickens, Charles. *Dickens's Dictionary of Paris*. London: Macmillan & Company, 1883.

Douglas, Robert Bruce. *The Life and Times of Madame du Barry*. London: Léonard Smithers, 1896.

Dumanoir, M. Philippe. *Léonard le perruquier: comédie, mêlée de couplets, en quatre actes*. Performed for the first time, Paris, April 22, 1847.

Dussieux, Louis. *Le Château de Versailles*. Versailles: L. Bernard, 1881.

Èze, Gabriel de. *Histoire de la coiffure des femmes en France*. Paris: Ollendorff, 1886.

Fausse-Lendry, Paysac Fars. *Mémoires: ou Souvenirs d'une octogénaire*. Paris: Le Doyen, 1830.

Flammermont, J. "Les Portraits de Marie-Antoinette." In *Marie-Antoinette: Her Early Youth*, by Helen Augusta Magniac. New York: Macmillan, 1912.

Fleischmann, Hector. *Marie-Antoinette Libertine*. Paris: Bibliothèque des Curieux, 1911.

Galignani, W. *Galignani's New Illustrated Paris Guide*. Paris: Galignani & Co., 1839.

Gleig, George. *Dictionary of Arts, Sciences and Miscellaneous Literature*. Edinburgh: Thompson Bonar, 1801.

Goncourt, Edmond de. *La femme au dix-huitième siècle*. Paris: Fasquelle, 1898.

Griffith, Thomas Waters. *My Scrapbook of the French Revolution*. Chicago: McClurg and Company, 1898.

Hamilton, Lord Frederick and Sir Douglas Straight. *Nash's Pall Mall Magazine*. Vol. 9. London: Charing Cross Road, 1896.

Hanson, John. *The Lost Prince*. New York: Putnam & Co., 1854.

Hardy, Blanche Christable. *The Princesse de Lamballe: A Biography*. London: Archibald Constable and Company, 1908.

Hervey, Charles. *The Theatres of Paris*. Paris: Galignani, 1847.

Hudson, Elisabeth Harriot. *The Life and Times of Louisa, Queen of Prussia*. London: Hatchards, 1876.

Hutton, Charles. *The Philosophical Transactions of the Royal Society of London*. "The Extract of M. Lessier's Letter to M. Magalthaens: 'I observed the transit of Venus, June 3, 1769, at the college of Louis le Grand at Paris.'" London: C. and R. Baldwin, 1809.

Jacob, P. L. *XVIIIme siècle: institutions, usages et costumes, France 1700–1789.* Paris: Firmin-Didot, 1875.

———. *The XVIIIth Century: Its Institutions, Customs, and Costumes.* London: Chapman and Hall, 1876.

La Rocheterie, Maxime de. *Histoire de Marie-Antoinette.* Paris: Perrin, 1890.

———. *The Life of Marie Antoinette.* New York: Dodd, Mead and Company, 1893.

———. *The Life of Marie Antoinette.* New York: Dodd, Mead and Company, 1906.

La Trémoille, Louis duc de. *Les La Trémoille pendant cinq siècles.* Nantes: Émile Grimaud, 1890.

Laclos, Choderlos de. "*Épitre à Margot.*" In *Poésies de Choderlos de Laclos.* Paris: Chez Dorbon, 1908.

Laclos, Choderlos de. *Les liaisons dangereuses.* Paris: Durand, 1782.

Lamartine, Alphonse de. *History of the Girondists.* London: Henry G. Bohn, 1848.

Lamballe, Marie Thérèse Louise de Savoie-Carignan. *Secret Memoirs of Princess de Lamballe.* New York: Walter Dunn, 1901.

Langlade, Émile. *Rose Bertin: The Creator of Fashion at the Court of Marie-Antoinette.* New York: Charles Scribner's Sons, 1913.

Lauzun, Duke de. "Gallantry and the Guillotine." *Gentleman's Magazine* 5 (1870): 109–17.

Legros, Le Sieur. *L'Art de la coëffure des dames françoises, avec des estampes où sont représentées les têtes coëffées.* Paris: A. Boudet, 1768.

Lenotre, G., Mrs. Rodolph Stawell, and BFS Hatchards. *The Last Days of Marie Antoinette: from the French of G. Lenotre.* Philadelphia: J. B. Lippincott Company, 1907.

———. *Romances of the French Revolution.* 2 Vols. London: William Heinemann, 1908.

Lescure, François Adolphe Mathurin de. *Correspondance secrète inédite sur Louis XVI, Marie-Antoinette la cour et la ville de 1777 à 1792.* Paris: Henri Plon, 1866.

Lippincott, J. B. *The Trianon Palaces.* Philadelphia: J. B. Lippincott & Co., 1874.

Littell, Eliakim and Robert S. *Littell's Living Age.* Boston: Littell & Company, 1886.

Lumbroso, Albert. *Revue Napoléonienne.* Vol. 3. Rome: Frascati, 1906.

Maleuvre, Louis. *Gustave III, Opéra d'Auber et Scribe: Costumes.* Paris: Martinet, 1834.

Marie Antoinette, *Correspondance inédite de Marie Antoinette.* Paris: E. Dentu, 1865.

———. *1755–1793, Testament de Sa Majesté Marie-Antoinette d'Autriche, reine de France et de Navarre, morte martyre le 16 octobre 1793, contenu dans la dernière lettre qu'elle écrivit à S. A. R. Madame Élisabeth, soeur de Louis XVI.* Paris: Gueffier, 1816.

Marie-Thérèse Impératrice Germanique. *1717–1780, Correspondance secrète entre Marie-Thérèse et le Comte de Mercy-Argenteau: avec les lettres de Marie-Thérèse et de Marie-Antoinette,* published with an introduction and notes by M. le chevalier Alfred d'Arneth et M. A. Geffroy. Paris: Firmin-Didot frères, fils et Cie, 1874.

McCarthy, Justin E. *The French Revolution.* New York: Harper & Brothers, 1898.

McGregor, John James. *History of the French Revolution.* Waterford: John Bull, 1816.

Mühlbach, Luise. *Joseph II and His Court.* London: H. S. Goetzel, 1864.

Mundt, Klara Müller. *Joseph II and His Court.* New York: McClure Company, 1873.

Percy, Reuben. *The Percy Anecdotes.* London: J. Cumberland, 1826.

Péricaud, Louis. *Théâtre de Monsieur.* Paris: Histoire de l'Histoire, 1908.

Podgorski, M. "Princess Ratazanoff." In *The Cosmopolitan* 11 (1892): 734.

Pottet, Eugène. *Histoire de la Conciergerie du Palais de Paris: depuis les origines jusqu'à nos jours.* Paris: Quantin, 1887.

Prothero, George Walter. "The Flight to Varennes." In *The Quarterly Review* 163 (1886): 86–115.

Rabaut, Jean-Paul. *The History of the Revolution of France.* London: J. Debrett, 1792.

Raigecourt, Charles de. *Exposé de la conduite de M. le C[om]te Charles de Raigecourt à l'affaire de Varennes.* Paris: Badouin, 1823.

Regnault-Warin, Jean-Josephe. *Le Cimetière de la Madeleine.* Paris: Lepetit, 1800.

Reiset, Tony Henri Auguste. *Anne de Caumont-La Force Comtesse de Balbi.* Paris: Émile Paul, 1908.

Religious Tract Society. *French Revolution: Sketches of its History.* London: Religious Tract Society, 1799.

Ritchie, Leitch. *Versailles.* London: Longman, 1839.

Saint-Amand, Imbert de. *Famous Women of the French Court.* New York: Charles Scribner's Sons, 1894.

———. *Marie Antoinette and the End of the Old Régime.* New York: Charles Scribner's Sons, 1898.

———. *The Last Years of Louis XV.* Boston: Club of Odd Volumes, 1893.

Sanderson, John. *Sketches of Paris.* Philadelphia: Carey & Hart, 1838.

Schaeper, Thomas J. *France and America in the Revolutionary Era*. New York: Berghan Books, 1995.

Smith, John Stores. *Mirabeau: Triumph!* 2 Vols. London: Smith, Elder and Company, 1848.

St. John, Bayle. *Purple Tints of Paris, Character and Manners in the New Empire*. 2 Vols. London: Chapman and Hall, 1854.

Stephen, Sir James. *Lectures on the History of France*. London: Longman, Brown, Green, Longmans, & Roberts, 1857.

Stephens, Henry Morse. *A History of the French Revolution*. 2 Vols. New York: Charles Scribner's Sons, 1905.

Talleyrand-Périgord, Charles Maurice de. *Memoirs*. New York: G. P. Putnam, 1892.

Theime, Hugo P. *Women of France*. Philadelphia: Rittenhouse Press, 1908.

Tourzel, Louise Elisabeth. *Mémoires de Madame la Duchesse de Tourzel*. Paris: Duc des Cars, 1883.

Tschudi, Clara. *Marie Antoinette*. London: Swan Sonnenschein, 1898.

Tytler, Sarah. *Marie Antoinette*. New York: G. P. Putnam's Sons, 1883.

Vigée-Lebrun, Louise-Elisabeth. *Memoirs of Madame Vigée-LeBrun*. New York: Doubleday, Page & Company, 1903.

Villemarest, Charles Maxime Catherinet de. *Life of Prince Talleyrand*. 2 Vols. Philadelphia: Carey, Lea & Blanchard, 1834.

Vizetelly, Henry. *The Story of the Diamond Necklace*. London: Tinsley Brothers, 1867.

Watson, Thomas Edward. *To the End of the Reign of Louis the Fifteenth*. New York: Macmillan Company, 1902.

Welch, Catherine. *The Little Dauphin*. London: Methuen & Co., 1908.

Whittaker, G. B. *The History of Paris from the Earliest period to the Present Day: Containing a description of its antiquities, public buildings, civil, religious, scientific, and commercial institutions*. Paris: A. and W. Galignani, 1827.

Wiel, Alethea. *The Story of Verona*. London: F. M. Dent & Company, 1907.

Williams, Hugh Noel. *Memoirs of Madame Du Barry of the Court of Louis XV*. New York: Collier & Son, 1910.

Wright, Thomas. *The History of France*. 2 Vols. London: London Printing Co., 1858.

Yonge, Charles Duke. *The Life of Marie Antoinette, Queen of France*. 2 Vols. London: Hurst and Blackett, 1876.

Younghusband, Lady Helen Augusta Magniac. *Marie-Antoinette, Her Early Youth, 1770–1774*. London: Macmillan & Co., 1912.

List of Illustrations & Credits

The illustrations found in this book originate from a variety of sources including books, newspapers, and government documents from the Bibliothèque Nationale de France. Those illustrations that were not identified are long since in the public domain due to their age, but every attempt will be made to identify their creators for future editions.

PROLOGUE

Scene at the Place de la République, October 16, 1793. Georg Heinrich Sieveking, copper engraving (1793). Work in the public domain; copyright has expired in countries copyrighting works for life plus 100 years or less.

PART ONE

The mania. Jules Fleury-Husson. *Histoire de la caricature: sous la Réforme et la Ligue: Louis XIII à Louis XVI* (Paris: Champfleury, 1880).

CHAPTER 1

Place Maubert. P. L. Jacob, *The XVIIIth Century: Its Institutions, Customs, and Costumes; France, 1700–1789* (London: Chapman and Hall, 1886).

Léonard Alexis Autié. *Souvenirs de Léonard, coiffeur de la reine Marie-Antoinette* (Paris: A. Fayard, 1905).

Drawing from *L'Art de la Coiffure des Dames Franchises*. Sieur Legros (Paris: Boudet, 1768).

Madame de Pompadour styled "à la tête de mouton." Saint-Amand, *Women of Versailles the Court of Louis XV* (London: Charles Scribner's Sons, 1896).

Hôtel de Langeac. Edmé Béguillet, *Description Historique de Paris* (Paris: Frantin, 1779). Courtesy of the Library of Congress.

CHAPTER 2

The royal coach. *Voiture qui a servie au sacre du Roi* (Prieur avec privilège du Roi, 1783). Bibliothèque Nationale de France.

Madame the Countess du Barry. Julia Kavanagh, *Women in France during the Eighteenth Century* (London: Smith, Elder and Co., 1850).

Mademoiselle Guimard. Hugh Noel Williams, *Later Queens of the French Stage* (London: Harper & Brothers, 1906).

CHAPTER 3

Madame the Countess du Barry in her boudoir. Hugh Williams, *Madame du Barry* (London: Charles Scribner's Sons, 1909).

Wedding celebration in the King's Chapel at Versailles. Claude-Louis Desrais (1770). Anonymous engraving.

Château de Versailles, eighteenth century. *Vuë du Château Royal de Trianon,* Le Pautre, dessinateur. Bibliothèque Nationale de France.

Countess de Noailles. *The Lady with the Mask.* Pierre Louis de Surugue (1746).

Dauphine Marie Antoinette. *Portrait of Marie-Antoinette.* Cathelin after Drouais (eighteenth century).

CHAPTER 4

Mademoiselle Rose Bertin, Dressmaker to Marie-Antoinette. Jean-François Janinet (1752–1814).

Monsieur the Duke of Chartres and his family. C. Le Peintre (1779).

Le Count of Artois, Charles-Philippe de France. Louis Jacques Cathelin (1773).

Gala ball, late eighteenth century. *Le bal paré.* Antoine Jean Duclos (1774).

Shepherdess, coachman, and harlequin costumes. *Gustave III, opéra d'Auber*, Maleuvre (1834). Bibliothèque Nationale de France.

The Dauphine Marie Antoinette. *Marie-Antoinette, reine de France*, 1755–1793. Collection Vinck. (ark:/12148/btv1b53028207g). Bibliothèque Nationale de France.

Journal des dames. *Journal des dames.* (L'imprimerie de Quillau, rue du Fouarre, 1774).

Rose Bertin's ques-à-co. *Histoire de la coiffure des femmes en France.* Gabriel d'Èze (Paris: Ollendorff, 1886).

CHAPTER 5

Pouf hairstyles worn by Marie Antoinette. Marie-Antoinette. Paris: Esnauts et Rapilly. (ark:/12148/btv1b53028207g). Bibliothèque Nationale de France.

Marie Antoinette's hedgehog pouf. Marie-Antoinette, à mi-corps, de face, cheveux en hérisson. (ark:/12148/btv1b69403193). Bibliothèque Nationale de France.

Marie Antoinette's coiffure à la Zephyr. *Marie-Antoinette.* Marie-Louise-Adélaïde Boizot (1775). Bibliothèque Nationale de France.

The coiffure à Belle-Poule. *Le négligé galant ornés de la coëffure à la Belle-Poule.* (ark:/12148/btv1b6940282h). Bibliothèque Nationale de France.

Duchesse of Chartres. Louise Marie Adelaide de Bourbon Penthièvre. Paris: Esnauts et Rapilly. (ark:/12148/btv1b6950004w). Bibliothèque Nationale de France.

France in tears, leaning on the medallion of Louis XV. Jean-Michel Moreau (1741–1814). (ark:/12148/btv1b84099140). Bibliothèque Nationale de France.

Happier days at Madame du Barry's Château Louveciennes, 1771. *Fête donné à Louveciennes.* Jean-Michel Moreau (1741–1814).

Le Petit Trianon. *Versailles*, Leicht Ritchie (London: Longman, Orme, Brown, Green and Longmans, 1839).

Coronation portrait of Louis XVI. Claude-Louis Desrais (1746–1816). (ark:/12148/btv1b6941584p). Bibliothèque Nationale de France.

Coronation of Louis XVI, Rheims Cathedral, June 11, 1775. (ark:/12148/btv1b8409969z). Bibliothèque Nationale de France.

PART TWO

The queen's confidant. *Weapons and Ornaments of Woman: Hairdressing and Head-Coverings,* Octave Uzanne in *Cosmopolitan*, Vol. XLI, 1906.

CHAPTER 6

Duke of Lauzun (Général Biron), *1791-1792: Correspondance intime.* Armand-Louis de Gontaut Biron (Paris: Perrin et Cie., 1906).

The Duchess of Polignac. *The Duchess of Polignac, (1787).* Louise Elisabeth Vigée-LeBrun.

Pamphlet depicting the queen's promiscuity (1789). *Je ne respire plus que pour toi . . . un baiser, mon bel Ange!* (ark:/12148/btv1b6942376r). Bibliothèque Nationale de France.

The Trianon Gardens. *Le Petit-Trianon, histoire et description* (1885). (ark:/12148/bpt6k841368w). Bibliothèque Nationale de France.

Coiffures during the reign of Marie Antoinette. P. L. Jacob, *The XVIIIth Century: Its Institutions, Customs, and Costumes; France, 1700–1789* (London: Chapman & Hall, 1876).

Marie Antoinette's "coiffure à l'enfant," *Maria Antonietta.* John Samuel Agar (1797). (ark:/12148/btv1b69417547). Bibliothèque Nationale de France.

Marie-Thérèse, Marie Antoinette, and Dauphin Louis. *Antoinette et ses enfants dans un parc.* Bataille. (ark:/12148/btv1b53028255n). Bibliothèque Nationale de France.

Marie Antoinette à la rose. *Marie-Antoinette,* Vigée-LeBrun, Louise-Élisabeth (1755–1842). (ark:/12148/btv1b53028278t). Bibliothèque Nationale de France.

CHAPTER 7

Madame Jeanne de la Motte. *Comtesse de La Motte,* François Bonneville (1796). (ark:/12148/btv1b6942346m). Bibliothèque Nationale de France.

Mademoiselle d'Oliva. *Mademoiselle Le Guet d'Oliva,* Romain Girard (1786). (ark:/12148/btv1b6942357d). Bibliothèque Nationale de France.

Boehmer's diamond necklace. Frantz Funck-Brentano, *L'affaire du collier* (Paris: Hachette, 1907).

Axel von Fersen. F. F. Flach, *Grefve Hans Axel von Fersen: minnesteckning jemte utdrag ur hans dagbok och* (Stockholm: Fritzes Kongl., 1896).

Assembly of Notables, 1787. *Assemblée des notables* (1802). Claude Niquet (1770–1830). (ark:/12148/btv1b6942559x). Bibliothèque Nationale de France.

CHAPTER 8

Receipts. Louise Emmanuelle de Châtillon, *Souvenirs de la princesse de Tarente, 1789–1792* (Paris: Honoré Champion, 1901).

Académie de coiffure on the rue de la Chaussée-d'Antin, 1788. *The Picture Magazine,* Vol. III, January to June, 1894.

Léonard's brother, Jean-François Autié. G. Lenotre, *Le Drame de Varennes* (Paris: Perrin et Cie., 1905).

Théâtre de Monsieur, Tuileries Palace. Imbert de Saint-Amand, *Marie Antoinette at the Tuileries, 1789–1791.* (New York: Charles Scribner's Sons, 1898).

Plan du Théâtre des Tuileries. Albert Babeau, *Le Théâtre des Tuileries sous Louis XIV, Louis XV et Louis XVI.* (Paris: Société de l'Histoire de Paris, 1895).

Giovanni Battista Viotti. *Viotti, célèbre violon et compositeur.* Pierre François Ducarme. (ark:/12148/btv1b84256252). Bibliothèque Nationale de France.

Favorite: The Count Decazes. *Pair de France, Chevalier Commandeur des Ordres du Roi.* (ark:/12148/btv1b69558061). Bibliothèque Nationale de France.

Louise-Marie-Joséphine de Savoie. Madame de Provence, wife of King Louis XVIII of France. Unidentified printmaker, ca. 1810.

Théâtre de Monsieur, formerly Salle de Machines, Tuileries Palace. Albert Babeau, *Le Théâtre des Tuileries sous Louis XIV, Louis XV et Louis XVI* (Paris: Société de l'Histoire de Paris, 1895).

Queen Marie Antoinette at Café du Théâtre. Louise-Élisabeth Vigée-LeBrun, *Café du Théâtre Français*. (ark:/12148/btv1b69416611). Bibliothèque Nationale de France.

Théâtre de Monsieur: Queen Marie-Antoinette's loge (lower left). *Couronnement de Voltaire*. Jean-Michel Moreau (1741–1814). (ark:/12148/btv1b8410068x). Bibliothèque Nationale de France.

Bienfaisance. *Journal de Paris* (Paris: 2 juin 1789).

PART THREE

The clouds of revolution. *Départ des femmes de la Halle pour Versailles*, after Scheffer. (ark:/12148/btv1b8431309z). Bibliothèque Nationale de France.

CHAPTER 9

Marie Antoinette's Portrait. *Marie Antoinette, reine de France*. Jean-Jacques-François Le Barbier (1738–1826). (ark:/12148/btv1b6941719s). Bibliothèque Nationale de France.

Dauphin Louis-Joseph with his sister Marie-Thérèse. *Louis Joseph Xavier François, premier Dauphin, en pied, de face, et Marie Thérèse*. Louise-Élisabeth Vigée-LeBrun, Louise-Élisabeth (1786). (ark:/12148/btv1b69419968). Bibliothèque Nationale de France.

The Princesse de Lamballe. Comtesse de Villermont, *Histoire de La Coiffure Féminine* (Paris: Henri Laurens, 1892).

Fall of the Bastille, 14th of July 1789. Thomas Carlyle, *The Bastille*, Vol. 1 (London: George Bell and Sons, 1902).

Baker François is hanged for the scarcity of bread. *Événement du 22 8.bre 1789: assassinat du nommé François, boulanger*. (ark:/12148/btv1b6944108v). Bibliothèque Nationale de France.

The Fatal Banquet. *Repas des gardes du corps*. (ark:/12148/btv1b69441706). Bibliothèque Nationale de France.

Women's March on Versailles. *A Versailles, à Versailles du 5 Octobre* (ark:/12148/btv1b8410839z). Bibliothèque Nationale de France.

CHAPTER 10

Palace of the Tuileries, Place Carrousel. George Lillie Craik, *Paris and Its Historical Scenes: of 1789. The Tuileries* (London: Charles Knight, 1831).

Duke of Orléans, Louis Philippe II. Antoine Louis François Sergent. (ark:/12148/btv1b6950012f). Bibliothèque Nationale de France.

Honoré Mirabeau. John Stores Smith, *Mirabeau: Triumph!* (London: Smith, Elder and Co., 1848).

Rue Saint-Honoré, area of Léonard's residence, circa 1789. Jean Duplessi-Bertaux, *Supplice de Gobel* (1819). (ark:/12148/btv1b6950499r). Bibliothèque Nationale de France.

Map of the route to Montmédy. Hilaire Belloc, *Marie Antoinette* (New York: Doubleday, Page and Co., 1903).

Coins minted in 1789 with the king's likeness. *American Journal of Numismatics*, Vols. 20–22, (American Numismatic Society, 1887).

CHAPTER 11

The Marquis de Lafayette. Hartwell James, *Military Heroes of the United States from Lexington to Santiago* (Philadelphia: Henry Altemus Co., 1899).

The Dauphin Louis, Queen Marie Antoinette, Madame Élisabeth, and Marie-Thérèse strolling in the Tuileries gardens. *Marie-Antoinette et le Dauphin, Madame Élisabeth et Madame Royale se promenant dans le jardin des Tuileries.* (ark:/12148/btv1b53009776j). Bibliothèque Nationale de France.

Paris to Varennes: approximate distances and times. Oscar Browning, *The Flight to Varennes* (London: Swan Sonnenschein, 1892).

Tuileries Palace and the Rue St. Honoré. Frank A. Munsey, *The Scrap Book* (New York: Frank A. Munsey Co., 1908).

Royal family's departure for Varennes. *Depart de Louis XVI le 21 juin* (1791). (ark:/12148/btv1b8411366f). Bibliothèque Nationale de France.

CHAPTER 12

King Louis XVI's likeness on revolutionary currency. NOTE: Assignat de Deux Cents Livres (1789). (Author's Collection)

The royal family in flight. *Arrestation du Roy Louis XVI à Varennes: Les habitants de cette ville ayant appris la qualité des voyageurs.* Mariano Bovi. (ark:/12148/btv1b84113777). Bibliothèque Nationale de France.

The royal family in Mayor Sauce's house. *Arrestation de Louis seize à Varennes: le 22 juin 1791.* (ark:/12148/btv1b8411384c). Bibliothèque Nationale de France.

Royal family escorted back to Paris. *Retour de Varennes. Arrivée de Louis Capet à Paris: le 25 juin 1791.* (ark:/12148/cb40248683r). Bibliothèque Nationale de France.

CHAPTER 13

The Princesse de Lamballe. Blanche Christabel Hardy, *The Princesse de Lamballe: A Biography* (London: Archibald Constable and Co., 1908).

Piccadilly in the eighteenth century. Henry Benjamin Wheatley, *Round about Piccadilly and Pall Mall* (London: Smith, Elder and Co., 1870).

PART FOUR

The struggles to survive. *The Persecuted Queen hurried at the Dead of Night into a common prison: The Queen is here delivered up to the keeper of the Conciergerie.* (ark:/12148/btv1b6949923v). Bibliothèque Nationale de France.

CHAPTER 14

Attack on the Tuileries, 10th of August 1792. *Dix août 1792. Siège et prise du château des Tuileries.* (ark:/12148/btv1b6948737w). Bibliothèque Nationale de France.

The royal family escorted to the Temple Prison. *La Tour du Temple.* (ark:/12148/btv1b84116637). Bibliothèque Nationale de France.

Docks of Dover. William Batcheller, *A Descriptive Picture of Dover* (Dover: Batcheller, 1851).

Madame Countess du Barry. Hugh Noel Williams, *Madame Du Barry* (New York: Charles Scribner's Sons, 1909).

Louis XVI bids farewell to his family. *The Last Interview between Lewis the Sixteenth and His Disconsolate Family.* (ark:/12148/btv1b69489617). Bibliothèque Nationale de France.

CHAPTER 15

List of victims of the Revolutionary Tribunal of Paris on the 25th of July 1794. Alphonse Picard, Liste des victimes du Tribunal révolutionnaire à Paris (Paris: Palais de Justice, 1911).

Marie Antoinette's prison cell in the Conciergerie. John S. C. Abbott, *The Life of Marie Antoinette, Queen of France* (London: Sampson Low, 1850).

The widow Capet. G. Lenotre, *The Last Days of Marie Antoinette* (Philadelphia: J. B. Lippincott Company, 1907).

The arrest of Madame du Barry. Maurice Alhoy & Louis Lurin, *Les Prisons de Paris* (Paris: Gustave Havard, 1846).

CHAPTER 16

Uncrowned Louis XVII in the Temple. G. Wappers, *Louis XVII in the Temple* (1871).

Marie-Thérèse, sole survivor of the Temple. Catherine Wormely, *The Ruin of a Princess: Marie-Thérèse Charlotte Angoulême* (Catherine Wormely, 1912).

Jelgava Palace in Mittau. Alexandre de Bar, *Jelgava Palace* (1884).

Louis XVIII, King of France. F. Lignon, *Louis XVIII. Roi de France.* (ark:/12148/btv1b6955027f). Bibliothèque Nationale de France.

Czar Paul I. Paul I of Russia (Издание И. В. Цветкова, 1896).

Maria Feodorovna. Nicholas Mikhailovich Romanov, *Russian Portraits of 18th and 19th Centuries* (1905).

St. Petersburg, Russia (eighteenth century). Mikhail Makhaev, *History of Saint Petersburg* (1753).

CHAPTER 17

The Reception of Louis XVIII. Theodor Hoffbauer. *Réception de Louis XVIII à l'Hôtel de Ville, 29 août 1814.*

The Restoration of the Bourbons. Gautier. *The French Royal Family, circa 1822.*

Léonard's creation, Feydeau Théâtre. Donnet et Orgiazzi. *Architectonographie des théâtres de Paris* (Paris: P. Didot, 1821).

CHAPTER 18

Madame d'Angoulême. F. Girard, *S. A. R. Madame Duchesse D'Angoulême* (1816). (ark:/12148/btv1b6955373q). Bibliothèque Nationale de France.

Count of Artois at the Tuileries. *Charles Philippe, Comte* (1814). (ark:/12148/btv1b69550728). Bibliothèque Nationale de France.

The Preposterous Headdress. Matthew Darly, "The Preposterous Headdress" (1776). Courtesy of the Lewis Walpole Library, Yale University.

Léonard Autié. *Galerie des modes,* Vol. 2. Bibliothèque Nationale de France.

Signature. Etienne Léon Lamothe-Langon et Léonard Autié. *Souvenirs de Léonard, coiffeur de la reine Marie-Antoinette* (1838).

Endnotes

A NOTE ON TITLES OF NOBILITY

1 Louis Chambaud, A. J. Des Carrières, *A Grammar of the French Tongue* (London: Cook and McGowan, 1816), 441. Nobility in France was hereditary and passed down through the male lineage. However, it was also possible to become noble by obtaining certain offices or by royal decree. The legal status of nobility was abolished during the Revolution in 1789, but titles were re-created in 1808, abolished in 1848, and restored again in 1852.

PROLOGUE

1 Claude-François Chauveau-Lagarde, *Note historique sur les procès de Marie-Antoinette d'Autriche, reine de France, et de Madame Élisabeth de France au Tribunal révolutionnaire* (Paris: Gide, 1816), 8–9.

2 Eugène Pottet, *Histoire de la Conciergerie du Palais de Paris: depuis les origines jusqu'à nos jours* (Paris: Quantin, 1887), 190–214. A very revealing declaration of Rosalie Lamortière.

3 Marie-Thérèse (Impératrice germanique, 1717–1780), *Correspondance secrète entre Marie-Thérèse et le Comte de Mercy-Argenteau: avec les lettres de Marie-Thérèse et de Marie-Antoinette,* publiée avec une introduction et des notes par M. le chevalier Alfred d'Arneth et M. A. Geffroy (Paris: Firmin-Didot frères, fils et Cie, 1874), 216–39.

4 F. Feuillet de Coches, *Marie-Antoinette et Madame Élisabeth* (Paris: Henri Pon, 1873), 532. "C'est à vous, ma sœur, que j'écris pour la dernière fois. Je viens d'être condamné non pas à une mort honteuse, elle ne l'est que pour les criminels, mais à aller rejoindre votre frère. Comme lui innocente, j'espère montrer la même fermeté que lui dans ses derniers moments. Je suis calme comme on l'est quand la conscience ne reproche rien; j'ai un profond regret d'abandonner mes pauvres enfants, vous savez que je n'existais que pour eux et vous ma bonne et tendre sœur. Vous qui avait par votre amitié tout sacrifié pour être avec nous, dans quelle position je vous laisse! J'ai appris par le plaidoyer même du procès que ma fille était séparée de vous."

5 Marie-Antoinette (reine de France; 1755–1793), *Testament de Sa Majesté Marie-Antoinette d'Autriche, reine de France et de Navarre, morte martyre le 16 octobre 1793, contenu dans la dernière lettre qu'elle écrivit à S. A. R. Madame Élisabeth, sœur de Louis XVI* (Paris: Gueffier, 1816).

6 Maxime de La Rocheterie, *Histoire de Marie-Antoinette* (Paris: Perrin, 1890). Indecent pamphlets flooded the court and the city; they were even attached to the door of Notre Dame or slipped under the king's dinner plate by servants.

7 John Hanson, *The Lost Prince* (New York: Putnam & Co., 1854), 69–70.

CHAPTER 1: LÉONARD THE MAGICIAN

1 Léonard Alexis Autié, *Souvenirs de Léonard, coiffeur de la reine Marie-Antoinette* (Paris: A. Levavasseur, 1838), 5–7. "J'avais fait ce jour-là douze lieues à pied; j'étais bien las, mais non pas résigné à le paraître; car j'apportais de ma province, pour tout bagage, une vanité que ne m'eût pas permis d'avouer que je venais de parcourir cent vingt lieues par le plus naturel de tous le moyens de locomotion."

2 Charles Hutton, *The Philosophical Transactions of the Royal Society of London*, "The Extract of M. Lessier's Letter to M. Magalthaens: 'I observed the transit of Venus, June 3, 1769, at the college of Louis le Grand at Paris'" (London: C. and R. Baldwin, 1809), 664.

3 George Gleig, *Dictionary of Arts, Sciences and Miscellaneous Literature* (Edinburgh: Thompson Bonar, 1801), 269.

4 G. Lenotre, *Romances of the French Revolution* (London: William Heinemann, 1908), Vol. 2, 81.

5 G. Lenotre, *Romances of the French Revolution* (London: William Heinemann, 1908), Vol. 1, 136. See also: *Metropolitan Magazine* (New York: J. Mason, XI, 1841) 92–94. "The Rue des Noyers stank worst of all, owing to its extreme narrowness, and the full state of the gutter, which runs down the middle of the street."

6 G. B. Whittaker, *The History of Paris from the Earliest Period to the Present Day: Containing a description of its antiquities, public buildings, civil, religious, scientific, and commercial institutions* (Paris: A. and W. Galignani, 1827, 516–17). This guide includes a listing of merchants: "The fashion of the waistcoat having become a peculiar object of attention to every gentleman who wishes to be distinguished for taste in dress, M. Blanc has devoted himself to this branch of his art exclusively, and brought it to the highest point of luxury and elegance. The greatest number of this portion of male attire which attracts notice at balls or parties in the evening, or in the morning promenade, for the gracefulness of their cut, is from the hands of Blanc."

7 Le Sieur Legros, *L'Art de la coëffure des dames françoises, avec des estampes où sont représentées les têtes coëffées* (Paris: A. Boudet, 1768).

8 The *Gazette de France* was the oldest newspaper in France, established in 1631 as the *Gazette*.

9 Reuben Percy, *The Percy Anecdotes* (London: J. Cumberland, 1826), 73. The lawsuit

of the ladies' hairdressers in Paris, which was brought before the highest court of judicature in January 1769, was entitled "For the *coëffeurs de dames* of Paris, against the corporation of master barbers, hairdressers and bath keepers." Percy wrote: "Those hair-dressers who presumed to dress both sexes, in this case maintained that it was their exclusive privilege to dress the ladies; and indeed they had several of their adversaries imprisoned, fined, etc. These in their turn defended themselves, and contended that the exclusive privilege was in their favor; because, first, the art of dressing ladies' hair is a liberal art, and foreign to the profession of the *maîtres perruquiers;* secondly, that the statute of the *perruquiers* does not give them the pretended exclusive right; and, thirdly, that they have hitherto oppressed them, and are indebted to them in considerable damages and interests."

10 G. B. Whittaker. Nicolet's Theatre was established about the year 1760. In 1772, Nicolet had the honor to perform before the king at Choisy, and his troupe then took the title of *Grands danseurs du roi.*

11 Léonard Alexis Autié, 23.

12 Charles Hervey, *The Theatres of Paris* (Paris: Galignani, 1847), 520.

13 P. L. Jacob, *The XVIIIth Century: Its institutions, Customs, and Costumes* (London, Chapman and Hall, 1876), 412.

14 Charles Maurice de Talleyrand-Périgord, *Memoirs* (New York: G. P. Putnam, 1892), 347. The king had shown some preference for the beautiful woman who married Choiseul's cousin, and Madame de Pompadour became very jealous. To cement his alliance with the Pompadour, Choiseul managed to show the king some passionate letters that his cousin's wife had written to himself.

CHAPTER 2: THE KING'S NEW MISTRESS

1 Augustin Challamel, *Histoire de la mode en France: la toilette des femmes depuis l'époque gallo-romaine jusqu'à nos jours* (Paris: Hennuyer, 1881).

2 Sir Archibald Alison, *History of Europe from the Commencement of the French Revolution* (London: Blackwood, 1870), 124–26.

3 Denis Bingham, *The Marriages of the Bourbons* (New York: Scribner and Welford, 1890). Madame d'Etiolles, created Marquise de Pompadour, was presented on the 14th of September at Versailles to the king and to the queen. On the 16th the king went to his house at Choisy, the ladies who accompanied him being the Duchess of Lauraguais, the Marquise de Bellefont, the Marquise d'Estrade, and the Marquise de Pompadour. On Sunday the queen, the dauphin, and the dauphine went to Choisy to dine, and Madame de Pompadour for the first time dined with the queen, who was very polite to her. In describing the reception of the Marquise de Pompadour, M. de Maurepas wrote, "There were a great number of people present when she went to pay her respects to the queen,

for all Paris was anxious to know what her Majesty would say to her." She only commented on the marquise's dress.

4   "C'est aux mortels d'adorer votre image; L'original était fait pour les Dieux," Verses addressed by Voltaire to Madame du Barry in 1773.

5   J. B. Ambs-Dalès, *Amours et intrigues des grisettes de Paris* (Paris: Roy-Terry, 1830). Author gives a description of the grisettes of the different quarters of Paris.

CHAPTER 3: THE COURT OF VERSAILLES

1   Leitch Ritchie, *Versailles* (London: Longman, 1839), 245. The royal family dined in public. In fact, the doorkeepers allowed everyone decently clothed to enter the chambers.

2   Clara Tschudi, *Marie Antoinette* (London: Swan Sonnenschein, 1902), 7. Marie Antoinette conquered all hearts in spite of French prejudice against her family's house of Habsburg in Austria. "Her grace and amiability called forth a perfect delirium of enthusiasm."

3   J. Flammermont, "Les Portraits de Marie-Antoinette, Gazette des Beaux Arts," in Helen Augusta Magniac Younghusband, *Marie-Antoinette: Her Early Youth* (New York: Macmillan, 1912), 100.

4   Ibid., 102.

5   Lady Helen Augusta Magniac Younghusband, *Marie-Antoinette, Her Early Youth (1770–1774)* (London: Macmillan & Co., 1912), 100.

6   Klara (Müller) Mundt, *Joseph II and His Court* (New York: McClure Company, 1873), 277. "She is a stiff and tiresome old dame, I grant you, but in France she presides over everything. Without her the royal family can neither sleep nor wake; they can neither take a meal if they be in health, nor a purge if they be indisposed, without her everlasting surveillance. She directs their dress, amusements, associates, and behavior; she presides over their pleasures, their weariness, their social hours, and their hours of solitude. This may be uncomfortable, but royalty cannot escape it, and it must be endured."

7   Madame Campan, *Mémoires sur la vie privée de Marie-Antoinette, Vol. 2,* (Paris: Badouin Frères, 1822), 139-54.

8   Augustin Cabanès, *Le cabinet secret de l'histoire* (Paris: Albin Michel, 1908, 49). Did this surgery actually take place? According to the memoirs of Madame Campan, the question is not resolved. "Vers les derniers mois de 1777, la reine, étant seule dans ses cabinets, nous fit appeler, mon beau-père et moi, et, nous présentant sa main à baiser, nous dit que nous regardant l'un et l'autre comme des gens bien occupés de son bonheur, elle voulait recevoir nos compliments; qu'enfin elle était reine de France et quelle espérait bientôt avoir des enfants; qu'elle avait, jusqu'à ce moment, su cacher ses peines, mais qu'en secret elle avait versé bien des

pleurs. À partir de ce moment heureux si longtemps attendu, l'attachement du roi pour la reine prit tout le caractère de l'amour. Le bon Lassone, premier médecin du roi et de la reine, me parlait souvent de la peine que lui avait faite un éloignement dont il avait longtemps à vaincre la cause, et ne me paraissait plus avoir alors que des inquiétudes d'un genre tout différent."

9   Louis Dussieux, *Le Château de Versailles* (Versailles: L. Bernard, 1881), 19. "Toutes les fautes de Marie-Antoinette sont du genre de celles que je viens de détailler. La volonté de substituer successivement la simplicité des usages de Vienne à ceux de Versailles, lui fut plus nuisible qu'elle n'aurait pu l'imaginer."

10 A. and W. Galignani, *Galignani's New Illustrated Paris Guide* (Paris: Galignani & Co., 1839), 516–17.

CHAPTER 4: CAPTIVATING A QUEEN AND HER SUBJECTS

1   Catherine Mary Charlton Bearne, *A Royal Quartet* (London: T. Fisher Unwin, 1908), 44.

2   Anna Bicknell, "The Dauphine Marie Antoinette," *The Century Magazine* (New York: Macmillan & Company, 1897), 857.

3   Clara Tschudi, *Marie Antoinette* (London: Swan Sonnenschein, 1898), 65.

4   According to the accounts of the queen's household, Léonard received commissions as early as 1779 as *premier valet de chambre-coiffeur*. Jean-François joined his brother at court in 1783. When Leguay passed away, Jean-François replaced him as *perruquier-baigneur-étuviste*, and Léonard retained the honorary title of *"Coiffeur de la reine,"* according to court records.

5   M. Dumanoir (Philippe), *Léonard le perruquier: comédie, mêlée de couplets, en quatre actes* (Performed for the first time in Paris, April 22, 1847).

6   Gustave Bord, *La Fin de Deux Legendes* (Paris: Henri Daragon, 1909). Marie-Anne Elisabeth, indeed the legitimate daughter of Léonard Alexis Autié, was baptized at Saint-Eustache.

7   Léonard Autié, 103.

8   Luise Mühlbach, *Joseph II and His Court* (London: H. S. Goetzel, 1864), 211.

9   Maxime de La Rocheterie, *The Life of Marie Antoinette* (Cambridge: John Wilson & Son, 1906), 76. Count Mercy, a powerful figure at court wrote: "Madame the Dauphiness is making herself adored here, and public opinion is so fixed on this point that some days ago on the occasion of a diminution of the price of bread the people of Paris said openly in the streets and markets that it was surely Madame the Dauphine who had solicited and obtained this reduction for the benefit of the poor people."

10 Émile Langlade, *Rose Bertin, the Creator of Fashion at the Court of Marie-Antoinette* (New York: Scribner, 1913), 15.

11 Louis Chambaud, *A Grammar of the French Tongue* (London: Cook & McGowan, 1816), 438.

12 Anna L. Bicknell, *The Story of Marie Antoinette* (New York: The Century Company, 1898), 33.

13 John Sanderson, *Sketches of Paris* (Philadelphia: Carey & Hart, 1838), 273.

CHAPTER 5: "LE POUF SENTIMENTAL"

1 Augustin Challamel, *The History of Fashion in France* (London: Sampson Low, Marston, Searle & Rivington, 1882), 161.

2 Ibid., 161–63.

3 Imbert de Saint-Amand, *The Last Years of Louis XV* (Boston: Club of Odd Volumes, 1893), 204.

4 Alphonse de Lamartine, *History of the Girondists* (London: Henry G. Bohn, 1848), 287.

5 Hugh Noel Williams, *Memoirs of Madame Du Barry of the Court of Louis XV* (New York: Collier & Son, 1910), 264.

6 Jean-Josephe Regnault-Warin, *Le Cimetière de la Madeleine* (Paris: Lepetit, 1800).

7 Léonard Autié, *Recollections of Léonard, Hairdresser to Queen Marie-Antoinette* (New York: Surgeon & Williams, 1909), 166.

8 W. H. Bidwell, *The Eclectic Magazine of Foreign Literature, Science, and Art*, Vol. 47 (New York: W. H. Bidwell, 1859), 102.

9 Léonard Autié, 168.

10 Jeanne-Louise-Henriette Campan, *Memoirs of the Private Life of Marie Antoinette* (London: Henri Colburn, 1822), 112.

CHAPTER 6: A HAIRDRESSER'S GOSSIP

1 Edmond et Jules de Goncourt, *Histoire de la société française pendant la révolution* (Paris: G. Charpentier, 1880), 33.

2 *The Gentleman's Magazine* (London: W. H. Allen, 1870), 109. "Lauzun, being young, handsome, saucy, and witty, with a certain dashing appearance of chivalrous manner, and immensely rich in the bargain—as soon as he became of age, all the gay ladies of the court of Louis XV made—if we accept his very indelicate narrative—love to him desperately, one after the other."

3 Madame Campan, Vol. 2, 330.

4 *Monthly Magazine and British Register*, Vol. 9, No. 55 (London: R. Phillips, 1800), 44.

5 *Essais historiques sur la vie de Marie-Antoinette, reine de France et de Navarre* (Versailles: Le Montensier, 1790):

De Coigny cependant rien ne défit l'ouvrage,
Les caresses de Jule et sa lascive main,
En vain de la nature insultent à l'ouvrage,
Au compte de Louis arrive un gros Dauphin,
Juste au bout de neuf mois, à dater de l'époque
Où Coigny le jetta dans le moule royal.

6 Edmond et Jules de Goncourt, 186. Louis XVI's younger brother, the Count of Artois, spitefully handed Louis a copy of this pamphlet, *Mes Pensées*, and later submitted papers to the Parliament of Paris, trying to establish the bastardy of the children of France and Louis XVI's impotence—thus hoping to procure the title of Regent of the kingdom for himself.

7 Marie Thérèse Louise de Savoie-Carignan Lamballe, *Secret Memoirs of Princess de Lamballe* (New York: Walter Dunn, 1901), 103.

8 Marie Antoinette, *Correspondance inédite de Marie Antoinette* (Paris: E. Dentu, 1865), 85–86.

9 Madame Campan, Vol. 2, 112–13.

10 Maxime de La Rocheterie, 194.

11 J. B. Lippincott, *The Trianon Palaces* (Philadelphia: J. B. Lippincott & Co., 1874), 28.

12 Gabriel d'Èze, *Histoire de la coiffure des femmes en France* (Paris: Ollendorff, 1886), 157.

13 Paysac Fars Fausse-Lendry, *Mémoires: ou Souvenirs d'une octogénaire* (Paris: Le Doyen, 1830), 176.

CHAPTER 7: THE QUEEN'S TEMPERAMENT

1 This pregnancy ended in miscarriage in November 1783.

2 Thomas J. Schaeper, *France and America in the Revolutionary Era* (New York: Berghan Books, 1995), 348. The livre, also called a franc, consisted of twenty sous, or pennies. Before the revolution, bread cost between eight and twelve sous, taking as much as half of a worker's earnings for a day. "One livre had a purchasing power equal to that of approximately 3.25 American dollars in 1994."

3 Charles Alexandre de Calonne, French statesman and controller-general in 1785, proved himself incompetent and extravagant, and was compelled to convene the Assembly of Notables in 1787, eventually losing favor and fleeing to England. The queen had disagreed with the appointment of Calonne, a member of the Duchess of Polignac's circle, to the post of controller-general. The intimate relationship between the queen and the duchess suffered immensely due to the duchess's role in the minister's appointment.

4 Choderlos de Laclos, *Les liaisons dangereuses* (Paris: Durand, 1782). Epistolary novel known to have exposed the perversions of the Bourbon regimes and the decadence of French aristocracy.

5 Choderlos de Laclos, "Épitre à Margot," April 1782.

6 Pierre-Augustin Caron de Beaumarchais, *La Folle journée ou le Mariage de Figaro, comédie en cinq actes* (Paris: A. Quantin, 1784).

7 Beaumarchais, xxvii. As a reply to his enemies, Beaumarchais wrote in the preface to *Mariage de Figaro*, "Quand j'ai dû vaincre lions et tigres pour faire jouer une comédie, pensez-vous, après son succès, me réduire, ainsi qu'une servante hollandaise, à battre l'osier tous les matins sur l'insecte vil de la nuit." The author's enemies persuaded the amiable locksmith king that he was the lion.

8 John Holmes Agnew, *The Eclectic Magazine: Foreign Literature* (New York: Bidwell, 1858), 406.

9 Sarah Tytler, *Marie Antoinette* (New York: G. P. Putnam's Sons, 1883), 136.

10 J. S. C. Abbott, *The Life of Marie Antoinette* (London: Sampson Low, 1850).

11 Sarah Tytler, 140.

12 Jeremy Bentham, *Rational of Judicial Evidence* (London: C. H. Reynell, 1827), 225.

13 Henry Vizetelly, *The Story of the Diamond Necklace* (London: Tinsley Brothers, 1867), 212.

14 François Adolphe Mathurin de Lescure, *Correspondance secrète inédite sur Louis xvi, Marie-Antoinette la cour et la ville de 1777 à 1792* (Paris: Henri Plon, 1866), 24.

15 Émile Campardon, *Marie-Antoinette et le procès du collier* (Paris: Henri Plon, 1863).

16 Hector Fleischmann, *Marie-Antoinette Libertine* (Paris: Bibliothèque des Curieux, 1911), 248.

> La Reine: Il te sied bien, vile catin,
>   De jouer le rôle de la reine!
> Mlle d'Oliva: Eh! Pourquoi non, ma souveraine?
>   Vous jouez si souvent le mien!

17 Maxime de La Rocheterie, 311.

18 Imbert de Saint-Amand, *Marie Antoinette and the End of the Old Régime* (New York: Charles Scribner's Sons, 1898), 196.

19 Léonard Autié, 233.

20 Ibid., 237.

21 Maxime de La Rocheterie, 341.

22 Madame Campan, Vol. 2, 202.

CHAPTER 8: THE MONSIEUR'S THEATER

1 Jean-Paul Rabaut, *The History of the Revolution of France* (London: J. Debrett, 1792), 57. "There lived, in the suburbs of Paris, a worthy citizen, named Réveillon, who employed at his manufactory a great number of workmen, to whom he was a benefactor and a father. He was the cause of their earning, yearly, two hundred thousand livres, and paid them from thirty to fifty sous a day. On a sudden, a report is spread, that this person had reduced the wages of his workmen to fifteen sous, that he had been heard to say, that bread was too good for them, and that he had been driven out of his district for his inhumane declarations."

2 La Comtesse D'Adhemar, *Souvenirs sur Marie-Antoinette* (Paris: L. Mame, 1836), 180.

3 Ibid., 181.

4 Gustave Bord, *La Fin de Deux Légendes* (Paris: Henri Daragon, 1899), 134.

5 Louis La Trémoille (duc de), *Les La Trémoïlle pendant cinq siècles* (Nantes: Émile Grimaud, 1890), 166.

6 Charles Dickens, *Dickens's Dictionary of Paris* (London: Macmillan & Company, 1883), 219.

7 Madame Campan, *Mémoires sur la vie privée de Marie-Antoinette* (Paris: Badouin Frères, 1826), 156. "Ce fut uniquement pour plaire à la reine que l'entrepreneur de l'Opéra fit venir à grands frais, à Paris, la première troupe de bouffons. Gluck, Piccini, Sacchini, y furent successivement attirés. Ces compositeurs célèbres, et particulièrement le premier, furent traités avec distinction à la cour."

8 *Note* (Paris: National Archives of France, carton 1683, 17 June 1788). "Le sieur Léonard Autié (cœffeur de la Reine) propose d'introduire un spectacle dans la Salle des Thuileries."

9 Albert Babeau, *Le Théâtre des Tuileries sous Louis XIV, Louis XV et Louis XVI* (Paris: Nogent-le-Rotrou, Daupeley-Gouverneur, 1895), 45.

10 Léonard Autié, 23 June 1788. "Le sieur Léonard Autié ose solliciter des bontés de Monseigneur le Comte d'Angivillers, la permission d'ouvrir le Théâtre de Monsieur, dans la salle des Thuileries, en attendant qu'il en ait fait bâtir une. Il a déjà obtenu l'agrément de M. le baron de Breteuil, et de M. de Champcenetz, et s'est arrangé avec le sieur Le Gros (M. Le Gros était le Directeur des Concerts spirituels qui se donnaient dans la Salle des Thuileries) de manière que les concerts spirituels, auront toujours lieu les jours accoutumés. Il ose attendre de Monseigneur, la permission qu'il prend la liberté de lui demander, sans laquelle il ne pourrait pas ouvrir son théâtre."

11 Chastenay-Lanty, Victorine de. *Mémoirés de Madame de Chastenay,* Vol. 1 (Paris: E. Plon, Nourrit et Cie, 1896), 89.

12 Antoine Vincent D'Arnault, *Souvenirs d'un Sexagénaire* (Paris: Librairie Dufey, 1833), 170. "Calomnié dans sa politique, il le fut aussi dans sa moralité. Les dames, qu'il ne courtisait que de propos, lui prêtèrent des goûts plus socratiques que platoniques. Cette imputation péchait par la base: là où il n'y a rien, le roi perd ses droits. Il a été toute sa vie chaste comme Origène."

13 Comtesse de Boigne, *Memoirs* (New York: Charles Scribner's Sons, 1908), 30.

14 Tony Henri Auguste Reiset, *Anne de Caumont-La Force Comtesse de Balbi* (Paris: Émile Paul, 1908), 272. The Count of Provence, later as king in exile, would one day refuse to admit Madame de Gourbillon to his court because of the vicious rumors of his wife's relationship with her.

15 Ibid., 25.

CHAPTER 9: THE FATAL BANQUET

1 Elisabeth Harriot Hudson, *The Life and Times of Louisa, Queen of Prussia* (London: Hatchards, 1876), 271.

2 Madame Campan, *Mémoires sur la vie privée de Marie-Antoinette* (Paris: Badouin Frères, 1826), 174.

3 François-Alphonse Aulard, *The French Revolution under the Monarchy* (New York: Charles Scribner's Sons, 1910), 137. "The retreat of Louis XVI at Marly, after the death of the Dauphin, had delivered him over absolutely to the influence of the Queen and the Comte d'Artois. He yielded to the supplications of the Nobles, and also to those of the Archbishop of Paris, and decided to resist the Third Estate, to annul the assembly's resolution, and to order the separation of the Orders in the Estates-General."

4 Catherine Welch, *The Little Dauphin* (London: Methuen & Co., 1908), 26.

5 John James McGregor, *History of the French Revolution* (Waterford: John Bull, 1816), 82.

6 Robert Chambers, *Popular Antiquities* (London: Chambers, 1832), 437.

7 Hugo P. Theime, *Women of France* (Philadelphia: Rittenhouse Press, 1908), 348.

8 Maxime de La Rocheterie, 334.

9 Charles Duke Yonge, *The Life of Marie Antoinette, Queen of France,* Vol. 2 (London, Hurst and Blackett, 1876), 47.

10 When the Revolution began it is well known that Liancourt walked into the king's bedroom, woke him, and told him about the storming of the Bastille. The king is said to exclaim, "Quelle revolte?" And Liancourt replied, "Non, sire, c'est une revolution!" Louis XVI also took Liancourt's advice and sent the troops away from Paris and Versailles; the king then went to the National Assembly alone.

11 Thomas Wright, *The History of France,* Vol. 2 (London: London Printing Co., 1858), 460.

12 Justin E. McCarthy, *The French Revolution* (New York: Harper & Brothers, 1898), 243.

13 Religious Tract Society, *French Revolution: Sketches of Its History* (London: Religious Tract Society, 1799), 65–66.

14 Maxime de La Rocheterie, *The Life of Marie Antoinette* (New York: Dodd, Mead and Company, 1893, 55).

CHAPTER 10: THE FLIGHT OF THE ROYAL FAMILY

1 Madame de Campan, Vol. 2, 253–57.

2 Ibid., 49.

3 Louis Barthou, *Mirabeau* (London: William Heinemann, 1913), 316.

4 Léonard Autié, Vol. 2, 33.

5 John Stores Smith, *Mirabeau: Triumph!,* Vol. 2 (London: Smith, Elder and Company, 1848), 292. "It was so rendered from expediency: there can be no doubt that the populace would have extorted a fearful revenge from somebody, had it been authoritatively stated that Mirabeau had been poisoned; and therefore the doctors judged it advisable to extinguish that idea. And now let us turn to a most suspicious circumstance. M. Koudel and the Baron Barbier were two pupils of the Professor Sue; and the former of the twain, on examination of the stomach, found many erosions (holes eaten into it by mineral poison), and having pointed them out to the latter, they both exclaimed that he had been poisoned: but their master, Sue, immediately drew them aside, and silenced them with these words, 'He was not poisoned—he cannot be poisoned—understand that, imprudence! Would you have them devour the King, the Queen, the Assembly, and all of us?' "

CHAPTER 11: THE OTHER LÉONARD

1 Claude-Antoine-Gabriel duc de Choiseul-Stainville, *Relation du départ de Louis XVI, le 20 juin, 1791* (Paris: Badouin Frères, 1822), 67–82.

2 Thomas Waters Griffith, *My Scrapbook of the French Revolution* (Chicago: McClurg and Company, 1898), 146.

CHAPTER 12: THE FATAL MESSAGE

1 Oscar Browning, *The Flight to Varennes* (London: Swan Sonnenschein, 1892), 68.

2 Henry Morse Stephens, *A History of the French Revolution,* Vol. 1 (New York: Charles Scribner's Sons, 1905), 449.

3 Louis de Bouillé, *Mémoires sur l'affaire de Varennes, comprenant le mémoire inédit de M. le Marquis de Bouillé* (Paris: Badouin, 1823), 161. See also: Thomas Edward Watson, *To the End of the Reign of Louis the Fifteenth* (New York: Macmillan Company, 1902), 530. "The faithful hair-dresser had appeared at Varennes also. He had told his story once more, that the king was not coming."

4   Le Marquis de Bouillé, *Collection des mémoires relatifs à la relatifs à la révolution française* (Paris: Badouin, 1823), 116.

5   Charles de Raigecourt, *Exposé de la conduite de M. le C[om]te Charles de Raigecourt à l'affaire de Varennes* (Paris: Badouin, 1823), 190. The young soldiers were thoroughly disgusted with the arrival of Jean-François.

6   Lenotre, p. 9.

7   Eliakim and Robert S. Littell, *Littell's Living Age* (Boston: Littell & Company, 1886), 740.

CHAPTER 13: LÉONARD IN EXILE

1   Blanche Christable Hardy, *The Princesse de Lamballe: A Biography* (London: Archibald Constable and Company), 1908, 225.

2   "Certifie conforme à Versailles le 9 Septembre, 1791, François Autié Léonard, cadet, coiffeur de la reine."—National Archives, 1077. National Archives, W. 432. "J'ai l'honneur de mettre sous les yeux de Messieurs les commissaires charges des scelles du château des Tuileries que moi, hautier [*sic*] coiffeur de la reine, que j'ait une chambre cour des princes bresil [?] du corridor noir, escalier No. 7, sous le comble dans laquelle chambre j'avais les effets que je soustrais a Messieurs les commissaires. Savoir: un habit et veste abilles rayes d'une rais jaune garnis de boutons d'acier,—un frac noir, boutons noirs,—un habit et veste d'uniforme du département de Versailles —une redingote de piquet blanc et son pantalon,—une épée de deuil, un manchon, un parasol de taffetas vert (etc. etc.)."

3   One louis (gold coin) = 20–24 livres.

4   Gustave Bord, *La Fin de Deux Legendes* (Paris: Henri Daragon, 1909), 64.

5   There was no official record of Pierre after 1792 in the National Archives. His first signature was recorded in 1786 when he married Marguerite-Rosalie le Guay, lady-in-waiting to Madame Élisabeth. The date of Pierre's wedding in 1786 is important because Pierre's brothers witnessed the ceremony with their signatures on the same day, thus providing information to track the Autié brothers' whereabouts.

6   The signatures are important: Léonard always signed his surname Autié. Jean-François and Pierre's signatures were Authier until 1787, when they began to sign Autié. Perhaps, as Léonard was devoting more time to the theater at this time, his brothers switched to the orthography of his last name, taking over his duties as hairdressers and thus taking advantage of his famous name. They would all three be referred to as "Léonard."

7   Edmond de Goncourt, *La femme au dix-huitième siècle* (Paris: Fasquelle, 1898), 347.

8   Léonard Autié, Vol. 2, 153.

CHAPTER 14: SORROWFUL EVENTS

1 Léonard Autié, Vol. 2, 167.
2 Ibid., 175–76. This letter was written to one of Count d'Artois's staff officers, Monsieur de Wicom, by his friend, Madame Le Bouhourn. The publishers of Léonard's memoirs reported that this letter was kept by Léonard and shown to them in 1816, and that they copied it word for word.
3 Lord Frederick Hamilton and Sir Douglas Straight, *Nash's Pall Mall Magazine*, Vol. 9 (London: Charing Cross Road, 1896), 304–9.
4 *La nuit porte conseil.*
5 Léonard Autié, Vol. 2, 191.
6 Ibid., 194.

CHAPTER 15: THE QUEEN IS NO MORE

1 Charles Maxime Catherinet de Villemarest, *Life of Prince Talleyrand*, Vol. 1 (Philadelphia: Carey, Lea & Blanchard, 1834), 211.
2 Léonard Autié, Vol. 2, 197.
3 Ibid., 215.
4 Ibid., 232.
5 Albert Lumbroso, *Revue Napoléonienne*, Vol. 3 (Rome: Frascati, 1906), 416.
6 G. Lenotre, Mrs. Rodolph Stawell, and BFS Hatchards, *The Last Days of Marie Antoinette: from the French of G. Lenotre* (Philadelphia: J. B. Lippincott Company, 1907), 144.
7 Clara Tschudi, *Marie Antoinette* (London: Swan Sonnenschein & Co., 1902), 274.
8 Léonard Autié, Vol. 2, 225.
9 Robert Bruce Douglas, *The Life and Times of Madame du Barry* (London: Leonard Smithers, 1896), 374–78.

CHAPTER 16: LÉONARD RESUMES THE COMB

1 Alethea Wiel, *The Story of Verona* (London: F. M. Dent & Company, 1907), 116. "The Comte de Provence had fixed his abode in Verona towards the end of the year 1794, under the incognito of 'Comte de Lille.' His mode of life was quiet and private, and though his suite recognized him as Louis XVIII, King of France, he himself avoided every outward semblance of majesty so as not to compromise the Venetian Republic, which had afforded him an asylum and hospitality in its territory."
2 Léonard Autié, Vol. 2, 117.
3 Ibid., 247.

4   Imbert de Saint-Amand, *Famous Women of the French Court* (New York: Charles Scribner's Sons, 1894), 191.
5   Léonard Autié, Vol. 2, 258.
6   Ibid., 289.
7   Ibid., 291.
8   Ibid., 301.
9   C. M. Podgorski, "Princess Ratazanoff" in *The Cosmopolitan*, Vol. 11 (New York: Cosmopolitan Publishing Company, 1892), 734.
10 Louise-Elisabeth Vigée-LeBrun, *Memoirs of Madame Vigée-LeBrun* (New York: Doubleday, Page & Company, 1903), 125.

CHAPTER 17: SIXTEEN YEARS LATER

1   Léonard Autié, Vol. 2, 302.
2   Ibid., 303.
3   Ibid.
4   Edward King, *My Paris: French Character Sketches* (Boston: Loring, 1868), 112.
5   Bayle St. John, *Purple Tints of Paris, Character and Manners in the New Empire*, Vol. 1 (London: Chapman and Hall, 1854), 257.
6   Ibid., 298.
7   Émile Langlade, *Rose Bertin: The Creator of Fashion at the Court of Marie-Antoinette* (New York: Charles Scribner's Sons, 1913), 303.
8   Léonard Autié, Vol. 2, 311.
9   Ibid., 312.

CHAPTER 18: LÉONARD'S FINAL RUSE

1   Ibid., 314.
2   Sponges were often used to wipe the blood off the faces of defeated soldiers; when they were no longer able to fight, it was said they "would throw up the sponge." This would be similar to the phrase "throw in the towel."
3   Léonard Autié, Vol. 2, 315.

AFTERWORD

1   Alfred Bégis, *l'Intermédiaire des chercheurs*, Vol. 23 (Paris: 1890), 408.
2   Albert Lumbroso, *Léonard le coiffeur de Marie-Antoinette est-il mort guillotiné?* (Paris: Picard et Fils, 1906), 10.
3   G. Lenotre, *The Flight of Marie Antoinette* (London: William Heinemann, 1906), 237.
4   Alfred Bégis, *l'Intermédiaire des chercheurs*, Vol. 51 (Paris, 1905), 291.

Index